Employment and Employee Rights

Foundations of Business Ethics

Series editors: W. Michael Hoffman and Robert E. Frederick

Written by an assembly of the most distinguished figures in business ethics, the Foundations of Business Ethics series aims to explain and assess the fundamental issues that motivate interest in each of the main subjects of contemporary research. In addition to a general introduction to business ethics, individual volumes cover key ethical issues in management, marketing, finance, accounting, and computing. The volumes, which are complementary yet complete in themselves, allow instructors maximum flexibility in the design and presentation of course materials without sacrificing either depth of coverage or the discipline-based focus of many business courses. The volumes can be used separately or in combination with anthologies and case studies, depending on the needs and interests of the instructors and students.

1 John R. Boatright: *Ethics in Finance*
2 Ronald F. Duska and Brenda Shay Duska: *Accounting Ethics*
3 Richard T. De George: *The Ethics of Information Technology and Business*
4 Patricia H. Werhane and Tara J. Radin with Norman E. Bowie: *Employment and Employee Rights*

Employment and Employee Rights

Patricia H. Werhane
and
Tara J. Radin
with
Norman E. Bowie

350 Main Street, Malden, MA 02148-5018, USA
108 Cowley Road, Oxford OX4 1JF, UK
550 Swanston Street, Carlton South, Melbourne, Victoria 3053, Australia

First published 2004 by Blackwell Publishing Ltd

Library of Congress Cataloging-in-Publication Data

Werhane, Patricia Hogue.
Employment and employee rights / Patricia H. Werhane, Tara J. Radin, and Norman E. Bowie.
p. cm. – (Foundations of business ethics ; 4)
Includes bibliographical references and index.
ISBN 0-631-21428-3 (hardcover : alk. paper) – ISBN 0-631-21429-1 (pbk. : alk. paper)
1. Employee rights. 2. Management rights. 3. Employee rights – United States. 4. Management rights – United States. I. Radin, Tara J. II. Bowie, Norman E., 1942– III. Title. IV. Series.

HD6971.8 .W468 2004
331′.01′1 – dc21

2002154330

A catalogue record for this title is available from the British Library.

Set in 10.5/12.5 Plantin
by SetSystems Ltd, Saffron Walden, Essex
Printed and bound in the United Kingdom
by MPG Books Ltd, Bodmin, Cornwall

For further information on
Blackwell Publishing, visit our website:
http:/www.blackwellpublishing.com

Contents

Part III The Evolving Workplace

Preface

This book is the outcome of a long series of studies on employee rights. In 1985, having written a book on employee rights, one of the authors optimistically speculated that many of the issues that book explored would no longer be relevant in 2000. Affirmative action and equal opportunity initiatives would have by and large solved inequalities in the workplace, and the "glass ceiling" phenomenon would be a thing of the past. Whistleblowing legislation would be in place, the Privacy Act would cover employers in the private as well as the public sectors, and threats to worker safety would occur only in the remotest parts of the economy. The elusive goal of workplace due process would have been achieved, and most places of work would encourage more participatory management.

Today, in 2002, these goals have not been achieved. While there is increased focus on diversity, and while there is much less discrimination in hiring, glass ceilings for women and minorities are still in place for senior positions in many firms. Due process in the private sector remains elusive, whistleblowers are often treated as pariahs, and privacy throughout the political economy in every area is practically nonexistent. We have seen an increased focus on employee teams, and more employee participation on the plant floors and assembly lines. The reduction and flattening of managerial hierarchies means that employees and middle managers have increased responsibilities. At the same time layoffs and other forms of workforce reductions have increased to such an extent that the notion of employee loyalty to a particular firm is no longer a consideration. The need for further work in this area has inspired us to write this book.

We want to thank the general editors of this series, Robert Frederick and Michael Hoffman, for their invitation to take on this project. We want especially to thank Robert for his tireless and meticulous editing of the first draft and John McCall for a careful review. We also want to acknowledge the contributions of Norman Bowie, Ronald Duska, R. Edward Freeman, and Donna Wood. Henry Tulloch is credited with fine copy-editing, and Jenny Mead did much of the research. We also thank the Olsson Center for Applied Ethics and the Darden Graduate School of Business Administration for their financial support, and Karen Musselman for administrative assistance. The shortcomings of the text are our own.

Acknowledgments

The authors and publisher gratefully acknowledge the permission granted to reproduce the copyright material in this book:

Some of the ideas in chapters 1, 3, 4, and 5 were originally developed from Patricia H. Werhane's 1985 book, *Persons, Rights and Corporations*. Englewood Cliffs, NJ: Prentice-Hall. Revised with permission of the author.

Parts of chapter 2 are revisions from Tara J. Radin and Patricia H. Werhane, "The Public/Private Distinction and the Political Status of Employment," *American Business Law Journal*, 34: 2 (1996), 245–60. Revised with permission of the journal and the authors.

Parts of chapter 3 are revisions from Patricia H. Werhane, "Employee and Employer Rights in an Institutional Context" in T. Donaldson and Patricia H. Werhane (eds.), *Ethical Issues in Business*, 4th edn. Englewood Cliffs, NJ: Prentice-Hall, 1993. Revised with permission of the author.

Parts of chapter 4 originally appeared in Patricia H. Werhane and Tara J. Radin, "Employment at Will and Due Process" in T. Donaldson and Patricia H. Werhane (eds.), *Ethical Issues in Business*, 5th and 6th edns. Englewood Cliffs, NJ: Prentice Hall, 1996, 1999. Reprinted in T. Beauchamp and N. Bowie (eds.), *Ethical Theory and Business*, 5th edn. Englewood Cliffs, NJ: Prentice-Hall, 1997. Revised with permission of the authors.

Parts of chapter 5 are revisions from chapter 2 of Patricia H. Werhane, *Moral Imagination and Management Decision-Making*. New York: Oxford University Press, 1999. Revised and reprinted with permission of the author and Oxford University Press.

Parts of chapter 9 are revisions from Tara J. Radin and Patricia H. Werhane, "Employment and Employee Rights: a Retrospective and Prospective" in *Business Ethics Quarterly*, forthcoming. Revised with permission of the journal and the authors.

Every effort has been made to trace copyright holders and to obtain their permission for the use of copyright material. The publisher apologizes for any errors or omissions in the above list and would be grateful to be notified of any corrections that should be incorporated in future reprints or editions of this book.

Introduction

This is a book about rights in the workplace. Although much of the literature on employment focuses on employee rights, we shall consider the rights of both employees and employers. We argue that the recognition and protection of employee and employer rights in the workplace, even in the absence of Constitutional or other legal directives, both coincides with our considered moral judgments and benefits multiple stakeholders, including employers, employees, shareholders, and firms themselves.

In particular, this book is about rights in employment in the United States. We defend this focus from two perspectives. First, because employment rights are not top priorities in the private sector of the economy in this country, it would be inappropriate for us, as American thinkers, to critique employment practices elsewhere. Second, it is important to target practices in the United States for analysis since these employment practices are commonly exported and copied around the world, not merely by American-based multinational corporations but also by other governments and other international and global corporations. As in other areas of commerce, the United States is often held up as a role model for free-market economic growth and well-being. A book such as this about the shortcomings as well as positive features of the American model for employment is an important step toward preventing the export of the employment-related ills that already plague the American workplace.

In the first part, Rights, Employee Rights, and Employment-at-Will, we discuss the moral and legal landscape and traditional assumptions about rights in employment. Chapter 1 begins with a theoretical exposition of rights theory interpreted through the lens of a postmodern conception of social construction. This point of view acknowledges that rights theory is a historically late Western framework for evaluating human behavior. We nevertheless argue that rights talk, while parochially developed, is a widely accepted mode of internal and cross-cultural evaluation, and human rights are thus provisional candidates for cross-cultural or global principles. Still, as we point out in the last section of the chapter, despite American political and legal preoccupations with rights, rights in the workplace are not part of that preoccupation. Indeed, employment is often thought of as a purely economic, even ahuman, phenomenon.

Chapter 2 focuses on the legal background for employee rights. We begin by sorting out traditional distinctions between the public and private sectors of our political economy, and the contemporary erosion of those distinctions. We point out that the Constitution and Bill of Rights protect political rights of individuals and corporations against the state, but do not apply, except with regard to egregious behavior, to private affairs such as within families or in employment in the private sector. This chapter sets the stage for chapter 3, which is devoted to a more extensive discussion of employment-at-will. Employment-at-will is a widely accepted common law American doctrine that, in the absence of contracts or laws, employment agreements are "at-will" arrangements that can be severed at any time, by either party, without any explanatory requirement or good reasons.

In the last chapter of this section, we show how employee rights, in particular the rights to due process and whistleblowing, can coexist with employment-at-will. Procedural due process is the requirement that some sort of mechanism be established to adjudicate employment practices, particularly those involving layoffs, firing, transfers and any practices for which there might not be mutual employee–employer consent. Substantive due process is the demand for good reasons for employment practices – reasons, we argue, that are required of any sound management activity. Chapter 4 ends with a discussion of Christopher McMahon's proposal for workplace democracy, a proposal that would circumvent the need for establishing separate employee and employer rights.

In part II, New Models of Employment and Employment Relationships, we explore arguments for guaranteeing rights, particularly for employees, which are derived from relational, developmental, and economic bases. Chapter 5 investigates the function of roles and role morality in employment. Recognizing the limits of role morality invites new thinking about employment practices that goes beyond traditional approaches and can serve as a basis for deriving employee rights. We suggest that employees are individuals with rights, not merely employees. As such, employees and employers not only have rights to be respected, but they also have responsibilities to each other and further obligations to act independently of their assigned roles.

Chapter 6 begins with an analysis of "meaningful work." The importance of work being meaningful for each individual is often discussed, but what "meaningful" signifies is different for different people and different occupations. This is a term that is often used with sufficient vagueness so as to be vacuous. We shall nevertheless attempt to arrive at a definition that defines meaningful work as work that an individual enjoys, excels in, and has some control over – work that creates a sense of satisfaction and preserves employee autonomy and employment choices. In response to a demand for meaningful work, in these turbulent times with changing labor conditions, employers have developed models of outplacement and employability with the idea that well-trained flexible employees and managers can find meaningful work in a number of employment settings. The chapter ends with an examination of such practices.

We end part II with chapter 7, written with Norman Bowie, depicting a series of arguments defending employee rights as economic value added for employers and companies. Appealing to the writings of Jeffrey Pfeffer and others, we argue that reasonable employment practices – including careful hiring, continuous training, team management, decentralization and participation in management decision-making, high compensation, financial transparency, and employment security – create more economic value for companies that employment practices to the contrary.

Finally, in part III, The Evolving Workplace, we conclude by exploring new dimensions of employment. Chapter 8 outlines challenges to diversity, and we defend the position that equitable employment practices are both fair and also, if carried out properly, contribute to economic value added. Recent changes in the workplace, resulting from variables such as technology and the changing economic climate, make it even more important for employees to exercise control over their careers. Even with employment-at-will as the default rule, it does not mean that employee rights must be ignored. In chapter 9 we propose a model that incorporates growing workplace diversity, builds upon our understanding of the legal landscape, and expands upon our justifications for recognizing and protecting rights. Such a model introduces the notion that every employee is his or her own contractor – that employment is not a matter of obedience or dependency, but should be thought of as a craft or profession with independent standards and justifications. The employee/professional in this model is neither a cost nor asset to the firm; rather he or she is an investor in a reciprocal employment exchange where independence, rights, and responsibilities of each party are equally respected. A professionalism approach to employment provides one vehicle through which employment rights can be protected. Professionalism not only ensures that employee rights, as well as employer rights, are protected, but also empowers employees to take charge of their careers so that they are able to protect their rights themselves. This creates economic value for the firm, and benefits multiple stakeholders as well.

part i

Rights, Employee Rights, and Employment-at-Will

The first section of this book discusses the American workplace and the underlying rationale for employee rights and presents some of the obstacles to their recognition and protection. Chapter 1 develops a theory of rights that takes into account postmodern theories of social construction and at the same time provides an evaluative mechanism for judging employee concerns. We will contend that morality does demand employee rights, but when employment is approached primarily as an economic phenomenon, that mindset does not always take into account the human dimensions of the phenomenon. In chapter 2 we will argue that the political distinction between the public and private sectors of our political economy contributes to thinking about private sector employment differently from civil service. This, in turn, affects how we think about employee rights in the private sector. In chapter 3 we analyze and critique the doctrine of employment-at-will (EAW), a common law principle that employment agreements are voluntary arrangements that can be terminated at any time, by either party, with or without reasons. Finally, chapter 4 explores the right to due process and develops the notion of a democratized workplace.

chapter one

Employment, Moral Rights, and Mental Models

We shall begin by laying out a theory of moral rights from which we can derive rights in employment. Moral rights theory is a somewhat recent Western philosophical construction – a mental model or way of framing our experiences that postulates moral rights as evaluative mechanisms for judging and improving upon human behavior. Despite the parochial roots of moral rights theory, and keeping that qualification in mind, we shall conclude that moral rights are candidates for general evaluative principles, justifiable standards by which to judge a range of human phenomena including employment and employment practices.

In the second part of this chapter we begin to address a simple question: if moral rights make sense, at least in an economically-developed Western democratic republic such as the United States, a republic founded on a clearly stated Bill of Rights, why are employee rights an issue, particularly in such a situation? In this chapter, we suggest that conflicting notions of rights, particularly as linked to freedom and property, underlie disparate treatment of employees and inconsistent recognition of employee rights.

RIGHTS TALK

Rights talk[1] has become a prevailing moral currency all around the world. In the United States, the Constitution and Bill of Rights outline protections for basic rights and freedoms for all citizens. This is not merely an American phenomenon, however. Similar protections surface on behalf of political rights to freedom and democratic participation, rights of the underrepresented such as women and minorities, religious freedoms, and even property rights in many countries around the world. Many of these rights are spelled out in the United Nations *Universal Declaration of Human Rights*. The *Declaration* also proposes more specific economic rights such as rights to work, to form unions, to choose employment, to have safe and decent working conditions, to receive equal and fair pay, and even to receive an annual holiday.

Rights talk is grounded on a set of assumptions derived from moral theory. Among these is that human beings have intrinsic value, that is, they are of value because of their human status, regardless of particular historical, religious, or cultural situations or abilities. Because human beings have intrinsic value, it follows that they have certain basic rights, ordinarily called *human rights* or *moral rights*, to which everyone should be entitled.[2] We call this set of rights moral rights or human rights because the rights involved are so fundamental and so inviolable that every person should be deemed to be entitled to them, regardless of his or her particular social, political, historical, or even cultural situation. According to rights theorists, they are universal equal rights (Werhane, 1985). The reality, though, is that human rights or moral rights often translate into entitlements that are not actually recognized and respected equally in every culture or society.

An assumption underlying the notion of rights concerns the classes of human beings for whom rights claims make sense.[3] As Rainer Forst states, "Every conception of human rights – by which I understand fundamental rights every human being can claim as a human being – presupposes . . . a conception of the moral person who is the author and addressee of such claims" (Forst, 1999: 43–4). We ordinarily restrict the expression "moral person" to a limited class of human beings, not merely to all those who are capable of interests, but rather to those who can make self-conscious choices based on some acceptable reasoning processes. Persons can self-consciously analyze their own actions; they can, to at least some extent, control and change their own lives; they can deliberately positively or negatively affect the lives of others; and they can engage in self-evaluation and in the deliberative evaluation of others. In addition, they can give reasons – reasons that make sense to others – for their judgments and decisions. Moral persons are thus those human beings who can be held responsible for their choices and actions (Gewirth, 1996).

We also extend intrinsic value to less rational human beings, such as children, the senile, the mentally ill, and the mentally handicapped, not merely because they are "look alikes," but because they were formerly or are potentially moral persons. They have emotions, they are capable of interests, they feel pain, and they sometimes even exhibit a modicum of choice. They are not considered full-fledged moral persons, however, because they do not exhibit sufficient rationality and self-awareness to identify them with adulthood and a broad capability for free choice.

This moral intuition is reflected in American law, where not all human beings are guaranteed the same rights. Full entitlement to all legal rights is restricted to legal persons, just as full entitlement to all moral rights is restricted to moral persons. Within the law, guardians are appointed to protect the interests of human beings such as children who are not considered legal persons. Children, for example, cannot commit to binding contracts. Parents, however, or comparable guardians, can engage in contracts on their behalf (Sterk, 1988).

It follows, according to defenders of rights, that basic moral rights are those entitlements intended to respect and protect what is uniquely characteristic of human beings. A more specific set of rights – basic liberties – is restricted to persons. The right to life, the right not to be enslaved, and the right not to be tortured are ordinarily classified as basic moral rights of all human beings since, without respect for life or pain, human existence would be intolerable.

The right not to be enslaved is linked to a right of considerable importance in our society, that is, the right to freedom or liberty. While liberty might be said, arguably, to be a Western socially constructed idea, it nevertheless captures what appear to be a set of important if not unique human characteristics: our abilities to make, write, and change our own histories; to change creatively our ingrained habits and our political, social and even religious beliefs, both positively and negatively; and to manipulate, for good or for ill, our natural environment. Freedom or liberty is a basic moral right for persons, because without being able to exercise free choice, we would not be able to develop our full capabilities. The ability to reason, in turn, implicitly underlies our notion of freedom or liberty, because without this ability, we could not exercise our freedom.

Another candidate for a basic moral right is the right to *equal consideration*. The right to equal consideration – or the right to be treated as an equal – is a crucial element in defining the recognition and exercise of rights. The right to equal consideration might be the most basic right, or it might merely be part of the definition of moral rights. Its ontological status in the family of rights will not be decided here, but its importance for the discussion of rights, in particular, as the philosophical basis for justifying equal opportunity, cannot be ignored (Dworkin, 1977).

Is liberty the most basic right? In a now classic text, *Basic Rights*, Henry Shue argues that security and subsistence preempt liberty:

> Security and subsistence are basic rights . . . because of the roles they play in both the enjoyment and the protection of all other rights. Other rights [such as liberty] could not be enjoyed in the absence of security or subsistence, even if the other rights were somehow miraculously protected in such a situation. And other rights could in any case not be protected if security or subsistence could credibly be threatened. (Shue, 1980: 30)

What Shue has done is to turn the rights not to be harmed and to be left alone into a practical claim that without minimum security from harm and basic subsistence needs met, the right to be left alone creates the possibility of not living at all or of living under conditions of constant threats to life and/or survival. Even if rights are thought to be Western constructions, the notion of living under threatening and starvation conditions is an abhorrent idea to almost everyone on the planet.

According to Amartya Sen, the "liberty v. basic needs" debate that Shue introduces is needlessly skewed. Liberty and basic needs overlap and are inexorably interconnected. Without liberty, communities commit unthinkable atrocities; without food and security, individual capabilities cannot develop. If a person is forced to remain narrowly focused on maintaining the basic safety of his or her family, for example, that person is rarely able to develop the sorts of skills that will enable him or her to flourish as a citizen within the community. Both of these sets of rights, together, form the basis for human existence, choice, and well-being (Sen, 1992).

Embedded in this discussion is an important distinction: the distinction between negative and positive rights (Berlin, 1969). A negative right is a right to be left alone or not to be interfered with in some way. Positive rights, on the other hand, are rights to something and involve action on the part of others. An example is the right to security, which encompasses rights to protection and implies the need for actions on the part of others to protect or maintain that security. Freedom or liberty is sometimes depicted as a negative right – the right to be left alone to pursue one's own interests and choices. Freedom can also be seen as a positive right. As a positive right, freedom or liberty involves others to enable those choices to be available. The negative right to be left alone, too, if extended to include the right to make unrestrained choices, includes the active component of having to exercise choice in order to realize that right.

The distinction between positive and negative rights is important to the subject matter of this book. Freedom might seem to translate simply into the negative right not to be coerced, the right to be left alone, or the right not to be forced into involuntary behavior. Construed in such a way, freedom does not necessarily require any positive action on the part of others except for restraint from interference. This interpretation of freedom emerges frequently in business, as corporations argue that they should be left alone to do as they choose and engage in voluntary mutual agreements, without being subject to governmental scrutiny, so long as laws and others' negative rights are not being violated (Nozick, 1974; Gauthier, 1987). What is particularly interesting is that many advocates of negative rights also defend the right to private ownership, an active right that requires involvement of other persons in order to protect property claims against counterclaims or infringements.

While mere noninterference might seem sufficient on its face, the reality is that people's exercise of their freedom inevitably interferes with other people's freedom when they are more aggressive than their peers in less propitious circumstances. For example, at the outset of the industrial revolution, adults were not literally forced into working in factories. Jobs were offered at certain wages, and people were "free" to choose for themselves whether or not to accept these offers. In addition, they were also "free" to quit if at any time they became dissatisfied with their wages or working conditions. Unfortunately, people were not truly "free" to reject or leave factory jobs, though, because the economic climate in the nineteenth century, in both Europe and the United States, was so difficult that people were compelled to take whatever positions they were able to find in order to survive.

Critics of the notion of positive rights argue that they infringe on a person's liberty by requiring active involvement in the achievement or the defense of the rights of others. Critics also contend that positive rights infringe on the right of the claimant by requiring rights protection, even when this is not desired by, or desirable to, that person. For example, the right to subsistence demands positive action on the part of all of us to help those in need who cannot help themselves. This requirement allegedly infringes on the rights of those not in need by forcing them to contribute to the needy, and it also allegedly infringes on the rights of the needy to control their own destiny (Nozick, 1974).

In response, other philosophers argue that the distribution of property, talents, resources, and accidents of birth or environment are such that, unless positive rights are explicitly recognized, some people will have none of their rights respected (Rawls, 1971; Gewirth, 1978; Gewirth, 1996). Other proponents go further and assert that freedom does not exist for the individual unless everyone is able to exercise his or her freedom, and exercise it equally (Marx, 1844, 1963). While positive liberty, at least according to one interpretation, includes the right "to participate in the process by which my life is to be controlled" (MacPherson, 1973: 108), it is also claimed that "the only sensible way to measure individual liberty is to measure the aggregate net liberty of all the individuals in a given society" (MacPherson, 1973: 117). In an unequal society, that is, a society where not everyone can exercise his or her choices and control his or her life to the same extent, C. B. MacPherson concludes that each of us is required to restrain his or her freedom and assist others to develop theirs.

Many readers will find that this egalitarian definition of positive freedom requires too much from each of us to be realized. Its failure lies in not acknowledging personal achievements, achievements that will often, and sometimes deservedly, create inequalities. There is, nevertheless, a valuable insight to be acquired from a more moderate notion of positive freedom. If freedom requires that we protect individuals from coercion, it also should safeguard our abilities to make choices. In other words, freedom can be seen as protecting "the desire of the individual to be his own master . . . to be self-directed[,] . . . to be moved by his own conscious purposes[, and] . . . to act and decide rather than be acted upon and decided for by others" (Berlin, 1969: 131).

Sen adopts a different approach. Sen develops a notion of "substantive freedoms – the capabilities – to choose a life one has reason to value," and he links freedom to "the extent of the freedom that a person actually has" (Sen, 1999: 74). This "extent" has to do with capabilities, that is, with what a person can actually achieve, given his or her abilities and the satisfaction (or lack thereof) of basic needs in a particular community. A handicapped person in a wealthy society will thus have fewer capabilities than others in his or her community, even when basic needs and security are addressed equally across the whole population. Moreover, the societal provisions for health and education will further influence these capabilities. In the United States, therefore, where healthcare is not universally guaranteed, those without insurance will be at a capabilities disadvantage, even though other basic needs are met (Sen, 1990).

While clearly arguing that a view of liberty as merely the right to be left alone is unsatisfactory, Sen, in developing this idea of substantive freedom, is not trying to make a value judgment about the necessity of equal freedoms. On the contrary, he wants us to take into account individual capabilities as well as equal access and equal opportunities in making judgments about the extent of freedom an individual may, is able to, or should enjoy.

Sen's notion of freedom has been adopted by many philosophers because it takes into account the fact that the presence of autonomy (the right not to be coerced or the right to be left alone) is not alone enough to encompass what we mean by freedom. Freedom can be seen as that which protects the individual's self-development, and this entails both the lack of coercion and opportunities for development. Interpreted in such a way, linking opportunities for positive enjoyment of autonomy and possibilities for self-development, turns freedom into an active right in that it imposes upon others the obligation to provide others access to the exercise of their freedom.

How, then, should freedom be defined? Freedom encompasses the right to autonomy, the right to be left alone, and the right not to be coerced. These are intrinsic to the exercise of free choice. Like all rights, though, freedom does not entail the right to do whatever one pleases. Freedom is an equal right circumscribed by the equal rights and interests of others. Freedom demands that people respect each other's right to an equal opportunity to exercise self-development. Failure to do this constitutes a form of interference with freedom in that it prevents others from being able to exercise their freedom. Whether this idea makes sense in all cultures, or whether it is the most important right in every culture, remains to be debated. It is nevertheless that concept that has been generally adopted in the United Nations *Universal Declaration of Human Rights*, and more specifically in many countries as an ideal to which every person and every nation should aspire.

PROPERTY RIGHTS

Property rights are human conventions that define a network of relationships outlining the parameters of, and limits to, possession, ownership, use, transfer, trade, and inheritance of physical, intellectual, and other forms of property (Kipnis, 1997). In every society, property and ownership are defined in some way or other, even if through communal ownership. John Locke, the seventeenth-century British philosopher whose writings influenced Jefferson's crafting of the American *Declaration of Independence*, argued that property rights, like the rights to life, survival, liberty and to work, are natural rights. Since Locke's time it has become more propitious to think of property rights as conventional rights, since in each society these are defined and laid out differently, depending on custom, tradition, religion, and particular laws, and it is not clear that one form of property convention is better, that is, morally better, than another.

We refer to Locke's ideas because, in spite of his controversial contention that property rights are "natural" rights, his thinking provides the foundation for the commonly-held view that ownership affords property owners rights to whatever happens to or on that property and rights to control or exclude the activities of whomever works on it. Property rights today are embedded in a network of laws, regulations, customs, and traditions that define and restrict ownership and transfer rights for individuals, companies, and even between nations. Yet there remains the nagging intuition that owners can do what they please with their property even with the dramatic changes in ownership structures and rules governing property rights we have developed during the last two centuries.

This notion of property rights is important for the purposes of this book for at least three reasons. First, property is one of the bases for free enterprise. That we have rights to buy, sell, trade, and inherit property allows the accumulation, development, sale and transfer of capital, stock, and properties necessary to build industries, create capital markets, and trade. Indeed, it is often argued that free enterprise with its concomitant property rights is the best economic system because it creates opportunities for economic growth and enhances well-being for more people than other systems (Smith, 1776, 1976; Friedman, 1952).

Second, however, and this point is equally important, it is important to understand property rights within the context of other rights.

Our preoccupation with property and the accumulation and distribution of wealth does not preempt other basic rights. In particular, property rights, however defined, do not preempt the more basic rights to life, liberty, and rights not to be harmed or enslaved. If it were the case that property rights were on a par with other basic rights, then wages below a minimum living standard, unsafe working conditions, child labor, and even slavery could be justified under certain desperate conditions. Thus those rights that protect what is crucial and unique to human existence could be usurped for the sake of the demands of property owners. Even Locke would never argue that property rights preempt rights to life, survival, liberty, or even the right to work.

Third, while we acknowledge ownership of physical and intellectual property, we sometimes neglect to think about property rights of employees. It is from Locke that we are able to derive an important property right, which we shall call the proprietary rights of employees. Locke argued that we have certain rights vis-à-vis our status as human beings. These rights extend to our bodies, and, therefore, to life, liberty, survival, and work. The right to work is significant because only through working are we able to provide for our independence and survival. At the same time, individuals acquire some sort of ownership in their work. Even as people contribute to their work environments by adding value to their employers, their actual contribution is the result of *their* efforts. According to Locke, this means that people have some sort of entitlement to the contributions of their work – what Locke called the "fruits of our labor." Proprietary rights, then, are non-exclusive rights to what people contribute or produce as a result of their labor contribution (Locke, 1690, 1963).

Building upon Locke's argument, Adam Smith later argued that a laborer's productivity is part of what makes slavery or serfdom wrong. Slavery or serfdom is an evil not only because it violates a right to liberty, but also because slave owners do not distinguish the slave from his or her contributions. In a slave society, productivity is often measured in terms of the number of slaves, not according to the degree of productivity of each worker. The practice of slavery therefore does not acknowledge the individual value of the slave either as a person or as a laborer.

Smith viewed the separability of a person from his or her productivity as something that contributes to his or her freedom. To deny this separability, as slavery does, would thus constitute the absence of freedom. Without that separation, the laborer is neither conscious of, nor in control of, his or her choices of work, and an identification of labor and labor productivity precludes even grasping what is meant by liberty. When each of us is free and able to work for wages, we are paid according to our contributions. Labor productivity is valued as a commodity and the laborer is consciously differentiated from his or her productivity. It is this, our productivity, that we "sell," and we have rights to do so, without sacrificing our individuality and individual liberty. It is only then that the laborer is conscious of and actually attains economic liberty (Smith, 1776, 1976; Werhane, 1991).[4]

The importance of all of these points is to make clear that daily and part-time workers, employees, managers, and executives, all have proprietary rights to their work contributions, in whatever situation or position, just as entrepreneurs, homeowners, and companies have property rights in whatever physical and/or intellectual property they own

CRITIQUES OF "RIGHTS TALK" 

Rights talk represents a commonly accepted way of defending political freedoms and providing standards to criticize atrocities that crop up all around the world. Still, rights theories are not without their critics. While we will not address all these objections in depth, three are important to mention in light of the project of this book. First, theories of human rights are a late development in the history of ideas. Moreover, rights theories are peculiarly Western ideas derived from Western Judeo-Christian theology and humanist philosophy. How, then, do they make universal claims, or when they do, what is the basis and status of those claims?[5]

Second, rights talk is allegedly over-individualistic. Theories of rights were developed during the seventeenth- and eighteenth-century enlightenment, a tradition that supposedly focused primarily on the individual and his or her rights, as if each of us were perfectly autonomous and independent of one other. Is rights talk, then, anything more than individual or group manifestos that ignore the social context in which this talk arises and takes place?

Third, at least since the late eighteenth century, many philosophers have argued that all human experience is socially constructed. All ideas, theories, concepts, and even scientific knowledge, are derived from mental models that frame, order, and organize the data of our experience. To claim, therefore, that human beings have *universal* rights that crosscut historical, social, or cultural origins belies this assertion. Is not then rights talk merely a socially constructed Western phenomenon, parochially derived, and of limited validity?

History of rights theories

According to Alan Gewirth, the idea that human beings have rights to life, liberty and, sometimes, property, just because they are human, probably stems from Roman law, where justice included the idea of "giving each his own" (Gewirth, 1992: 1101). The bases for rights theories were further developed from the medieval tradition of natural law. Medieval philosophers by and large defined rights as powers to act, to be in self-control, and/or as powers to influence the actions of others. Somewhat later, during the sixteenth century, thinkers such as Mazzolini linked rights to duties by depicting them not simply as powers over oneself and others, but also as claims that required recognition or respect from others (Gewirth, 1992).

The more contemporary notion of a right as a liberty to act (where there is no prohibition or obligation not to do so) probably comes from the seventeenth-century philosopher, Thomas Hobbes. Hobbes argued that, in a state of nature where there are no laws or governmental bodies, everyone has the natural liberty to do as he or she pleases (Tuck, 1979: 5–7). It is from a Hobbesian notion of liberty that John Locke developed his notion of natural rights. While arguing that each of us has natural rights to liberty, Hobbes recognized that without laws and enforcement mechanisms, most of us would not develop the rational skills to recognize our duty to others to respect their rights. He thus proposed a fairly coercive form of government to restrict our exercise of rights and protect us from each other (Tuck, 1979: 5–7, 119–42). A critic of Hobbes, Samuel Pufendorf, then introduced the argument that rights, by definition, entail duties to respect the rights of others, thus distancing rights theory from the necessity of coercive government (Tuck, 1979: 156–62).

Our present Bill of Rights derives, through Jefferson and others, from Locke. In setting out to distinguish rights of individual citizens from the alleged divine rights of monarchs, Locke links the origin of rights to the "nature" of human beings. While the language of natural rights is disturbing today to some, Locke's arguments form the basis of many of our moral intuitions about rights in general, and, in particular, as we saw in an earlier section, property rights. According to Locke,

> Every man has a property in his own person; this no body has any right to but himself. The labor of his body and the work of his hands we may say are properly his. Whatsoever then he removes out of the state that nature has provided and left it in, he hath mixed his labor with, and joined to it something that is his own, and thereby makes it his property. . . . For this labor being the unquestionable property of the laborer, no man but he can have a right to what this is once joined to, at least where there is enough, and as good left in common for others. (Locke, 1690, 1963: 328–9)

Locke was an early critic of slavery in any form and an early proponent of the argument that, because my work is mine, I cannot be forced to work for another. It is from Locke, then, that the contemporary idea that each of us has rights to ourselves, to survival, to liberty, to our work, and to property derives.

It is thus true that the notions of rights and human rights arrived late in the history of philosophy, and in its present contemporary form, even in the United Nations *Declaration*, certainly originated in Western thinking. This, in itself, is not an argument for or against the universality of rights. In this age of globalization and the pluralism of global communities, however, it does raise cautionary flags that rights talk might not be acceptable in all cultures or have the absolute universal applicability we in the West might imagine.

Individualism, community, rights, and duties

A second critique of rights talk, in particular American rights talk, is "its absoluteness, its hyper-individualism, its insularity, and its silence with respect to personal, civic, and collective responsibilities" (Glendon, 1991). According to Mary Ann Glendon, a critic of rights theory, rights theorists allegedly assume that one of the distinguishing features of a human being is his or her autonomy – the ability to develop and live as an independent "unencumbered" self (Sandel, 1982), a self that has or should enjoy a set of rights. One of these rights is the right to exercise individual liberties as each of us sees fit (Berlin, 1969; Nozick, 1974). Each of us is, or should be, the final authority on who we are, what we care about, and how we direct and focus our lives and projects. This insular individualism, it is contended, flies in the face of the notion that we are social beings, created, nurtured, and dependent upon family, social, community, and cultural relationships (Taylor, 2000: 39–61). A completely independent and unencumbered self would be an empty notion since who we are and how we experience the world depends upon our social encounters (Sandel, 1982). Even the concept "self" is a socially constructed idea, dating back to a tradition beginning probably with the ancient Greek philosopher, Plato.

Rights theorists do not, though, need to rely on radical or insular individualism, and indeed they do not and cannot. Rights make no sense except within social contexts. Someone alone on a desert island could be said to have rights, but it would not matter one way or another, since there would be no one else there either to interfere with or recognize those rights. Rights talk stems from social interrelationships where survival, liberties, security, opportunities, and property either thrive or are threatened. Such interrelationships create obligations between rights claimants and others in two respects. First, rights claims often entail claims against others, that is, one person's rights are often connected with obligations or duties of other persons either to respect those rights or, at a minimum, to leave claimants alone to exercise their liberties. This connection between rights (first-party claims to entitlements or to respect) and obligations of others (second-party duties) contributes to the contention that "when one person has a moral right, some other person or persons have corresponding obligations" (Bentham, 1789, 1950).

Although a number of philosophers contend that every right is defined by, or at least correlated in some way with, a duty of other persons, there are noted exceptions. For example, two equally qualified persons who apply for a job might both have an equal right to that job. If the employer has only one position available, though, he or she does not have an obligation to hire both candidates. Similarly, although a person might feel an obligation to contribute to a charitable organization, such as the Red Cross, that organization does not necessarily have a correlative right to that contribution.

A second way in which rights talk entails interrelated responsibilities and obligations to others is embedded in the very notion of rights. As rights talk has been conceived, a right is an entitlement made on behalf of myself and thus implicitly of every human being, or, in the case of freedom, of every person. In order to legitimize that entitlement, a rights claimant must, therefore, acknowledge that everyone else in his or her community has those same rights, and is entitled to them equally.

To put it another way, "the author [of a rights claim] may not demand any rights or privileges that he or she denies his or her addressee" (Forst, 1999: 44). If so, rights talk would become a form of group or individual manifesto, without regard to the claims or entitlements of others. That would undermine its legitimacy as a generalizable *rights* claim. Rights claims are thus based on social reciprocity of recognizing the equal rights of others as well as generality of application. Any legitimate moral rights claim develops out of and defines boundaries and normative limitations of socially interactive relationships. Rights, therefore, are not merely socially dependent, but are inherently social phenomena that set parameters and standards for our interrelationships in a community (Werhane, 1985; Gewirth, 1978).

Most rights theorists argue that individual rights claims "trump" community interests, at least in the majority of instances (Rawls, 1971; Dworkin, 1977). For example, according to this point of view, it would be wrong to lock up, punish, or kill one innocent person in order to enhance community interests or well being (Dennett, 1978). This is not an argument for hyper-individualism, though, but an argument that contends that in most communities that defend human rights, individual rights claims and the protection of individual rights of all community members usually preempt utilitarian concerns of that community.

Where there does exist a seeming contradiction between individual rights and community interests, rights talk does not inherently undermine or ignore community interests. In times of national security or extreme scarcity rights are often suspended to assure the survival and protection of a community. Rainer Forst nevertheless argues that, even in these crises and even in closed communities, members of that community have what he calls "the right to justification," a right to be given good reasons for what that society practices, enforces, and demands (Forst, 1999). Moreover, the importance of the establishment of individual rights, Sen has argued repeatedly, plays a critical role in national survival. Only through the recognition and protection of individual rights can the communities, in which those individuals exercise their rights, thrive. In fact, studies of less developed countries demonstrate that in those countries that have a functioning democracy that recognizes moral rights, such as India and Botswana, there have never been famines, even though they are poorer than some other countries such as Ethiopia or China (Sen, 1994).

Social construction and mental models

A third criticism of rights talk is linked to the first. Not only is rights theory a late development, but rights talk is also a theoretical construct – based on Western philosophy – that frames our experiences, moral intuitions, and moral judgments. Because individuals are guided by mental models or mindsets that are grounded in their particularized experiences, it might seem that rights talk would be limited to people who share similar mental models.

Since the eighteenth century, when Immanuel Kant postulated that categories or principles of the understanding order and organize our experiences, it has become commonplace to argue that human beings deal with the world through mindsets or mental models, such that "our conceptual scheme[s] mediate even our most basic perceptual experiences" (Railton, 1986: 172). Kant contended that we do not create or construct the content of our experiences, a content that is in constant flux. "Experience" is not merely that ever-changing flow of perceived data in constant flux, for such an ever-changing flow could not constitute experience or knowledge. On the contrary, what we call "experience" is organized, structured, and interconnected by categories of understanding in our minds and imagination. Kant pointed out that a person can never actually *experience* ordering principles such as space, time, cause, effect, size; rather, he or she orders, organizes, and recalls his or her experience according to these principles. According to Kant, these are frames, or "categories," in the mind that organize our experiences spatially and sequentially, synthesize and identify repetitions, account for comparative identifications, and make memory possible. Kant went so far as to argue that what we call knowledge and the source of scientific principles and laws (but not the data of science) are cognitive constructions built into, and thus derived from, our minds (Kant, 1781, 1970).

While contemporary philosophers debate whether our minds are "hard-wired" as Kant envisioned, it is nevertheless commonly (although not universally) concluded that human beings deal with the world through mindsets or mental models. Although the term is not always clearly defined, "mental model" encompasses the notion that human beings have mental representations, or cognitive frames, that model the stimuli or data with which they interact, and these frameworks set up parameters though which experience, or a certain set of experiences, is organized or filtered (Senge, 1990: ch. 10;

Gentner and Whitley, 1997: 210–11; Gorman, 1992; Johnson, 1993; Werhane, 1999). Mental models take the form of schemata that frame the experiences through which individuals process information, conduct experiments, and formulate theories.

Mental models frame all our experiences and pervade our thinking. They enable us to make sense of our experiences and engage in abstract thinking. We do not simply take in experiences as if our minds were receptacles or "blank tablets." Rather, we focus, organize, select, and censor even our simplest perceptions so that all our experiences are framed by complex mindsets or cognitive frames. This is why small children do not learn merely from associating a word with an object. They are unable to use color words correctly, for instance, until they have understood the model or rule that pointing to an object is a reference to a quality – color, not to the object that is colored. Children eventually learn a complex of rules for organizing and ordering their experiences that shape perceptions, focus their experiences, and influence their conceptualization.

Although mental models order our experiences individually, because they are socially learned and constructed, they remain subject to revision and change, from either internal or external stimuli. Because schemata we employ are socially learned and altered through religion, socialization, culture, educational upbringing, and other experiences, they are shared ways of perceiving, organizing, and learning. We are constantly exposed to a myriad of socially constructed mental models that frame, shape, color, and even distort our perceptions, opinions, reasons, and points of view. These include images, theories, assumptions, and perspectives that we are exposed to culturally, socially, through religious and educational training, parental upbringing, peer pressure, media, art, and so on.

Because of the variety and diversity of mental models, "there are multiple possible framings of any given situation" (Johnson, 1993: 202). No mental model is complete in and of itself, so that we end up incorporating multiple overlapping mental models into our thinking and sensemaking. We are able to frame situations, events, and phenomena in multiple ways. How we frame these situations, events, and phenomena matters, though, because "[t]here are . . . different moral consequences depending on the way we frame the situation" (Johnson, 1993: 214). Mental models thus have normative dimensions, because each, as a selective process, is a boundary-creating or boundary-maintaining process. These forms of sensemaking limit the scope, scale, and focus of what we experience, and what is included or left out creates the frame that can also be evaluated from a normative perspective (Weick, 1995; Werhane, 1999).

It thus follows that our rights theories and reasoning about rights have developed from a set of mental models derived from a historically late Western point of view, which is, itself, a collection of mental models. Rights talk is, therefore, one way, but not the only way, to conceptualize our experiences and our moral intuitions, engage in evaluations, and form moral judgments about what we can and should claim for others and ourselves. To argue that moral rights are universal claims to which every human being is entitled is an example of an incomplete, socially constructed, normative frame on which we base our rights claims and judgment about others and other cultures.

MENTAL MODELS AND THE STATUS OF RIGHTS

These three indictments against rights theory, while prescient, are not fatal. One way to think about rights is to argue that rights talk is one evaluative means for attempting to make cross-cultural, cross-historical judgments. At a minimum, moral rights are concepts that help us make judgments about what most of us in every part of the world consider deplorable activities and situations. In other words, they capture what Michael Walzer has called a "thin thread" of agreement, that is, that there is general global (although not absolute) agreement about moral minimums, a consensus about what is "wrongdoing." For example, while we might argue endlessly about what is fairness and what forms of justice are appropriate in various settings, there is widespread agreement about what constitutes injustice. This allows us to set up minimum standards that apply across boundaries and cultures and mental models. Murder, torture, gratuitous imprisonment, slavery and serfdom, not honoring promises or contracts, and disrespect for law and national boundaries are all acts that are commonly thought to be and treated as evil or wrong in almost every culture. Committing these acts is, then, going below a globally agreed upon (although not absolute) moral minimum (Walzer, 1994). While some of that thinking originates from Western philosophy, the result is one that transcends such boundaries.

If there is consensus about these "bads," we can provisionally defend the universal applicability of negative rights – the right not to be harmed, rights not to be murdered, tortured, wrongly imprisoned, enslaved, and so on – as protecting moral minimums. Negative rights are often perceived as minimalist rights because they appear to demand only that each of us refrains from committing such evils. A number of philosophers argue that *only* negative rights are candidates for moral rights, because only negative rights allow the maximum exercise of rights with minimum demands or restraints on the part of others (Nozick, 1974; Maitland, 1990). Even the notion of minimum negative rights raises questions about responsibilities, in particular, the question as to whether or not each of us has responsibilities beyond simply not committing heinous acts ourselves, but also obligations to protect or rescue others when their negative rights are trampled. Moreover, even the minimal exercise of negative rights requires that each of us is capable of choice so as to enjoy a modicum of liberty.

Rights talk, we conclude, is a form of intercultural dialogue aimed at reducing harms and abuses, making human existence tolerable, and establishing those liberties that enable us to develop and enhance our lives. One test for whether a given rights claim should be considered legitimates to ask whether that claim could and/or should be generalizable, that is, whether it could be a candidate for a global moral standard (Hare, 1981). Rights are universal entitlements. Basic rights are provisional candidates for universal principles or standards, standards that are often revised to become more inclusive and farther reaching over time. The United Nations *Universal Declaration on Human Rights* is a normative proposal to be adapted (or not) by all its member countries as a set of standards that serves to ground cross-cultural moral judgments concerning individual, social, institutional, cultural and national conduct. The *Declaration* nevertheless does not claim to defend absolute rights "written in stone," and its rights list is subject to further modification and revision as new concerns rise to global attention.

LEGAL RIGHTS AND MORAL RIGHTS

It is sometimes argued that rights claims make no sense unless they are ideals that people are willing to formalize in law and defend against other ideals or intrusions (Brandt, 1983). We can, though, still distinguish legal rights from moral rights, at least in a secular society such as our own in the United States. Legal and moral rules are not the same, and many laws are derived from our moral intuitions. A difference is that legal rights are identified in rules, laws, or constitutional systems and supported in jurisprudence, case decisions, and through enforcement mechanisms. Where legal rights are not explicitly defined, claims are often made on the basis of legal interpretation – that is, by determination of what should be encompassed by rules or legal systems. The so-called "right to privacy" is a prime example. Although a right to privacy has been interpreted as being implied by the Constitution, no such right is explicitly stated there. Privacy rights have thus been created out of Constitutional interpretations and case law (Warren and Brandeis, 1890).

The difficulty is that laws that spell out legal rights are not always just or fitting laws themselves. Indeed, we must often use other principles in order to understand, justify, or criticize a certain rule or law. For example, despite wording in the Constitution guaranteeing the right to vote for everyone, suffrage for women was not established in the United States until 1922. Moral rights often function as principles or standards to which we can appeal in evaluating laws, legal systems, or legally granted rights. Conversely, not all moral principles we espouse are protected by legal codes (Paine, 1999). Rights talk thus often serves to support challenges to laws.

In the chapters to follow we will argue in defense of employee rights, which, in the United States, have largely not been codified into law or protected by the Constitution. We are therefore arguing from the basis of moral, not legal claims, that employees should be afforded these rights. Such rights might also be legislated, and this would strengthen their enforceability, but that is only the second part of our argument. Our initial concern is for the development of the moral basis for employee rights. If this moral basis is established, then the presence or absence of legal enforceability becomes a secondary concern.

RIGHTS TALK AND THE EMPLOYMENT ANOMALY

We have argued that rights talk derives from socially constructed mental models that ordinarily arise out of social relationships where survival, freedom, property, and other entitlements are at stake. Discussions of rights have tended to focus on individuals interacting with one another, although it is possible to make arguments defending secondary rights claims for institutions and nation states as well (Werhane, 1985). There is often substantial agreement, at least in the United States, about the sorts of rights to which individuals should be entitled. Few people today argue that basic political rights, such as life, freedom, due process, and assembly should not be protected. Interestingly, these rights are assumed to exist between individuals or between individuals and the state. The result is an anomaly in rights talk, at least in the United States. Constitutional guarantees do not extend to private places, such as the home, religious institutions, or the private sector workplace except when there are blatant infractions. Why is this the case?

Reasoning about employment is an outcome of the ways we frame our thinking about political and economic life. This, in turn, is an outcome of another framing or modeling effect. In the United States we tend to compartmentalize or divide our economic life from political life. As we shall point out in chapter 2, the Constitution and Bill of Rights are political documents dealing with civil rights of citizens. Economic phenomena, including employment, are private arrangements not subject to the same constraints as political rights. This results in a dichotomy in the protection and preservation of rights, according to whether the context is considered political (public) or private. This is the so-called public/private distinction, which provides for separate legal treatment depending upon whether rights claims occur in public (political) or private situations. While we value the right to free speech, for example, it is protected only in political/public arenas.

The protection, or lack of protection, afforded free speech has proved particularly controversial. Although public and political free speech is protected, because we do not have similar protections for whistleblowers in many states, they may be summarily fired for uncovering damaging activities, even when those employees are correct. For example, according to court records, Michael Haddle was fired from Healthmaster Inc. for helping federal agents to uncover evidence of corporate fraud. Although the Supreme Court eventually overturned the case, the District Court for the Southern District of Georgia and the Court of Appeals upheld the firing because Haddle was an "at will" employee, under no specific contract with Healthmaster, and could be fired at any time for any reason (*Haddle* v. *Garrison*, 525 U.S. 121, 119 S. Ct. 489, 142 L. Ed. 2d 502 (1999)).

The way we think about, and treat, employees derives, in part, from the distinction between the public and private sectors of the political economy and an economic mental model that has permeated our thinking for some time. What is this model? The language of employment is a language of economic phenomena. Employees are often referred to as "human resources," much like natural resources or manufacturing resources. "Human resource management" is discussed in the same way as agricultural management, forestry, operations management, or financial management. In business schools, faculty teach courses on "Human Resource Management" or "Strategic Human Resource Management," as if we could develop strategies for dealing with people just as we develop strategies for dealing with finance or markets or even race horses. We often tend think of employees as a statistical phenomenon, and, in doing so, we measure them accordingly. When we downsize, therefore, we downsize groups of employees, not individuals.

There is something disturbing about such economic language being used about people. It nevertheless illustrates that, in many companies, employees are measured in at least two ways. First, we hire, promote, transfer, lay off, and fire on the basis of qualifications, job skills, competency, productivity, fit with the organization, retrainability, loyalty, and performance. These are all worthwhile criteria that make sense in the workplace, and, indeed, failure to meet these criteria could serve as good reason for layoffs or firing. At the same time, however, we hire and lay off employees by and large on the basis of costs and savings, and costs of hiring, promotion, demotion, transfer, or layoffs are calculated in terms of gross dollars saved or expended in hiring or laying off x numbers of people. In other words, there are no names or faces when layoffs are done "en masse" (McVea and Freeman, forthcoming).

The "buzzword problems" of the moment are downsizing, rightsizing, and layoffs. In times of economic exigency, layoffs make sense, and can sometimes be justified with good reasons. Such changes are not always justifiable, though, and can often be linked to inadequate foresight. When a company shifts its focus, reorganizes, reengineers, divests or acquires other divisions or companies, or simply streamlines itself, it tends to lay off hoards of employees, as evidenced in the series of layoffs during the past five years. From an economic perspective, employees become the logical target, because they are the largest cost and the easiest to divest. Layoffs are possible when employers do not have specific legal or contractual obligations to employees, and the absence of due process to precede the layoffs is based on conceptions of employees as economic phenomena measured in monetary and statistical terms. But such an approach is inconsistent with measuring the productivity and performance of employees, because layoffs for restructuring reasons are usually conducted on the basis of job redundancy, last hired, obsolete skills, or simply on the basis of reorganization rather than productivity. In these cases, reasons for hiring, promoting, and retaining – ordinarily good reasons – are set aside, and employees are treated as statistical quantitative phenomena measured in terms of their cost.

That this is an anomaly is reflected in the annual report of AT&T, which, in 1996, laid off approximately 40,000 managers. According to CEO Bob Allen, quoted in AT&T's annual report,

> Perhaps most important, [are] the values of Our Common Bond as a guide to doing business. One of those values is Respect for Individuals. We are making an intense effort to live that value now as we go through the difficult process of reducing our skilled and capable work force by about 40,000 jobs, or about 13 percent. (Allen, 1996: 6)

In addition, Allen noted, "It was a year of record sales" (Allen, 1996: 4). AT&T's profits were down, but only because they took a one-time $5 billion charge against earnings "to prepare . . . for the future." As Allen explained, "Good and talented people will be leaving us because they are not a match for our future needs and size" (Allen, 1996: 6).

When a quantitative mental model frames employment thinking, some businesses tend to place employees at the bottom of stakeholder concerns, and rank them in importance after shareholders, customers, and sometimes, even, after top management. There are exceptions, of course. Some small companies, such as Ben and Jerry's and Johnsonville Sausage, and many large companies, such as Motorola, IBM, and Johnson and Johnson, do rank their employees as important stakeholders. There are still companies, though, even those that pay close attention to their employees, such as IBM, who will, in times of restructuring – even without economic exigency – lay off large numbers of employees as the first line of retrenchment.

The compartmentalization of rights talk as political rights, the mental model of employment as an economic phenomenon, and the public/private distinction appear to preclude making sense of rights talk in private sector employment. In the chapters that follow, we will challenge that compartmentalization and inconsistency in applying rights talk, and, in our final chapter, we shall offer an alternative that preserves employee rights by circumventing these prevailing mindsets.

CONCLUSION

The theoretical assumptions of rights theory underlie the project of this book. The workplace is not separate from other spheres of life. Employees everywhere, in every country and culture, whether they are executives, managers, assembly line workers, piece workers, or contingent part-time consultants, share at least one common characteristic: they are all human beings, usually adult moral persons. It thus follows, from the perspective of rights talk, that all employees share and are entitled to certain rights – moral rights – regardless of the particulars of their working conditions, economic exigencies, cultural biases, religious prohibitions, and so on.

If individuals cherish rights in their personal and political lives, should these rights not be valued in their work lives as well? It only makes sense that employees should have the same moral rights to which they are entitled as private individuals, for it is not clear how the process of employment should deprive a person of his or her basic rights.

In the workplace, certain conditions are necessary in order for employees to have rights, construed as the absence of coercion, due process, and self-development. Safety is obviously necessary for self-preservation. Free speech and association (such as through unions) enable development and self-protection. Privacy is also important, as it indicates limiting access to information that influences the individual's future choices. In addition, equal opportunity and procedural due process serve to protect the choices that employees are free to make. At the same time, there are parallel responsibilities of employees not to harm, defame, or subvert the workplace, and thereby interfere with the freedom of other employees or the organization.

While this seems fairly straightforward in theory, the reality is that the American workplace today often fails to recognize even the most basic employee rights. Our purpose in the pages that follow is to emphasize the importance of such rights and show how they can be recognized, preserved, and protected. We shall explore how we can change prevailing mindsets, so that both employees and employers can move toward instituting and protecting important rights of all individuals in the employment context.

NOTES

1. We borrow this term from Mary Ann Glendon from her 1991 book *Rights Talk*.
2. Rights, or at least basic rights, are sometimes called *natural rights*. A natural right is a right that is neither conventional nor institutional (Locke, 1690, 1963). It can neither be created nor artificially conferred – it is a right that everyone possesses just because he or she is human. Natural rights were once thought to be God-given, or somehow genetically instilled in the nature of human beings. Since to engage in such discussion is highly speculative and would distract us from our purposes here, we refer to *natural rights* simply as *human rights* (see Tuck, 1979, for more information regarding the origins of rights).
3. There are some who also defend rights of animals and other sentient beings. Although these might be worthwhile arguments, we are not addressing such arguments here.
4. It follows that providing company housing and paying workers in script to be redeemed at company stores, a common practice in the mining industry in the late nineteenth and early twentieth centuries in this country, represent forms of serfdom, because a person could not choose to do what he or she would like to do with his or her earnings.
5. Some who argue from this line of thinking push the analogy to claim that rights talk is a form of neocolonialism, "a tool which Western, capitalist states use to politically and culturally dominate other societies" (Forst, 1999: 35). Whether or not this claim has any validity is not addressed, since we are focused here on discussing employment primarily within an American (i.e., Western) context.

REFERENCES

Articles, books, and other similar publications

Allen, Robert. 1996. *AT&T 1995 Annual Report.*

Bentham, Jeremy. 1789, 1950. *Theory of Legislation.* London: Routledge and Kegan Paul.

Berlin, Isaiah. 1969. *Four Essays on Liberty.* London: Oxford University Press.

Brandt, Richard. 1983. "The Concept of a Moral Right and its Function." *Journal of Philosophy*, vol. 80: 40–8.

Dennett, Daniel. 1978. *Brainstorms.* Montgomery, VT: Bradford Books.

Dworkin, Ronald. 1977. *Taking Rights Seriously.* Cambridge, MA: Harvard University Press.

Forst, Rainer. 1999. "The Basic Right to Justification: Toward a Constructivist Conception of Human Rights." *Constellations*, vol. 6: 35–60.

Friedman, Milton. 1952. *Capitalism and Freedom.* Chicago: University of Chicago Press.

Gauthier, David. 1987. *Morals by Agreement.* New York: Oxford University Press.

Gentner, Dedre and Whitley Eric W. 1997. "Mental Models of Population Growth." In Max Bazerman, David Messick, Ann Tenbrunsel, and Kimberley A. Wade-Benzoni, eds., *Environment, Ethics, and Behavior.* San Francisco: New Lexington Press, 209–33 .

Gewirth, Alan. 1978. *Reason and Morality.* Chicago: University of Chicago Press.

Gewirth, Alan. 1992. "Right, Concepts of." In Lawrence C. Becker and Charlotte B. Becker, eds., *Encyclopedia of Ethics.* New York: Garland, 1101–9.

Gewirth, Alan. 1996. *The Community of Rights.* Chicago: University of Chicago Press.

Glendon, Mary Ann. 1991. *Rights Talk.* New York: Free Press.

Gorman, Michael. 1992. *Simulating Science.* Bloomington, IN: Indiana University Press.

Hare, R. M. 1981. *Moral Thinking.* Oxford: Oxford University Press.

Johnson, Mark. 1993. *Moral Imagination.* Chicago: University of Chicago Press.

Kant, Immanuel. 1781; 1970. *Critique of Pure Reason.* Trans. Norman Kemp Smith. London: Macmillan.

Kipnis, Kenneth. 1997. "Property, Rights to." In Patricia H. Werhane and R. Edward Freeman, eds. *The Encyclopedic Dictionary of Business Ethics.* Oxford: Blackwell, 523–6.

Locke, John. 1690, 1963. *Two Treatises f Government*, ed. Peter Laslett. Cambridge: Cambridge University Press.

MacPherson, C. B. 1973. *Democratic Theory.* Oxford: Clarendon Press.

Maitland, Ian. 1990. "Rights in the Workplace: A Nozickian Argument." In Lisa Newton and Maureen Ford, eds., *Taking Sides.* Guilford, CT: Dushkin Publishing Group, 33–7.

Marx, Karl. 1844, 1963. *The Economic and Philosophic Manuscripts of 1844.* New York: McGraw-Hill Book Company.

McVea, John and R. Edward Freeman. Forthcoming. "Names and Faces."

Nozick, Robert. 1974. *Anarchy, State, and Utopia.* New York: Basic Books.

Paine, Lynn S. 1999. "Law, Ethics, and Managerial Judgment." In Robert E. Frederick, ed., *A Companion to Business Ethics.* Malden, MA: Blackwell, 194–206.

Railton, Peter. 1986. "Moral Realism." *Philosophical Review*, vol. 95: 168–75.

Rawls, John. 1971. *A Theory of Justice*. Cambridge, MA: Harvard University Press.

Sandel, Michael J. 1982. *Democracy's Discontent*. Cambridge, MA: Harvard University Press.

Sen, Amartya. 1990. "Justice: Means versus Freedoms." *Philosophy and Public Affairs*, vol. 19: 111–22.

Sen, Amartya. 1992. *Inequality Reexamined*. Cambridge: Cambridge University Press.

Sen, Amartya. 1994. "Freedom and Needs." *The New Republic*, January 10–17: 31–8.

Sen, Amartya. 1999. *Development as Freedom*. New York: Oxford University Press.

Senge, Peter. 1990. *The Fifth Discipline*. New York: Doubleday.

Shue, Henry. 1980. *Basic Rights*. Princeton, NJ: Princeton University Press.

Smith, Adam, 1776, 1976. *The Wealth of Nations*. Ed. R. H. Campbell and A. S. Skinner. Oxford: Oxford University Press.

Sterk, Stewart E. "The Continuity of Legislatures: Of Contracts and the Contracts Clause." *Columbia Law Review*, vol. 88: 647–722.

Taylor, Humphrey. 2000. "The Mood of American Workers," *The Harris Poll*, 4, January 19: http:/www.harrisinteractive.com/harris_poll/index.asp?PID=5.

Tuck, Richard. 1979. *Natural Rights Theories*. Cambridge: Cambridge University Press.

Tully, James. 1980. *A Discourse on Property: John Locke and His Adversaries*. Cambridge: Cambridge University Press.

Walzer, Michael. 1994. *Thick and Thin*. Notre Dame, IN: Notre Dame University Press.

Warren, Samuel D. and Louis D. Brandeis. 1890. "The Right to Privacy." *Harvard Law Review*, vol. 4: 193–220.

Weick, Karl. 1995. *Sensemaking in Organizations*. Thousand Oaks, CA: Sage Publications.

Werhane, Patricia H. 1985. *Persons, Rights, and Corporations*. Englewood Cliffs, New Jersey: Prentice-Hall, Inc.

Werhane, Patricia H. 1991. *Adam Smith and his Legacy for Modern Capitalism*. New York: Oxford University Press.

Werhane, Patricia H. 1999. "Justice and Trust." *Journal of Business Ethics*, vol. 21: 237–49.

Case

Haddle v. *Garrison*, 525 U.S. 121, 119 S. Ct. 489, 142 L. Ed. 2d 502 (1999).

chapter two

The Public/Private Distinction and Its Influence on Employment Practices

At the heart of the way we think about the American workplace lies the public/private distinction. This distinction between the public and private spheres of life is deeply rooted in American tradition. It circumscribes our relations with one another and frames our expectations of the government, just as it emerged out of our forefathers' preconceptions about what government could and should be. The public/private distinction defines our legal existence:

> Nothing is more central to our experience in American culture than the split between public and private. It is the premise, which lies at the foundation of American legal thought, and it shapes the way in which we relate to each other in our daily lives. We consistently take for granted that there is both a public realm and a private realm. In the private realm we assume that we operate within a protected sphere of autonomy, free to make self-willed individual choices and to feel secure against the encroachment of others. Private law, for example contract law, serves as a helpmate in this realm, facilitating and securing the autonomous world of private decision-making. In contrast, the public realm is a world of government institutions, obliged to serve the public interest rather than private aims. For the most part the public realm is accountable to the private and obligated to limit its intrusion into the world of private choice. Occasionally, however, it is supposed to override the private sphere, either to serve a greater public good or to solve problems that are poorly handled by private decision-making. (Freeman and Mensch, 1987: 237)

This distinction divides a person's life into a "public" sphere, which falls within the bounds of government purview and regulation, and a "private" sphere, which falls outside those bounds. This notion undergirds much of the thinking upon which the Constitution is based, and reveals our forefathers' concern with protecting the individual from state encroachment. The distinction gained momentum and became more prevalent with the industrial revolution, as private corporations, distinguishing themselves from state institutions, struggled to find their footing within the American legal system. The public/private distinction has become a model that we accept and perpetuate through our culture, jurisprudence, and practices.

The public/private distinction dates back several centuries. As the power of the state increased with the emergence of the nation-state during the sixteenth and seventeenth centuries, so did the quest to stake out a private sphere of life protected from state intrusion. It grew out of the desire to distinguish individuals from the state and to protect them and their property from public, governmental interference. Political philosophers such as John Locke and John Stuart Mill articulated theories that drew heavily upon the alleged public/private distinction in order to constrain state power, particularly with regard to religion and property (Horwitz, 1982; Locke, 1764, 1986; Mill, 1859, 1963; Mill, 1848, 1963).

It was not until the nineteenth century, though, that the public/private distinction began to play a particularly influential role in American legal discourse. The tension between the "private" business corporation and the "public" governmental institution culminated in the landmark case, *Trustees of Dartmouth College* v. *Woodward*, 17 U.S. (4 Wheat.) 518, 559, 669–73 (1819), decided in 1819. In *Dartmouth*, Justice Story offered a memorable concurring opinion directed at liberating private enterprises from public scrutiny:

> Another division of corporations is into public and private. Public corporations are generally esteemed such as exist for public political purposes only, such as towns, cities, parishes, and counties; and in many respects they are so, although they involve some private interests; but strictly speaking, public corporations are such only as are founded by the government for public purposes, where the whole interests belong also to the government. (*Dartmouth College* at 668–9)

Prior to this decision, municipal and trading corporations had been treated alike as arms of the state and regulated by public law.

While the public/private distinction was originally intended to protect the individual from the state, it underlies much of our thinking about life and society in general. It is a mental model that has infiltrated many of our early views about property arrangements and about how institutions and individuals interact. It has since been used to distinguish between public and private ownership, free enterprise and public policy, publicly- and privately-held corporations, and even between public and private employees. In addition, it has played a significant part in the shaping of the American workplace. Employment law and business law are predicated upon this model. And it is because of this model that we have attempted to treat dimensions of our lives, such as public and private workplaces, according to different standards.

On the one hand, the public/private distinction has served to insulate private employers from excessive governmental scrutiny or regulation. Unfortunately, it has also translated into a license for private employers to treat their employees however they choose, without regard for the constitutional rights provided to public employees. The result is a serious, and arguably inequitable, dichotomy between public and private employment. While, in most cases, the public and private sectors can be virtually indistinguishable as business enterprises, their treatment of employees can be quite different.

PROPERTY INTERESTS AND THE PUBLIC/PRIVATE DISTINCTION

The primary contribution of the public/private distinction has been to divide the workplace into disparate "public" and "private" sectors. The distinction frames, and, some will argue, limits, our thinking about employment. While the same sort of work takes place in both types of workplaces, the nature of the employment relationships in each sector differs markedly. Despite some degree of overlap, the actual rights and responsibilities differ between the two sectors. "Public" employment, that is, employment in local, state, and national government departments and their agencies, falls within the province of the Constitution and federal oversight. "Private" employment, on the other hand – employment in non-government-owned entities such as for-profit corporations – remains virtually immune to Constitutional considerations and many legislative strictures.

From a philosophical perspective, theories of property and contract underlie this dichotomy. Private property interests are rooted in the financial investment of corporate shareholders along with corporations' development and acquisition of tangible and intangible property. At the same time, employment is inherently contractual – an agreement between rational adults that entails a promise by an employer to pay for services the employee promises to perform. The presence of private property interests and the emergence of free enterprise have led American courts to adopt a relatively hands-off attitude toward corporate activities, and to fall back upon contractual treatment of the employer–employee relationship.

The United States free enterprise system is, in part, originally based on a Lockean notion of private property, although property arrangements today are dramatically different from what Locke had in mind. Today, it is often unclear where "private" property and ownership end and "public" property and ownership begin. "The process of drawing the line between private and public is neither natural nor automatic," asserts Alan Wolfe. "The line is drawn differently in different times and different places, and law, including corporate law, is one of the major mechanisms by which it is drawn" (Wolfe, 1993: 1683).

Similarly, within the workplace, ownership and control are often divided – at least ostensibly. The truth of the matter is that there tends to be significant overlap between those who own stock, and those who participate in corporations as employees and managers. Corporate assets are nevertheless "held" by an ever-changing group of individual and institutional shareholders, some of whom are also employees. It is no longer always true that owners exercise any real sense of control over their property and its management. Moreover, such complex property relationships are spelled out and guaranteed by the state. This has prompted at least one scholar to argue that "private property" should be defined as "certain patterns of human interaction underwritten by public power" (Cohen, 1933, 1954; Hale, 1923; Brest, 1982).

This fuzziness surrounding the "privacy" of property is exacerbated by the way we use the term "public" in analyzing the status of businesses, and, in particular, corporations. For example, we distinguish between privately owned business corporations and government-owned or controlled, "public" institutions. Among those companies that are *not* government-owned, we distinguish between regulated "public" utilities, whose stock is owned by private individuals and institutions, and "publicly held" corporations, those corporations whose stock is traded publicly, who are governed by special Securities and Exchange Commission (SEC) regulations and whose financial statements are public knowledge. We also distinguish between publicly-held enterprises and privately-held companies, entrepreneurships, and small businesses, which are owned by an individual or group of individuals, and are not available for public stock purchase.

There are also substantive similarities between government-owned, public institutions and privately owned organizations. When the air controllers went on strike in the 1980s, Ronald Reagan fired them, and declared that, as public employees, they could not strike because it jeopardized the public safety (Johnson, 1981). More recently, President Bush and his administration have interceded in various ways subsequent to the hijackings of American airplanes on September 11, 2001, in an effort to ensure public safety. Business-people and homeowners were temporarily prevented from accessing their property and possessions, and travel in downtown New York, even for residents, was severely limited. Since September 11, airports have suffered from increased oversight – the American Airlines terminal at JFK International Airport was even closed temporarily on several occasions during late October and early November of 2001, when it was determined that proper safety precautions were not being followed.

Such actions underscore the inherent interconnectedness of the public and private spheres of our lives. The government intervenes not only where physical safety is at stake, but for other societal reasons as well. For example, Congress recently approved public funds to be donated to the airline industry in order to help bail it out of the financial obstacles it currently faces. While the events of September 11 certainly exacerbated the situation, the truth of the matter is that the industry was already struggling in the wake of increasing fuel costs and decreased travel. The government intervened because, while the airlines are privately owned, they serve the public and everyone is hurt – not just the airlines themselves – when they suffer.

An interesting debate in this regard stems from "public/private" takings, which conflate the distinction between public and private even further. A "taking" occurs when the government appropriates private property, such as when a new road is being built and the homeowners living on that land are compelled to sell their homes to the local government and move. The American legal principle of "eminent domain" provides for this sort of usurpation of private property when for the public good. As it was originally conceived, eminent domain is a legal construct taken from the Constitutional right of the local, state, and federal governments "to take private property for public use . . . following the payment of just compensation to the owner of that property" (Timmons and Womack, 1999/2000: 44). According to the Fifth Amendment, government may take over private property, as long as it is for a public purpose and fair compensation is paid.

In a growing number of instances, the definition of "public use" has been expanded to justify taking private property from one group of people for use by another private entity. In what have been labeled "public/private takings," private property (land) is taken by a municipality, and then handed over to another private entity for economic development. Technically, these fall within the category of legal "takings" by the government, provided for by the Fifth Amendment. They are non-traditional, though, in that they are "public/private" takings, because it is not the government who actually uses the property it takes over.

This occurred most notably in 1981, when General Motors (GM) wanted to expand by building a plant in what was called the "Poletown" area of Detroit. Poletown was an old Detroit Polish neighborhood. The site was favorable because it was near transportation facilities and there was a good supply of labor. To build the plant, however, GM had to displace residents in a nine-block area. The Poletown Neighborhood Council objected, but the Supreme Court of Michigan decided in favor of GM, and held that the state could condemn property for private use, with proper compensation to owners, when it served public interests (*Poletown Neighborhood Council* v. *Detroit*, 410 Mich. 616, 304 N.W.2d 455 (1981)). What is particularly interesting about this case is that GM is not a government-owned corporation, and its primary goal is profitability, not the common good. The Supreme Court of Michigan nevertheless decided that it was in the public interest for Detroit to use its authority to allow a company to take over property in spite of the protesting of the property owners (Lebowitz, 1983).

Since the Poletown decision a number of eminent domain cases have been decided in favor of invoking the right to eminent domain to take property from one group of individuals in order to hand it over to another group or entity. In 1997, Hurst, Texas allowed a few hundred homeowners to be displaced, with compensation for a new shopping mall, even though the displaced homeowners protested (Mansnerus, 1997). In Kansas, the courts ruled that Kansas City could use eminent domain to condemn private property to allow a private company to build a NASCAR race track (Dauner and Nicely, 1998).

In another case, the New Jersey Supreme Court acknowledged the trickiness of these "public/private" takings and asserted that, even where a public purpose is served, existing property interests must be carefully examined before the implementation of a proposed taking:

> Generally, when the exercise of eminent domain results in a substantial benefit to specific and identifiable private parties, "a court must inspect with heightened scrutiny a claim that the public interest is the predominant interest being advanced" . . . The power of eminent domain must always be exercised in the public interest and without favor to private interests [citations omitted]. (*City of Atlantic City* v. *Cynwynd Investments*, 148 N.J. 55 (1997))

In spite of the demand for careful consideration, the property in question was condemned and the owners were compelled to relinquish their land in favor of the improved road access to the Sands Casino.

More recently, in July 2001, seven property owners in New London, Connecticut, confronted the notion of "public/private takings" head on. They went to court, for their own reasons, but also to challenge the widespread use of eminent domain in cities across the country to force property owners to turn over their land to private developers (Mansnerus, 2001a). In this instance, it was a good tiding that has turned sour. In 1998, Pfizer, a large and prosperous pharmaceutical *Fortune* 20 company, had moved to the area – the fourth poorest city in Connecticut – and agreed to develop an abandoned industrial site to house a research division (Mansnerus, 2001b). The city then decided to take advantage of this initiative to redevelop surrounding areas for the existing population as well as the population to arrive. An agent for the city negotiated with as many property owners as could be convinced to sell their land and an attempt was made to remove the rest of the property owners through the exercise of eminent domain.

Although this case is still being litigated, it is mirrored across the country by similar situations. Regardless of the outcome, it evidences the continued "scrambling" of public and private interests (Lebowitz, 1983). This sort of approach is setting a precedent, according to which many municipalities are operating, and it is framing the expectations of many private individuals and entities. Even though not every situation gets to court, and not every initiative is sanctioned by the court, the conflation of public and private interests is increasing. Donald Trump even tried (though he ultimately failed) to get private shop-owners to relinquish their property in Atlantic City for his casino by appealing to eminent domain (Danitz, 1998). Such situations underscore the reality that there is no longer, if there ever was, a bright-line dichotomy between what is "private" and what is "public."

THE ROLE OF TECHNOLOGY IN PROPERTY INTERESTS AND PRIVACY

Advances in technology further complicate the scenario. Our growing dependence on technology and our increasing reliance upon it for both personal and professional applications create significant challenges to our traditional notions of individual privacy. Several decades ago, Gerald Frug commented "developments in the twentieth century have significantly undermined the 'privateness' of modern business corporations, with the result that the traditional bases for distinguishing them from public corporations have largely disappeared" (Frug, 1980: 1129). Technology adds to the confusion of these distinctions.

The rise of Internet and e-mail has enhanced communication in ways we barely anticipated. We can now engage in real-time communication that transcends both temporal and geographic barriers. People are able to remain in contact with a wider range of friends, family, and colleagues, and the nature of that contact is tremendously enhanced. E-mail enables the transmission of multimedia presentations, in addition to text, documents, and images, and a wide array of business transactions can be taken care of over the Internet. Although e-mail was introduced as an intra-organizational mechanism, it has since evolved into a unifying device for individuals and organizations around the world (Beeson, 1998).

As a result of the prevalence of the Internet, in both the public and private arenas, most workplaces today are "wired." Many firms regularly conduct business via e-mail and the Internet. Leading corporations, such as Sony and Palm, conduct real time customer service through "chat" lines. In addition, virtually every financial institution offers customers the opportunity to make transactions over the Internet. E-mail plays a valued role in business settings in that it enables employees to maximize workplace efficiency. It allows them to interact more efficiently and effectively with clients, fellow employees, and business associates, such as through the exchange of group memos and business plans (Griffin, 1991). The use of e-mail by people for non-business related purposes is increasing as well (Schnaitman, 1998/1999). Not only is e-mail instantaneous, like a phone call, and available day and night, but it also allows for the same message to be sent simultaneously to multiple recipients, no matter where they are located or when they will have the opportunity to view the message (Lewin, 1996).

Although e-mail offers an array of benefits, it is accompanied by a number of potential drawbacks. A controversy has emerged between employees who regard their e-mail messages as personal and, therefore, private, and employers who contend that they have legitimate business justifications for monitoring (Lehman, 1997). In addition, concerns surrounding e-mail in the workplace relate to its universal application and the security of the content of the message. Like telephone communication, e-mail often takes place throughout the day, and this causes employees' public and private lives to become intertwined. It is no longer the case that what is "personal" is left behind when employees enter the workplace. This is especially true in situations where employees work long hours at the office, which forces them to conduct some of their personal business from the workplace (Higgins, 1999). Tension is thus created between employees who want to keep their personal lives (and messages) private, and employers who seek to keep the work environment free from any situation that might affect the company adversely (White, 1997).

These problems translate into tangible costs for employers. Citibank, for example, spent more than $10 million to restore its computer network after it was compromised by a Russian crime group (Goodman, 1997; Gripman, 1997). Real dollars are also lost in employee time. According to a 1999 survey by SurfWatch Software, an Internet filtering firm, nearly a third of employees' Internet use in the workplace is recreational. Companies pay for Internet access twice: they spend $3.5 billion for Internet access on the job, and then lose up to $1.1 billion a year in lost productivity (Westover, 2001). In addition, according to a survey by myjob-search.com, three out of four workers admitted to sending personal e-mails from work, and they indicated they absolutely did not want their bosses to see more than 50 percent of those messages (Westover, 2001).

Employee e-mail monitoring procedures have been implemented by employers largely to minimize their exposure to, and insulate them from liability for, employee wrongdoing, such as that which occurs through sexually harassing messages (Kaplan, 1998), excessive use of e-mail for personal reasons, and illegal activities conducted via the Internet (White, 1997). Employers are becoming increasingly concerned about their employees' conduct, because an employer can be held responsible for the acts of employees' negligent activities (Nowak, 1999). For example, an employer can be held liable for a sexually charged work environment, caused or exacerbated by sexually explicit e-mail messages exchanged between employees, even if the employer has no actual knowledge of those messages. E-mail messages provide a record of proof of conduct (Araneo, 1996). In addition, since an estimated $370 billion a year is lost through employee theft, employers often use electronic monitoring to prevent such conduct, and to protect trade secrets and other intangible property (Flanagan, 1994).

The result is that employers have taken it upon themselves to monitor employees' e-mail and Internet usage. The same technology that enables employees to make use of e-mail and the Internet, enables employers to both limit that usage and to monitor it (Brown and Raysman, 1998; *Restuccia* v. *Burk Technology, Inc.*, 95-2125 Lexis 367 (Mass. Super. Aug. 12, 1996)).

Although electronic monitoring, or "snooping," calls into question the privacy rights of employees, the courts and legislatures have determined that employers do have the right to monitor their employees (*Bourke* v. *Nissan Motor Co.*, No. B068704 (Cal. Ct. App. July 26, 1993)). The right is technically linked to the employer's ownership (or management) of the technology equipment (i.e., computer, server, telephone lines, and so on). In this way, employers have been afforded a virtual carte blanche.

The controversy persists. Employers continue to assert their right to monitor their workplaces, and employees continue to argue that such measures violate their privacy. And questions emerge regarding how this affects trust, loyalty, and good faith in the workplace. Regardless, according to a survey by Websense.com, a provider of Internet management solutions, 82 percent of companies have a written Internet use policy, and more than 50 percent of all companies now monitor Internet use and e-mail (Westover, 2001). Many employees are on notice that, since they do not own the technology, they do not have electronic privacy in the workplace, and they should adjust their behavior accordingly.

While any number of objections can be made, it is important to notice how the situation reflects the underlying conflation of the private and public spheres of our lives. The controversy erupting regarding workplace electronic monitoring is merely symptomatic of a much larger problem, that is, our continuing reliance on a dichotomy that is no longer applicable.

FURTHER EVIDENCE OF THE BLURRINESS OF THE DISTINCTION

Both private and public institutions run transportation, control banks, and own property. While the goals of private and public institutions differ somewhat, in that public institutions supposedly place the public good ahead of profit maximization, trends in business are pointing toward socially responsible business practices. Interestingly, businesses are finding out first-hand that they can actually achieve profit maximization by focusing their private efforts outward – to the public. "Doing well by doing good" seems to be a management mantra that is rapidly gaining momentum, both in scholarship and in practice (Collins and Porras, 1994).

The actual gap between private enterprises and governmental organizations is narrowing. In addition to the support for socially responsible business practices, public institutions are looking toward private organizations as role models in their effort to become more efficient and increasingly accountable. PricewaterhouseCoopers has even set up an endowment, "The Business of Government," that explores and exploits this interconnectivity through the ongoing sponsorship of scholarly research and conferences at the intersection of the supposed public/private "distinction."

James B. Atleson underscores this basic untenability of the public/private distinction:

> The essence of the public/private distinction is the conviction that it is possible to conceive of social and economic life apart from government and law, indeed that it is impossible or dangerous to conceive of it any other way. The core ideological function served by the public/private distinction is to deny that the practices comprising the private

> sphere of life – the worlds of business, education and culture, the community, and the family – are inextricably linked to and at least partially constituted by politics and law. Denying the role of politics – the processes by which communities organize and institutionalize their self-directive capacities – in constituting the forms and structure of social life is a way of impeding access to an understanding of the role of human agency in constructing the world. The primary effect of the public/private distinction is thus to inhibit the perception that the institutions in which we live are the product of human design and can therefore be changed. (Atleson, 1985: 841)

The public and private spheres of our lives overlap and interconnect. In many ways, it is counterintuitive even to try to divide our lives into separate spheres.

 PRIVATE VS. PUBLIC EMPLOYMENT 

In spite of the shortcomings of the public/private distinction, it continues to frame our disparate treatment of employees in the United States. Private employees who do not have protection from dismissal without cause are considered "employees-at-will." This means that for these cases employers and employees are treated as potential bargainers who have the opportunity to negotiate whatever sorts of arrangements they believe will further their interests and create satisfactory employment relationships. American courts see it as their responsibility to interpret and enforce the terms of such arrangements, since the majority of all employees in the private sector are "at-will" employees.

In the absence of employment contracts, collective bargaining arrangements, or applicable legislation, however, "employment-at-will" (EAW) usually precludes court intervention. The assumption is that the potential bargainers have elected not to agree to a specific arrangement, and, therefore, that there are no contractual terms to enforce. The de facto agreed-to relationship is then one where neither the employer nor the employee has any unusual rights or duties, and one where either the employer or the employee can terminate the employment relationship at any time without justification or notice. In *Gladden* v. *Arkansas Children's Hospital*, 728 S.W.2d 501 (Ark. 1987), for example, an Arkansas court held that hospital employees were "at-will" and could be fired at any time for any reason, even though the employer hospital's manuals described methods for dismissal under certain circumstances.

More recently, the California Supreme Court, usually known for favoring employees, upheld an arrangement as "at-will." According to the case, John Guz was terminated by Bechtel in 1993, after 22 years of service, allegedly as part of a workforce restructuring. At Bechtel, Guz had earned merit raises, received promotions, and earned favorable performance evaluations. Guz, age 50 at the time of the dismissal, claimed that he was fired because of his age. The California Supreme Court, overturning the Court of Appeals, ruled that Guz was an "at-will" employee, and, in the absence of a contract with Bechtel, the dismissal was justified (*Guz* v. *Bechtel Nat'l Inc.*, 8 P. 3d 1089 (Cal. 2000)).

Public employment relationships differ from private employment relationships in that public employers (local, county, state, and national governments) are required to abide by government mandates such as those spelled out in the Constitution. Public employers are, for example, required to respect employee rights to free speech. Justification and notice are required by employees and employers prior to termination of public employment relationships by either party. When conflicts arise regarding public employees, courts intervene not only with regard to specific contractual terms but also to protect rights afforded by federal and state legislation, as in *Messano* v. *Board of Education*, 161 A.2d 475 (N.J. 1960), where a New Jersey court invalidated a mandatory retirement age for noninstructional employees.

The nature of employment in the United States thus varies according to its status as private or public. Private employment is dictated primarily by EAW, limited only by specific state statutes and small number of federal regulations. Private employees are not considered to have many protected rights. Public employees, on the other hand, are protected by the Constitution and Bill of Rights, along with other federal and state statutes.

CONSTITUTIONAL GUARANTEES AND FEDERAL LEGISLATION

Many people mistakenly suppose that the rights enumerated in the United States Constitution, including the rights to free speech, assembly, and a fair trial, ordinarily thought of as moral as well as legal rights, automatically extend to the workplace. This is not the case, however. In the United States, constitutional guarantees apply only to interactions between persons or institutions and the state – they do not extend to the private sector or to the home, except in extreme instances. Employment relationships, and, in particular, relationships between employers and employees in the private sector of the economy, are considered voluntary private contractual relationships between consenting parties, and the Constitution was not intended to interfere with these sorts of relationships.

It is important to keep in mind the historical context within which the Constitution was drafted. At that time, government was feared. The bicameral system of federalism was introduced to combat some of that fear. The clear intent of the drafters was to keep the government in check. The role of the Constitution, then, was to protect people from encroachments by the government – the need to protect individuals from one another was simply not anticipated, at least not by that document.

The Constitution and Bill of Rights bind public employers and at least offer guidance for private employers. Employers, particularly public employers, must adhere to the dictates of the Constitution. For an employee, public or private, to be able to make a successful Constitutional claim, though, he or she must be able to show the involvement of state action. While this is clearly not an insurmountable barrier, it is one with content. In addition, the employee must be able to identify a private right of action implied in the particular Constitutional provision, and it must not be barred by sovereign immunity (Larson, 2001).

The Fifth and Fourteenth Amendments of the Constitution are usually interpreted as creating a property interest in employment under certain circumstances. In the absence of contrary legislation, an employee can be said to have a protected property interest in employment where rules exist that stem from independent sources, such as state law, the terms of an employment contract, or guarantees contained in a firm manual. Where such rules exist, an employee can be said to have a legitimate entitlement to his or her job through a property interest protected against deprivation without due process.

The Fourth Amendment is called upon for protection from unreasonable searches and seizures. This right is most frequently asserted to protect public employees from mandatory drug and alcohol testing. Employees are protected from the searches themselves, as well as from the consequences of such searches, which could involve undesirable employment decisions.

Courts have also recognized privacy claims emanating from the various penumbras of the Bill of Rights and the Fourteenth Amendment. Such a right protects employees from employers' interference regarding decisions such as marriage, child-bearing, polygraph testing, and so on. This right can also be asserted with regard to drug and alcohol testing.

A number of federal pieces of legislation have been enacted by Congress that also govern employment relationships. A wave of federal legislation that has had a significant impact on private employment began with the passing of Title VII of the Civil Rights Act of 1964, which prohibits the discrimination of employees on the basis of "race, color, religion, sex, or national origin" (*Title VII of the Civil Rights Act of 1964*, 42 U.S.C.S. 2000e-2(a)). It was followed by the *Age Discrimination in Employment Act* (ADEA), 29 U.S.C.S. 621-634, the *Pregnancy Discrimination Act* (PDA), 42 U.S.C.S. 2000e(k), and the employment provisions of the *Americans with Disabilities Act* (ADA), 42 U.S.C.S. 12112. Together, such legislation demonstrates Congress' recognition that there are limits to EAW, and that the default rule cannot, and should not, be used as a license to disregard fundamental rights. All of these acts, and others, such as the *Family and Medical Leave Act* (FMLA), 29 U.S.C.S. 2601, afford degrees of protection to both public and private employees. In other words, while employers are afforded a significant amount of leeway with regard to how they design and regulate their workplaces, they are not completely free to trample upon every right of their employees.

Sections 1981 and 1985 of the Reconstruction Statute also offer protection to employees – public, and, to some degree, private as well. Section 1981 protects employees from discrimination, including harassment and discriminatory termination, in situations that occur subsequent to the formation of the employment relationship. The court in *Taitt* v. *Chemical Bank*, 849 F.2d 775 (2d Cir. 1988) found in favor of the employee, who had performed well for more than 20 years, but was then rated poorly and discharged shortly after he objected to two successive settlement offers to a class action suit brought by a fellow employee on behalf of black bank officers. Section 1981 was also invoked in *Spriggs* v. *Diamond Auto Glass*, 165 F.3d 1015 (4th Cir. 1999) with regard to racial harassment and retaliation against an at-will employee. Similarly, in *Fadeyi* v. *Planned*

Parenthood Assoc. of Lubbock, 160 F.3d 1048 (5th Cir. 1998), the court held that an at-will is sufficient for the sort of "contractual" relationship necessary to enable an employee to maintain an action under Section 1981. It remains interesting, though, how EAW, which is essentially the absence of a contract, is interpreted as a contract for the purposes here.

Section 1985, rarely invoked in employment-related situations, nevertheless operates to afford protection from interference by conspiracies with civil rights, including the right to hold and discharge the duties of any office of the United States, the right to participate freely in federal court proceedings as a party, witness, or juror, and the right to equal protection of the laws.

In *Haddle v. Garrison*, for example, an at-will employee was fired as a result of his having participated in grand jury proceedings, through a conspiracy intended to deter him from testifying in the federal court trial (*Haddle* v. *Garrison*, 525 U.S. 121, 119 S. Ct. 489, 142 L. Ed. 2d 502 (1999)). The United States Supreme Court held that an employee, even an at-will employee, could not be fired where the goal was to interfere with rights protected by Section 1985, such as the right to participate freely in federal court proceedings.

THE ROLE OF STATE REGULATION 

The public/private distinction in employment is further complicated by our system of federalism. While public employment is regulated on the federal level, private employment is regulated primarily by the states. Different states have thus contributed to the legal framework that governs public and private employment. A number of states have passed legislation that parallels federal guarantees. There are, for example, state statutes that protect employees' free speech and privacy. In addition, a number of states have passed civil rights legislation that protect employees from discrimination on the basis of race, sex, color, religion, or national origin. Some states have gone even further than the federal legislation, in protecting employees from discrimination on the basis of their sexual orientation.

Many states have side-stepped EAW to recognize employee rights, such as in the area of privacy, by passing statutes on issues ranging from workplace discrimination to drug-testing. A few states, such as Colorado, North Dakota, and Nevada, have enacted statutes barring employers from firing employees for legal off-work activity. A handful of jurisdictions have experimented with legislative alternatives to employment-at-will. Montana and the Virgin Islands have both enacted "just cause" statutes, which put standards in place that must be met in order for unilateral (by the employer) employment changes and terminations to be deemed "just." Similarly, a statute in Puerto Rico imposes mandatory severance pay for "unjust" terminations.

In 1987, Montana became the first state, and the only one so far, to pass a comprehensive statute rejecting EAW in favor of "just cause" terminations. Contrary to EAW, the "just cause" standard requires that the reasons offered in termination decisions be defensible. Montana currently stands alone in demanding "just cause" dismissals (Daglish, 2000: 308).

DUE PROCESS

The distinction between public and private employment is most clearly delineated in the presence and absence of due process. Due process is a distinctive vehicle through which the rights of employees are safeguarded. Due process provides for "[a]n orderly proceeding wherein a person is served with notice, actual or constructive, and has an opportunity to be heard and to enforce and protect his [or her] rights before a court having power to hear and determine the case" (Nolan and Connolly, 1979). The Fifth and Fourteenth Amendments protect liberty and property rights, and guarantee that any alleged governmental violation or deprivation may be challenged through some form of due process. According to the Fifth Amendment, "No person shall be . . . deprived of life, liberty, or property without due process of law; nor shall private property be taken for public use, without just compensation." This constitutes the right known as "due process." In addition, according to the Fourteenth Amendment, "[N]or shall any State deprive any person of life, liberty, or property, without due process of law."

In general, due process ensures that the state will not encroach upon individuals by passing legislation that impinges on Constitutional guarantees or by denying individuals their opportunities for a fair hearing where such rights are in jeopardy. There are two types of due process: *substantive due process* refers to the protection of fundamental rights, and *procedural due process* refers to the equitable administration of the protection of such rights. Together, these two types of due process are guaranteed for public employees.

Due process is, however, guaranteed only for permanent full-time workers in the public sectors of the economy, that is, for workers in local, state, and national government positions. The reason given for this is that the Constitution was intended to protect individuals, including private corporations, from governmental intrusions, not from each other – it was not anticipated that private individuals would need protection with regard to private, freely-made arrangements such as employment contracts.

In chapter 4 we will argue that employee rights, and in particular, due process, should not vary according to the political status of employment. It is not necessarily the case that EAW must be abandoned, but it is important that additional safeguards be implemented (such as federal legislation including mandated due process for private as well as public employees). In the alternative, the employment relationship might be overhauled altogether.

CONCLUSION

The longstanding public/private distinction has contributed to a lack of consistency and an element of arbitrariness in the treatment of employees in various types of employment situations. The amount of protection an employee receives for his or her work-related rights depends both on the public or private status of the employment relationship and on the state in which the relationship exists.

The absence of constitutional protection is not problematic, in and of itself. Neither the Constitution nor the Bill of Rights denies rights to employees in the private sector – they just do not afford explicit protection. Some private employers, though, have tended to turn the absence of explicit guarantees into a basis for their neglect of such rights. It is thus important that employers understand the legal context, so that they can come to understand that the lack of legal oversight does not imply that the rights of both public and private sectors of employment should not be safeguarded. In fact, there are numerous strong business arguments in favor of enhanced protection, as we shall point out in chapter 7.

If the public/private distinction ever accurately depicted American life, it is becoming increasingly apparent that it no longer does. It remains an influential artifact, though, as it continues to dominate legal thinking, in terms of how employment relationships and workplaces are governed. As long as it does remain intact, it is particularly important to recognize it for what it is – a vehicle that guides rule-making.

It is essential to keep in mind the distinction between rules and practice. Rules are created often for their ease of administration. This means that rules, particularly legal rules, are favored because of their clarity and consistency. The fact that a rule exists does not mean that it is intended to direct behavior. The legal framework regulating electronic monitoring is thus, arguably, not aimed at encouraging employers to monitor, but to clarify the legal rights. It is then for employers and employees to either adjust their behavior or bargain around the rules. This can be said of many legal rules. They are merely starting points, and should be treated as such.

REFERENCES

Articles, books, and other similar publications

Araneo, John. 1996. "Pandora's (E-Mail) Box: E-Mail Monitoring in the Workplace," *Hofstra Labor Law Journal*, vol. 14: 339.

Atleson, James B. 1985. "Reflections on Labor, Power, and Society," *Maryland Law Review*, vol. 44: 841.

Beeson, Jared D. 1998. "Cyberprivacy on the Corporate Intranet: Does the Law Allow Private Sector Employers to Read Their Employees' E-mail?" *University of Hawaii Law Review*, vol. 20: 165.

Brest, Paul. 1982. "State Action and Liberal Theory," *University of Pennsylvania Law Review*: 1296–1329.

Brown, Peter and Raysman, Richard. 1998. "Developing Corporate Internet, Intranet and E-Mail Policies." *New York Law Journal*, vol. 219, no. 109: 3–7.

Cohen, Morris R. 1933. *Law and the Social Order: Essays in Legal Philosophy*. Archon Books.

Cohen, Morris R. 1954. "Dialogue on Private Property," *Rutgers Law Review*, vol. 9: 357.

Collins, James C. and Porras, Jerry I. 1994. *Built to Last*. New York: Harper Business.

Daglish, Richard. 2000. "Avoiding the Legal Pitfalls of Hiring and Firing," *Jewelers' Circular-Keystone*, vol. 6: 306–13.

Danitz, Tiffany. 1998. "When Private Land is Public Property," *Insight*: 14.

Dauner, John and Nicely, Steve. 1998. "Speedway Wins High-Court Test," *Kansas City Star*, July 11: A1.

Flanagan, Julie. 1994. "Restricting Electronic Monitoring in the Private Workplace," *Duke Law Journal*, vol. 43: 1256.

Freeman, Alan and Elizabeth Mensch. 1987. "The Public-Private Distinction in American Law and Life," *Buffalo Law Review*, vol. 36: 237.

Frug, Gerald. 1980. "The City as a Legal Concept," *Harvard Law Review*, vol. 93: 1129.

Goodman, Marc D. 1997. "Why the Police Don't Care About Computer Crime," *Harvard Journal of Law and Technology*, vol. 10: 465.

Griffin, Jennifer J. 1991. "The Monitoring of Electronic Mail in the Private Sector Workplace: An Electronic Assault on Employee Privacy Rights," *Software Law Journal*, vol. 4: 493.

Gripman, David L. 1997. "The Doors are Locked but the Thieves and Vandals are Still Getting In: A Proposal in Tort to Alleviate Corporate America's Cyber-Crime Problem," *John Marhall Journal of Computer and Information Law*, vol. 16: 167.

Hale, Robert. 1923. "Coercion and Distribution in a supposedly non-Coercive State," *Political Science Quarterly*, vol. 38: 470.

Higgins, Michael v. *High Tech, Low Privacy. American Bar Assocation Journal* (1999).

Horwitz, Morton J. 1982. "The History of the Public/Private Distinction," *University of Pennsylvania Law Review*, vol. 130: 1423.

Johnson, Haines. 1981. "A Strike Against the Controller's Union and the President," *Washington Post*, August 9: A3.

Kaplan, Stuart J. 1998. "E-mail Policies in the Public Sector Workplace: Balancing Management Responsibilities with Employee Privacy Interests," *LERC Monograph Series*, vol. 15: 103.

Larson, Lex K. 2001. *Unjust Dismissal.* Newark, NJ: Matthew Bender and Company, Inc.

Lebowitz, Neil H. 1983. "*Poletown Neighborhood Council* v. *City of Detroit*: Economic Instability. Relativism, and the Eminent Domain Public Use Limitation," *Washington University Journal of Urban and Contemporary Law*, vol. 24: 215.

Lehman, Anne L. 1997. "E-Mail in the Workplace: Question of Privacy, Property or Principle?" *Commercial Law Conspectus*, vol. 5: 99.

Lewin, Lucien G. 1996. "The Evolution of E-Mail/Are You a Subscriber of Technet Yet?" *West Virginia Law Review*, vol. 9: 10.

Locke, John. 1764, 1986. *The Second Treatise of Government.* New York: Macmillan.

Mansnerus, Laura. 1997. "The Mall's Expanding – and You're Evicted," *U.S. News and World Report*, September 15: 43.

Mansnerus, Laura. 2001a. "Refusing to Let Go, Property Owners Test Eminent Domain's Limits." *New York Times*, July 23: B1.

Mansnerus, Laura. 2001b. "Ties to a Neighborhood At Root of Court Fight," *New York Times*, July 24: B5.

Mill, John Stuart. 1859, 1963. *On Liberty. Collected Works of J. S. Mill.* Toronto: University of Toronto Press.

Mill, John Stuart. 1848, 1963. *Utilitarianism. Collected Works of J. S. Mill.* Toronto: University of Toronto Press.

Nolan, Joseph R. and Connolly, M. J. 1979. *Black's Law Dictionary*, 5th edn. St. Paul, MN: West Publishing Co.

Nowak, Jeffrey S. 1999. "Employer Liability for Employee Online Criminal Acts," *Federal Communications Law Journal*, vol. 51: 467.

Schnaitman, Peter. 1998/1999. "Building a Community Through Workplace E-Mail: The New Privacy Frontier," *Michigan Telecommunications Technology Law Review*, vol. 5: 177.

Timmons, Douglas and Womack, Lara. 1999/2000. "Eminent Domain or Domination?" vol. Real Estate Issues, no. Winter: 44–52.

Westover, Jeff. 2001. "People at Work Internet's Dark Side," *Philippine Daily Inquirer*, September 12.

White, Jarrod J. 1997. "E-mail@Work.com: Employer Monitoring of Employee E-mail," *Alabama Law Review*, vol. 48: 1079.

Wolfe, Alan. 1993. "The Modern Corporation: Private Agent or Public Actor?" *Washington & Lee Law Review*, vol. 50: 1673–96.

Cases

Bourke v. *Nissan Motor Co.*, No. B068704 (Cal. Ct. App. July 26, 1993).

City of Atlantic City v. *Cynwynd Investments*, 148 N.J. 55 (1997).

Fadeyi v. *Planned Parenthood Assoc. of Lubbock*, 160 F.3d 1048 (5th Cir. 1998).

Gladden v. *Arkansas Children's Hospital*, 728 S.W.2d 501 (Ark. 1987).

Guz v. *Bechtel Nat'l Inc.*, 8 P. 3d 1089 (Cal. 2000).

Haddle v. *Garrison*, 525 U.S. 121, 119 S. Ct. 489, 142 L. Ed. 2d 502 (1999).

Messano v. *Board of Education*, 161 A.2d 475 (N.J. 1960).

Poletown Neighborhood Council v. *Detroit*, 410 Mich. 616, 304 N.W.2d 455 (1981).

Restuccia v. *Burk Technology, Inc.*, 95–2125 Lexis 367 (Mass. Super. Aug. 12, 1996).

Spriggs v. *Diamond Auto Glass*, 165 F.3d 1015 (4th Cir. 1999).

Taitt v. *Chemical Bank*, 849 F.2d 775 (2d Cir. 1988).

Trustees of Dartmouth College v. *Woodward*, 17 U.S. (4 Wheat.) 518, 559, 669–73 (1819).

Legislation

Americans with Disabilities Act (ADA), 42 U.S.C.S. 12112.

Age Discrimination in Employment Act (ADEA), 29 U.S.C.S. 621–634.

Family and Medical Leave Act (FMLA), 29 U.S.C.S. 2601.

Pregnancy Discrimination Act (PDA), 42 U.S.C.S. 2000e(k).

Title VII of the Civil Rights Act of 1964, 42 U.S.C.S. 2000e-2(a).

chapter three

Employment-at-Will: History, Evolution, and Current Applications

Although the legal and philosophical landscape governing employment situations is somewhat murky, there is a prevalent theme: the American workplace exhibits a strong presupposition toward employment-at-will (EAW). Legally speaking, 55 percent of all employees in the private sector are at-will employees. What this means is that these employees are working with no assurances regarding the conditions or term of their employment, which can be unilaterally altered or terminated at any time, for good reasons, no reason, or even immoral reasons. Although government employees, union employees, tenured faculty, and employees covered by specific contracts or law, are afforded varying degrees of employment security and rights, the majority of employees in the private sector in the United States have none.

At-will employees range from part-time contract workers to CEOs. This category includes all those workers, managers, and executives in the private and public sectors of the economy not covered by agreements, statutes, or contracts. According to EAW these employees enjoy rights parallel to employer prerogatives, because employees may quit their jobs for any reason whatsoever (or no reason) without having to give any notice to their employers. While many companies have grievance procedures and other protections for at-will employees, these employees have no rights to due process or to appeal employment decisions, and the employer does not have any obligation to give reasons for demotions, transfers, or dismissals. This does not mean that these employees are, in fact, mistreated on a regular basis. The reality is that most employees, particularly those who perform at least adequately, are generally unaffected by their at-will status. It is often not until something out-of-the ordinary occurs, such as an unforeseen altercation, corporate restructuring, layoffs, economic downturns, or a corporate merger, that people become aware of their status.

While changes are taking place with regard to how employment is regulated, these changes do not significantly alter the fact that our default legal framework and mindset about employment is rooted firmly in employment-at-will. We continue to argue against employment-at-will as a useful regulatory model, but it nevertheless remains a common practice in employment. In this chapter we will trace the legal history of EAW and outline its current legal and business practice. We will then examine philosophical arguments in defense of EAW and counterarguments by its critics. We will conclude that legal practices are merely starting points and default rules, and, more importantly, that good employment practices coincide with fair and equitable treatment of employees, regardless of what those default rules or starting points are.

HISTORICAL CONTEXT OF EAW

The principle of EAW, the philosophical underpinning of employment practices in the United States, reinforces, and is reinforced by, the public/private distinction. EAW is a doctrine that holds that, in the absence of law or contract, employers have the right to hire, promote, demote, and fire whomever and whenever they please. In this country, EAW has been interpreted as the rule that employers whose employees are not specifically covered by statute or contract "may dismiss their employees at will . . . for good cause, for no cause, or even for causes morally wrong, without being thereby guilty of legal wrong" (Blades, 1967: 1405). Interestingly, EAW is neither a common law doctrine, nor a policy imported from England. At the time that EAW emerged in the United States, the traditional English rule of employment was that, where the term of employment was not explicitly defined, it was presumed to be employment for the term of a year. Indeed, the American rule of EAW, as distinguishable from the English rule, varies from the rules applicable in most other industrialized countries of the world today.

Prior to the emergence of EAW, American courts adjudicated employment cases on virtually a case-by-case basis. They rejected the English presumption of a year, for they were opposed to imposing the intended duration of employment arbitrarily. Instead of applying the English rule, early American courts preferred to inquire into specific circumstances, looking to extract a duration based upon the details of each particular situation. This led to a variety of decisions. In *Babcock & Wilcox Co.* v. *Moore*, 62 Md. 161 (1884), for example, the court determined that a provision for payment of excess commissions to the employee "at end of year" implied a contract for a year. Then, in *The Hudson*, (C.C.S.D.N.Y. 1846) (No. 6831), the court held that the duration of employment was for a month where wages were paid monthly. This prevented the employer from being able to terminate the employee in less than a month, but it also did not extend the employment for an entire season.

Not all cases were as straightforward, however. In *Franklin Mining Co.* v. *Harris*, 24 Mich. 115 (1871), there was evidence that Harris accepted a position with Franklin Mining Co. because he wanted a yearly contract. An agent of the employer replied that he would make sure that Harris was "all right." There was, then, an express agreement made for a salary to be paid to Harris in the amount of $1,800 per year. When Harris was fired after only eight months, and he brought an action for breach of contract, the court found in favor of Harris and held that the duration of the employment relationship was intended to be for a year. Then, in *Tatterson* v. *Suffolk Manufacturing Co.*, 106 Mass. 56 (1870), the court stated that: "[The term of the contract] depended upon the understanding and intent of the parties; which could be ascertained only by inference from their written and oral negotiations, the usages of the business, the situation of the parties, the nature of the employment, and all the circumstances of the case."

The result was a mishmash of decisions, which provided little guidance for subsequent decisions. American courts were frustrated and confused, but they remained unwilling to adopt the English rule, and there was no other existing alternative. Then, in 1887, a principle appeared in a treatise by H. G. Wood entitled, *Master and Servant*.[1] The term "master–servant," a medieval expression referring to employer–employee relationships, persists in some areas of the law even today. According to Wood, "A general or indefinite hiring is prima facie a hiring at will" (1887: 134). American courts began applying the principle, even though its basis was a treatise not firmly rooted in legal jurisprudence, because it offered clear and predictable guidance. The treatise was attractive, even in the absence of binding precedent, because it enabled courts from that point forward to exhibit uniformity in the rendering of employment decisions. The introduction of Wood's rule reflected a major change in American jurisprudence. It shifted the burden of proof away from the employer onto the employee. Whereas, according to the English rule, it was for the employer to provide evidence that the employment relationship was intended for a term other than a year, according to the new rule, it was the onus of the employee to provide evidence of the length of the contract. And so the so-called "American rule" of employment was born.

EARLY APPLICATIONS

Popular sentiment was not in favor of EAW even at its inception. It was nevertheless adopted by the courts, in spite of its shortcomings, most likely because it did at least add an element of consistency, without imposing the requirement of elaborate case-by-case analysis. If that were considered burdensome then, imagine how courts would fare today under such circumstances!

The court in *Martin* v. *New York Life Insurance Co.*, 148 N.Y. 117, 42 N.E. 416 (1895), indicated that such thinking perhaps lay behind the adoption of Wood's rule, and stated that "[t]he decisions on this point in the lower courts have not been uniform, but we think the rule is correctly stated by Mr. Wood." Similarly, the court in *Watson* v. *Gugino*, 204 N.Y. 535, 98 N.E. 18 (1912), echoed that sentiment in explaining that the adoption of the Wood rule enabled the settling of the differences of opinion that had bogged down the lower courts in previous cases.

Understanding this context plays a significant role in our evaluation of employment-at-will. It is not difficult to understand the rationale for such a legal rule. It offered clarity and consistency where there was none. Placed within the historical context, it becomes clear why the rule was adopted, and how it could play a beneficial role in society. It is important to remember, though, that it is a rule based on the administration of justice, not on management practices. It is a rule in place in order to streamline the legal process, which should not be interpreted as a blank check for employers. It is, then, not the rule that is flawed, but our application, or, rather, misapplication of it, as managers.

At its formation, the policy of EAW also served to liberate employees. When it was initially introduced, EAW did actually liberate employees, who, according to the English rule, were bound to their employer for a year, unless a clear alternative term were specified. That is exactly what the American rule did: it provided that neither party be bound by any sort of prescribed term, unless it were determined that it was the intent of the parties to be bound by such a term.

Although Wood's rule lacked precedential jurisprudential authority, it continued to be repeatedly applied by the courts, until a body of case law had developed that stood as its own precedent. In 1934, in *Putnam* v. *Producers' Live Stock Mktg. Ass'n*, 256 Ky. 196, 75 S.W.2d 1075, 100 A.L.R. 828 (1934), the highest court in Kentucky pointed out that Wood's rule was without support, but stated that "there is now quite respectable authority establishing that [rule] to be a proper rule of construction" (*Putnam* at 831). In other words, enough courts, in enough jurisdictions, had applied the rule so often as to turn it into "law." By the 1970s, the rule of law with regard to employment was considered settled. In 1976, in *Singh* v. *City Serv. Oil Co.*, 554 P.2d 1367, 93 A.L.R.3d 654 (1976), the Supreme Court of Oklahoma unanimously adhered to the "American doctrine," supported by all but a handful of jurisdictions in the United States.

In many ways, ironically, the Wood rule was perceived as favoring employees and their right to choose the terms of their labor. It was also during this era that an array of cases were decided so as to remove restrictions on labor. In *Lochner* v. *New York*, 198 U.S. 45 (1905) the Court held unconstitutional state legislation that restricted the number of hours that bakers could work. In *Adair* v. *United States*, 208 U.S. 161 (1908), the Court struck down as unconstitutional a federal statute that prohibited the firing of union members and in *Coppage* v. *Kansas*, 236 U.S. 1 (1915), the Court decided that a state statute preventing the firing of union members was unconstitutional.

LEGISLATIVE ACTIONS

In 1935, in the wake of the accepted adoption of the Wood rule, the United States Congress and state legislatures began enacting a range of statutes to institute across-the-board federal exceptions to at-will employment, beginning with the *National Labor Relations Act of 1935*.

The NLRA represented a significant change in that it gave employees a protected bargaining voice: it explicitly prevented employees from being fired for union activity, and it established protection for collective bargaining by employees for contracts to limit employers' right to fire employees. As a result, while private, non-union employees tend to remain at-will, many union members have been able to secure limitations on terminations, such as through "just cause" provisions, which prevent employers from firing employees without "just cause."

The NLRA was followed by numerous state initiatives, but the next significant wave of federal legislation that affected employment emerged in the 1960s with civil rights legislation that prohibited discrimination on the basis of such factors as race, sex, color, religion, national origin, age, or handicap. The first piece of such legislation was *Title VII of the Civil Rights Act of 1964*, but, as mentioned in chapter 2, a number of other acts, such as the Americans with Disabilities Act (ADA), the *Family and Medical Leave Act* (FMLA), the *Age Discrimination in Employment Act* (ADEA), and the *Pregnancy Discrimination Act* (PDA), have also been passed. In addition, private employees are also protected by provisions of a wide range of additional legislation, such as the *Employee Retirement Income Security Act* (ERISA) and *Racketeer Influenced and Corrupt Organizations Act* (RICO). The catch, though, is that such legislation affords avenues of redress only under particular circumstances, and an employee's situation must fit within those circumstances for the acts to apply.

STATE INTERPRETATIONS AND LIMITATIONS ON EAW

Employment in the United States is ostensibly regulated by the states. What this means is that states are allowed to determine for themselves the specific legal framework within which employment relationships are permitted to operate. Interestingly, though, there is little variety across state boundaries. The default rule in almost every state is EAW (Larson, 2001). The real limiting power of EAW lies in the hands of state and local legislatures and courts. During the past 50 years or so, state legislatures and courts have stepped in to carve out exceptions to EAW. They have evaluated local norms, and determined the rules best suited to the environment. Jurisdictions have varied with regard to which combination of circumstances they have recognized as exceptions to EAW, and to whether they are identified by statute or in case law. In addition, the legal landscape is still evolving. Cases are still being handed down, and legislation is still being passed. Jurisdictions are learning from one another, and are observing patterns and trends in the federal arena as well. While, according to the American system of federalism, regulation of employment technically falls within the realm of state control, it was not until the middle of the twentieth century that states began shaping the EAW doctrine to reflect local standards and practices through judicially carved out exceptions.

Public policy exceptions

The California Court of Appeals is responsible for the initial two non-statutory inroads into EAW. First, in 1949, in *Kouff* v. *Bethlehem-Alameda Shipyard, Inc.*, 90 Cal. App. 2d 322, 202 P.2d 1059 (1949), the court established that EAW is subject to statutory limitation. In *Kouff*, although the employer argued that EAW trumped express statutory prohibitions, the court held that this was not the case and enforced a statute that prohibited the discharge of employees who served as election officers.

Then, a decade later, in *Petermann* v. *International Brotherhood of Teamsters*, 174 Cal. App. 2d 184, 344 P.2d 25 (Cal. App. 1959), the court carved out the first significant exception to EAW in holding that EAW is limited not only by statute, but also by considerations of "public policy." Although, in *Petermann*, the court specifically addressed a situation where an employee was unjustly fired for refusing to commit perjury, the underlying message was that EAW is subject to public policy considerations in general – though the specific content of those considerations is determined by the states. The court in *Petermann* thus laid the groundwork for a public policy exception to EAW:

> The public policy of this state . . . would be seriously impaired if it were to be held that one could be discharged by reason of his refusal to commit perjury. To hold that one's continued employment could be made contingent upon his commission of a felonious act at the instance of his employer would be to encourage criminal conduct upon the part of both the employee and employer and would serve to contaminate the honest administration of public affairs. This is patently contrary to the public welfare. (*Petermann* at 189)

The next major inroad was ironically not through a court decision but a law review article, by Lawrence Blades, which illuminated an additional consideration, that is the power imbalance between employers and employees (Blades, 1967). Whereas the Wood rule might have initially operated to equalize power between the parties, EAW in the latter half of the twentieth century was situated quite differently. Blades pointed out the potential for abuses of managerial or ownership power, and suggested that courts should recognize a tortuous cause of action for abusive discharge. To illustrate the need for such a cause of action, Blades pointed to cases such as *Comerford* v. *International Harvester Co.*, 235 Ala. 376, 178 So. 894 (1938), where an employee was fired because of his supervisor's inability to woo the employee's wife, and *Christy* v. *Petrus*, 365 Mo. 1187, 295 S.W.2d 122 (1956), where an employee was fired for filing a workers' compensation claim. According to Blades, such situations reflected an employer/employee power imbalance. They clearly ran counter to the principles encompassed by the origins of EAW, but were not accounted for according to the current legal framework.

In spite of the strength of the argument contained in *Petermann* and reflected in Blades' analysis, it was not until 1973 that the next judicial inroad was carved out of EAW. In *Frampton* v. *Central Indiana Gas Co.*, 260 Ind. 249, 297 N.E.2d 425 (1973), the Supreme Court of Indiana recognized an exception based on "wrongful discharge." In that case, the court held that a woman could not be discharged for filing a workers' compensation claim:

> If employers are permitted to penalize employees for filing workmen's compensation claims, a most important public policy will be undermined. The fear of discharge would have a deleterious effect on the exercise of a statutory right. Employees will not file claims for justly deserved compensation . . . [and] the employer is effectively relieved of his obligation. . . . Since the Act embraces such a fundamental . . . policy, strict employer adherence is required. (*Frampton* at 252)

Such decisions clearly demonstrate the court's unwillingness to stand by without doing anything as employers attempted to interfere with fundamental liberties. Interestingly, though, the court based its analysis primarily on analogies to landlord–tenant cases, without citing either *Petermann* or Blades.

With this decision, the public policy exception gained momentum and acquired a degree of national recognition. This line of cases established that it was not acceptable for employers to prevent their employees from exercising fundamental liberties. The next year, the highest court in New Hampshire recognized a cause of action for wrongful discharge in *Monge* v. *Beebe Rubber Co.*, 114 N.H. 130, 316 A.2d 549 (1974), along with the Supreme Court of Pennsylvania in *Geary* v. *United States Steel Corp.*, 456 Pa. 171, 319 A.2d 174 (1974), and followed by the Oregon court in *Nees* v. *Hocks*, 272 Or. 210, 536 P.2d 512 (1975). Interestingly, both these cases referred to *Petermann* or Blades in pointing out that EAW could be overridden in order to respond to or deter tortuous behavior on the part of the employer (Werhane, 1985, 1999).

The public policy exceptions have been applied widely. While not every state has adopted them, they have been applied in an overwhelming majority of states, and only a small handful of states have not evidenced leanings toward them. A range of other public policy exceptions has been grounded on fundamental liberties, many of which are protected by statute as well. While not all courts recognize all statutes as preempting EAW, most courts in most jurisdictions protect activities such as jury service and voting. In addition, most courts protect employees from undue influence by employers attempting to compel illegal or unethical behavior by employees, such as perjury.

Exceptions derived from contract theory

A broad category of exceptions involves those lodged on contract theory. Many employers and employees opt to alter the employment relationship through contractual agreements. Since evidence of such agreements is not always lodged in an explicit arrangement, courts often find it necessary to delve further in order to determine the reasonable assurances and expectations of employers and employees.

There are two sorts of contractual causes of actions that have emerged, the first with regard to positive representations, as through the vehicle of employee handbooks, the second through implied covenants of good faith and/or fair dealing, through which the court interprets the existence of contractual obligations through the behavior or spoken words of employers.

Implied-in-fact contractual obligations

The first set of contractually-based actions that have emerged concern representations made by employers. These representations, either oral or written, are sometimes construed as creating the basis for contractual-type obligations. Courts prevent employers from treating employees as at-will employees where there is evidence that employees have relied on these representations to their detriment, particularly when those representations concerned duration of employment.

Courts have held that an employment contract exists, even where it exists only as a result of assumed behavior, through a so-called "implied-in-fact" contract. In such instances, the court weighs the circumstances and determines whether the behavior of the parties indicated that a contractual understanding existed, or should have existed. Such a situation arises where there is deemed to be "promissory estoppel." Promissory estoppel occurs where a party relies upon the inducements of the other party to his or her detriment, and the only way to avoid the injustice is to enforce the promise. Such a case would arise if an employee accepted one position instead of another because of a commitment for a longer term of employment.

The foundation was laid for a "personnel handbook" exception in 1972. In that year, the United States Supreme Court heard *Perry* v. *Sinderman*, 408 U.S. 593 (1972), which involved a junior college professor who claimed that the personnel handbook of that college provided protectable assurances to employees. Although the Court had earlier refused to protect employees under the rubric of substantive due process, at this time it held that it was conceivable for a public employee to be entitled to procedural due process. The Court held that a professor who asserted reliance upon the college's Faculty Guide might be able to "justify his legitimate claim of entitlement to continued employment absent 'sufficient cause'" (*Perry* at 602–3). According to the Faculty Guide:

> Odessa College has no tenure system. The Administration of the College wishes the faculty member to feel that he has permanent tenure as long as his teaching services are satisfactory and as long as he displays a cooperative attitude toward his co-workers and his superiors, and as long as he is happy in his work. (*Perry* at 600)

The court determined that, in light of the express language contained in the Faculty Guide, coupled with the professor's record of ongoing satisfactory service for the past decade, the professor might have acquired a property interest in his continued employment. While this employment could be terminated, the Court determined that, in order to refuse to renew such a professor's contract, the college might be subject to the requirement of granting "a hearing at his request, where he could be informed of the grounds for his nonretention and challenge their sufficiency" (*Perry* at 603).

Reliance upon employee manuals has been determined to give rise to reasonable employment expectations in a number of jurisdictions. In *Woolley* v. *Hoffmann-La Roche, Inc.*, 491 A.2d 1257, *modified*, 499 A.2d 515 (1985), the court held that companies are contractually bound by the statements in their employment manuals. In *Woolley*, the employment manual implicitly provided that employees would not be terminated without good cause: "It is the policy of Hoffmann-La Roche to retain to the extent consistent with company requirements, the services of all employees who perform their duties efficiently and effectively." The court thus held that an employee at Hoffmann-La Roche could not be dismissed without good cause and due process. *Woolley* is but one of many decisions that demonstrate that employers are accountable to employees for what is contained in employment manuals, because, the court determined, the manual is part of an implicit employment contract.

Implied-in-fact situations are also said to arise where additional commitments are made that are construed as contractual. For example, several courts have provided for an exception to EAW where the employer made oral assurances. While not all jurisdictions agree, a number of other courts have found an exception to EAW to exist where an employee manual contains information, such as assurances of permanent employment, inconsistent with the discharge.

Implied-in-law or quasi contracts

"Implied-in-law" contracts differ from the implied-in-fact situations in that there is no presumption of the existence of any sort of contract. Also called "quasi contracts," these situations are treated as obligations, even though it is recognized that they are non-contractual. Situations that fall into this category tend to be based either on implied covenants of good faith and fair dealing or on public policy considerations.

Implied-in-law contracts, or quasi contracts, fall in the cracks between torts and contracts. They are not actually contracts, because they do not involve the *actual* agreement of the parties, but, instead, reflect the court's assessment of what *should have been* the agreement, according to what transpired. The quasi contract contains an obligation imposed by law that serves justice in the absence of a promise made, or even intended. The quasi contract is thus a non-contractual obligation, treated by law, for procedural purposes, as if it were a contract, and it is based on the fulfillment of obligations consistent with good faith and fair dealing.

California was one of the first jurisdictions to recognize quasi contracts in the employment setting. In 1980, in *Cleary* v. *American Airlines, Inc.*, 111 Cal. App. 3d 443, 168 Cal. Rptr. 722 (1980), the state court of appeals determined that the longevity of the employee's service ("18 years of apparently satisfactory performance") coupled with the airline's adoption of a procedure for due process created the presence of an implied-in-law contract. The court stated: "While the contents of the regulation are not before us, its existence compels the conclusion that this employer had recognized its responsibility to engage in good faith and fair dealing rather than in arbitrary conduct with respect to all of its employees" (*Cleary* at 455).

In *Pugh* v. *See's Candies, Inc.*, 171 Ca. Rptr. 917 (1981), the California court ruled that 32 years of service gave rise to an implied covenant of good faith and fair dealing, even in the absence of a specific termination procedure promulgated by the employer. In *Pugh*, the employee was fired without explanation. Although no contract existed that specified the duration of employment, the court determined that the implied corporate policy was not to discharge employees without good reasons. The court in *Pugh* held: "[T]here were facts in evidence from which the jury could determine the existence of such an implied promise: the duration of appellant's employment, the commendations and promotions he received, the apparent lack of any direct criticism of his work, the assurances he was given, and the employer's acknowledged policies" (*Pugh* at 329). Where an employer's behavior and/or policies encourage an employee's reliance upon employment, according to this decision, the employer cannot dismiss that employee without a good reason.

A host of cases across the country have further elaborated upon this exception. In some states, it can be considered a breach of contract to fire a long-term employee without sufficient cause, under normal economic conditions, even when the implied contract is only a verbal one. In California, for example, the majority of recent implied contract cases have been decided in favor of the employee (Bastress, 1988).

The quasi contract has also been used in other jurisdictions as a vehicle for the prevention of additional identified abuses. Some states have applied such a covenant in order to fashion a remedy against specific employer abuses, such as the deprivation of monetary compensation. In 1977, for example, a Massachusetts court intervened in *Fortune* v. *National Cash Register Co.*, 373 Mass. 96, 364 N.E.2d 1251 (1977), where there was evidence that an employee was fired to prevent him from receiving a commission of more than $90,000, which he was to earn on a multimillion dollar sale. The rule has been expanded to cover not only wrongful discharges, but also to allow employees to receive deferred compensation even after they are rightfully discharged (*Gram* v. *Liberty Mut. Ins. Co.*, 384 Mass. 659, 429 N.E.2d 21 (1981), *appeal after remand*, 391 Mass. 333, 461 N.E.2d 796 (1984)).

Exceptions derived from tort theory

Exceptions to EAW are also derived from tort theory. These exceptions fall into a number of broad categories. Most of these situations target either the right of the employer to discharge the employee or the manner in which an employee is discharged.

Wrongful discharge based on public policy is clearly the most successful argument in many jurisdictions, as we discussed earlier. Such actions contend that the employer is preempted from discharging the employee, generally on the basis of a contrary federal or state regulation. Similarly, arguments for outrage, fraud, intentional infliction of emotional distress, and intentional interference with contract, while less successful, are also based on claims of improper motivation for discharge.

Claims based on allegations of retaliatory discharge also fall within this category. In *Bowman* v. *State Bank of Keysville*, 229 Va. 534 (1985), a Virginia court asserted its refusal to condone retaliatory discharges. In *Bowman*, a couple of employee-shareholders of a bank voted for a merger at request of the bank's officers. After the vote was counted, the employee-shareholders subsequently retracted their votes and contended that their vote had been coerced. They alleged that the bank officers had warned them that they would lose their jobs if they did not vote in favor of the merger. They were then fired. The court in *Bowman* found in favor of the employee-shareholders.

According to the *Bowman* court, "Virginia has not deviated from the common law doctrine of employment-at-will. . . . And we do not alter the traditional rule today. Nonetheless, the rule is not absolute" (*Bowman* at 539). In this way, the *Bowman* court demonstrated that EAW is subject to limitations and exceptions. Even where the EAW doctrine still appears to "thrive," it does so within definite restrictive legal and policy constraints.

Defamation, on the other hand, is based on the manner in which the discharge takes place. A number of employees have brought successful claims based on statements made publicly regarding their discharge. Indeed, it has even been argued that the discharge itself can constitute defamation.

Whistleblowing statutes

The 1970s and 1980s witnessed the emergence of both judicial and statutory exceptions in the area of whistleblowing. Whistleblowing statutes began to be enacted in many states to prevent employer abuses by providing remedies to employees for reporting, or threatening to report, illegal or unethical behavior by the employer. A number of jurisdictions have held that employees cannot be discharged for reporting unethical, illegal, or disruptive behavior. Some courts require the presence of applicable statutes to find in favor of the employee, others do not.

In *Pierce* v. *Ortho Pharmaceutical Corporation*, 845 N.J. 58, 417 A.2d 505 (1980), for example, the court reinstated a physician who was fired from a company for refusing to seek approval to test a certain drug on human subjects. The court held that safety clearly lies in the interest of public welfare, and that employees are not to be fired for refusing to jeopardize public safety. Similarly, in *Palmateer* v. *International Harvester Corporation*, 85 Ill. App. 2d 124 (1981), the court reinstated an employee who was fired for reporting theft at his plant on the grounds that criminal conduct requires such reporting.

Other exceptions

In addition, an increasing number of jurisdictions have enacted statutes aimed at preventing discrimination based on sexual orientation (Cal. Lab. Code § 1102.1; Con. Gen Stat. Ann § 46a-814c; Hawaii Rev. Stat. § 368–1; Mass. Gen. L. ch. 151B § 4.). This is an important development because federal protection in this area is still lacking.

Privacy interests have also been recognized and protected by legislatures as well as the judiciary. In *Luck* v. *Southern Pacific Transportation Co.*, 267 Cal. Rptr. 618 (1990), *modified on denial of rehearing* (March 23, 1990), the California court held that an employee could not be fired for refusing to take a drug test. The court determined that such a claim constituted a breach of an implied covenant of good faith and fair dealing, based on a violation of privacy right, in this instance embodied in the state's constitution.

Fraudulent inducement of hiring

In addition to the exceptions to EAW, a number of jurisdictions have moved in a completely different direction in instituting a tortuous claim for an action for fraud. This claim arises not as a result of employment or discharge, but on the basis of promises made prior to acceptance of employment. Where an ex-employee can show that his or her employer made intentional misrepresentations at the time of employment, such a claim is said to arise. Theories for recovery include intentional infliction of emotional distress and tortuous interference with contract.

Exceptions to EAW

Together, the exceptions reflect the varying and variable application of EAW. While EAW retains a strong foothold in American employment practices, it is not absolute. State legislatures and courts have demonstrated that they have the power, and are willing to exercise it, to limit the application of EAW in order to recognize and protect employee rights.

PHILOSOPHICAL ARGUMENTS IN DEFENSE AND AGAINST EAW

EAW is not merely a doctrine that serves as the basis for legal procedures in this counter. As a principle, it represents a prevailing mindset about employment, one shared by public policy makers as well as by employers, managers, and many employees, which encompasses the idea that employment is a voluntary agreement that can be terminated at any time by either party.

While the principle of EAW may appear unjust in some instances where it is invoked, it has been strongly defended not only by jurists but also by economists, political thinkers, and philosophers. The principle is often justified for one or more of the following reasons (Werhane, 1985):

1 The proprietary rights of employers guarantee that they should be allowed to employ or dismiss whomever and whenever they wish.
2 EAW defends employee and employer rights equally, such as through the protection of the right to freedom of contract, because employees voluntarily contract to be hired and can quit at any time as well.
3 In choosing to take jobs, employees voluntarily commit themselves to certain responsibilities and conditions, including "at-will" employment.
4 Extending due process rights to the workplace possibly threatens the efficiency and productivity of business organizations.
5 Legislation, or regulation, of employment relationships further undermines an already over-regulated economy.

While such defenses ostensibly make sense, it is important to examine them in greater detail. The principle of EAW is sometimes maintained purely on the basis of proprietary rights of employers and corporations. In dismissing or demoting employees, the employer is not denying rights to *persons*; rather, the employer is simply excluding that person's *labor* from the organization. Entrepreneurs and employers often justify such actions on the basis of their ownership of the property where work takes place. Similarly, managers cite their representation of shareholder ownership interests as the basis for their right to control – even arbitrarily – access and activities at that company or place of employment.

These are not altogether faulty arguments. Accepting them, though, necessitates consideration of the proprietary rights of employees as well as those of employers. To understand what "proprietary rights of employees" means it is useful to consider first what is meant by the term "labor." "Labor" is sometimes used collectively to refer to the workforce as a whole: the "labor" force. It also refers to the activity of working, "laboring." Other times it refers to the productivity or "fruits" of that activity. Productivity, labor in the third sense, might be thought of as a form of property, or, at least, as something convertible into property, because the productivity of working is what is "sold" or traded for remuneration in employee–employer work agreements. For example, suppose an advertising agency hires an expert known for his or her creativity in developing new commercials. This person trades his or her ideas, the product of his or her work (thinking), for pay. The ideas are not literally property, but they are tradable items because, when presented on paper or on television, they are sellable by their creator and generate income, even though the activity of working (thinking in this case) cannot be sold or transferred (Werhane, 1983).

Caution is necessary in relating productivity to tangible property, because there is an obvious difference between productivity and material property. Productivity requires the past or present activity of working, and thus the presence of the person performing this activity. Person, property, labor, and productivity are all different in this important sense. A person can be distinguished from his or her possessions, a distinction that allows for the creation of legally fictional persons such as corporations or trusts that can "own" property. Persons cannot, however, be distinguished from their working, and this activity is necessary for creating productivity, the tradable product of working.

In dismissing an employee, a well-intentioned employer aims to reduce the costs of generating that employee's work products. Ordinarily, however, terminating that cost entails terminating that employee. In those cases the justification for the at-will firing is presumably proprietary, that is, based on the presumption that owners and employers have rights to control what happens on their property or in the companies for which they are agents. What is not always taken into account, though, is that there are employer *and* employee proprietary interests, both of which need to be taken into account.

Ordinarily, companies give reasons, usually good economic reasons, for layoffs and dismissals. EAW, however, permits arbitrary layoffs, and this leeway is problematic. When I get rid of a robot, I do not have to give reasons, because a robot is not a rational being. It has no emotions and no use for reasons. On the other hand, people do reason and feel, and they feel an entire range of emotions. If I fire a person arbitrarily, I am making the assumption that he or she does not need reasons. But if I have hired people, then, in firing them, I should treat them as such, with respect, throughout the termination process. This does not preclude firing or layoffs. It merely proposes that it is appropriate for employers to give reasons for their actions, because reasons are appropriate when people are dealing with other people.

This reasoning leads to a second defense and critique of EAW. It is contended that EAW defends employee and employer rights equally. A worker's right to accept or reject employment balances an employer's right to hire and fire at will. The institution of any employee *right* that restricts at-will hiring and firing would be unfair, unless this restriction were balanced by a similar restriction controlling employee job choice. Either program would do irreparable damage by preventing both employees and employers from continuing in voluntary employment arrangements. These arrangements are guaranteed by freedom of contract. Limiting EAW practices or requiring due process would negatively affect the right of persons or organizations to enter into any voluntary agreement with which all parties of the agreement were in accord. Both are thus clearly coercive, because in either case persons and organizations are forced to accept behavioral restraints that place unnecessary constraints on voluntary employment agreements.

This second line of reasoning in defense of EAW, like the first, presents some solid arguments. A basic presupposition upon which EAW is grounded is that of protecting equal freedoms of both employees and employers. The purpose of EAW is to provide a guaranteed balance of these freedoms. But arbitrary treatment of employees extends prerogatives to managers that are not equally available to employees, and such treatment may unduly interfere with a fired employee's prospects for future employment if that employee has no avenue for defense or appeal. This is equally true when an employee quits without notice or good reason. Arbitrary behavior either by employees *or* employers that affects the other party therefore violates the spirit of EAW, that of protecting the freedoms of both employees and employers.

The third justification of EAW defends the freedom of employment contracts. If these are agreements between consenting adults, such agreements imply reciprocal obligations between the parties in question for which both are accountable. It is obvious that, in an employment contract, people are rewarded for their performance. What is seldom noticed is that if part of the employment contract is an expectation of loyalty, trust, and respect on the part of an employee, the employer must, in return, treat the employee with respect as well. The obligations required by employment agreements, if these are free and non-coercive agreements, must be equally obligatory and mutually restrictive on both parties. Otherwise, one party cannot expect, *morally* expect, loyalty, trust, or respect from the other.

EAW is most often defended on practical grounds. From a utilitarian perspective, hiring and firing at will is deemed necessary in productive organizations to ensure maximum efficiency and productivity. In the absence of EAW, unproductive employees, workers who are no longer needed, and even trouble-makers, would be able to keep their jobs. Even if a business could rid itself of undesirable employees, lengthy grievance procedures required by an extension of employee rights would be costly and time-consuming, and would likely prove distracting to other employees. This would probably slow production and, more likely than not, prove harmful to the morale of other employees (Maitland, 1990).

Companies that have grievance procedures, for example, such as Motorola and Volkswagen, are nevertheless as efficient and productive as those that do not – if not more so. At Motorola, layoffs occur only with documented, transparent, economic data, and if an employee has been with the company ten years or more, he or she cannot be fired without extensive due process and a decision by the Board of Directors. Motorola still achieves Six Sigma quality (one defect in every six million pieces) in almost every plant. Companies that have flattened the power hierarchy and encourage free speech, such as Intel and Cisco Systems, are highly successful, and morale in those companies is extraordinarily positive.

The strongest reasons for allowing abuses of EAW and for not instituting a full set of employee rights in the workplace, at least in the private sector of the economy, have to do with the nature of business in a free society. Businesses are privately-owned, voluntary organizations of all sizes, from small entrepreneurships to large corporations. As such, they are not subject to the restrictions governing public and political institutions. Political procedures such as due process, needed to safeguard the public against the arbitrary exercise of power by the state, do not apply to private organizations. Guaranteeing such rights in the workplace would require restrictive legislation and regulation. Voluntary market arrangements, so vital to free enterprise and guaranteed by freedom of contract, would be sacrificed for the alleged public interest of employee claims, and the public/private distinction, so central to protect individuals and institutions against the state, would be blurred. The public/private distinction is, though, at best, already confused, except with regard to employment, and questioning EAW does not require legislation – it requires only voluntary, consistent treatment of employees, which corresponds with the way we treat public employees and fellow citizens.

Even if it were possible to defend EAW on the basis of equal rights, freedom of contracts, voluntarism, and/or fear of legislation, in practice, EAW supports inconsistent and even irrational management behavior by permitting arbitrary treatment of employees, behavior that is not tolerated as best management practice (Radin and Werhane, 1996; Werhane, 1999). The most telling argument against at-will employment does not the question the principle itself but rather raises issue about its abuses. Such practices allow managers or boards to make arbitrary employment decisions, and sanction decisions that do not have to be justified. This sanction violates the managerial ideal of rationality and consistency. Most companies do not tolerate management decisions for which good reasons cannot be given, nor do they permit inconsistent decision-making. That such arbitrariness could be tolerated, even in principle, in employment decisions, then, is inconsistent with good management practice. Now in fact ordinarily employees are treated pretty well. Most companies have reasons, often good economic reasons, for employment decisions. But there are lingering feelings of distrust when employees are not consulted, or indeed are kept in the dark, about their employment future, when choices that radically affect their lives are made for them without their knowledge, or when good long-term employees are transferred, demoted, or laid off under what appear to be less than exigent circumstances.

If at-will employment is problematic, why do people agree to such employment by accepting jobs? Sometimes a person must take a job for economic reasons, because jobs are scarce, or because his or her talents are limited. In such cases the prospective employee often thinks he is not in a position to bargain for his rights at the time of employment. Sometimes employees are simply not fully informed about their rights as at-will employees. Employment is often accepted because a potential employee enters into the employment agreement in good faith, and assumes good faith and fair treatment in return on the part of the employer. Or perhaps it is that people need jobs, and they take it as a given phenomenon that they will not have many rights at work. Or perhaps it is that there is a prevailing mindset, a "boss" mentality, and a belief that managers and employers have some proprietary rights that employees are not entitled to. None of these reasons justifies subsequent arbitrary treatment of employees by employers.

CONCLUSION

The lack of constitutional guarantees and EAW have traditionally contributed toward the mindset that employees do not have rights in the workplace. Parallels can nevertheless be drawn between public and private employment, and the body of law restricting EAW is growing. Recent years have witnessed a significant trend in American law toward the judiciary carving out exceptions to EAW, which afford protection to employees by giving them claims for action that trump the underlying default rule. While these are still not many, and not nationally adopted, they do exist and their mere existence is significant within the historical context of employment law in the United States. It is important to examine the range of case law available in order to determine the extent of the exceptions, but jurisdictions are changing their approaches, often toward the identification of additional exceptions. In addition, in response to increased case law, legislatures are interceding to establish even clearer rules.

While, philosophically, according to Locke, employees acquire property interests in their work through the input of their labor, American law has yet to recognize this as giving rise to a protected legal claim. In fact, courts have frequently stated that the at-will employee does not acquire a property interest in employment. This contradicts our moral intuitions, and it is in defiance of the recognition that public employees do have such proprietary interests.

It is inappropriate, in terms of morality or, pragmatically, for legal consistency or firm performance, to substitute legal constructs and default rules for a moral compass. It is neither morally right nor good business sense to deprive employees of workplace rights simply because those rights are not explicitly guaranteed by law. Individuals do not lose their personhood simply by going to work. In the remaining chapters, we will make some positive arguments in defense of such employee rights.

NOTE

1. Until 1980 this unfortunate expression was used in the *Index of Legal Periodicals* to refer to articles on employee–employer relationships.

REFERENCES

Articles, books, and other similar publications

Bastress, R. M. 1988. "A Synthesis and a Proposal for Reform of the Employment at Will Doctrine." *West Virginia Law Review*, vol. 90: 319–51.

Blades, Lawrence. 1967. "Employment at Will vs. Individual Freedom: On Limiting the Abusive Exercise of Employer Power." *Columbia Law Review*, vol. 67: 1405.

Larson, Lex K. 2001. *Unjust Dismissal.* Newark, NJ: Matthew Bender and Company, Inc.

Maitland, Ian. 1990. "Rights in the Workplace: A Nozickian Argument." In Lisa Newton and Maureen Ford, eds., *Taking Sides*. Guilford, CT: Dushkin Publishing Group, 33–7.

Radin, T. J. and Werhane, P. H. 1996. "The Public/Private Distinction and the Political Status of Employment." *American Business Law Journal*, vol. 34, no. 2: 245–60.

Werhane, Patricia. 1983. "Individual Rights in Business." In Tom Regan, ed., *Just Business.*. New York: Random House. 100–28.

Werhane, Patricia H. 1985. *Persons, Rights and Corporations.* Englewood Cliffs, NJ: Prentice Hall.

Werhane, Patricia H. 1999. "Justice and Trust." *Journal of Business Ethics*, vol. 21: 237–49.

Wood, H. G. 1887. *A Treatise on the Law of Master and Servant.* Albany, NY: John D. Parsons, Jr.

Cases

Adair v. *United States*, 208 U.S. 161 (1908).

Babcock & Wilcox Co. v. *Moore*, 62 Md. 161 (1884).

Bowman v. *State Bank of Keysville*, 229 Va. 534 (1985).

Christy v. *Petrus*, 365 Mo. 1187, 295 S.W.2d 122 (1956).

Cleary v. *American Airlines, Inc.*, 111 Cal. App. 3d 443, 168 Cal. Rptr. 722 (1980).

Comerford v. *International Harvester Co.*, 235 Ala. 376, 178 So. 894 (1938).

Coppage v. *Kansas*, 236 U.S. 1 (1915).

Fortune v. *National Cash Register Co.*, 373 Mass. 96, 364 N.E.2d 1251 (1977).

Frampton v. *Central Indiana Gas Co.*, 260 Ind. 249, 297 N.E.2d 425 (1973).

Franklin Mining Co. v. *Harris*, 24 Mich. 115 (1871).

Geary v. *United States Steel Corp.*, 456 Pa. 171, 319 A.2d 174 (1974).

Gram v. *Liberty Mut. Ins. Co.*, 384 Mass. 659, 429 N.E.2d 21 (1981), *appeal after remand*, 391 Mass. 333, 461 N.E.2d 796 (1984).

Kouff v. *Bethlehem-Alameda Shipyard, Inc.*, 90 Cal. App. 2d 322, 202 P.2d 1059 (1949).

Lochner v. *New York*, 198 U.S. 45 (1905).

Luck v. *Southern Pacific Transportation Co.*, 267 Cal. Rptr. 618 (1990), *modified on denial of rehearing*(March 23, 1990).

Martin v. *New York Life Insurance Co.*, 148 N.Y. 117, 42 N.E. 416 (1895).

Monge v. *Beebe Rubber Co.*, 114 N.H. 130, 316 A.2d 549 (1974).

Nees v. *Hocks*, 272 Or. 210, 536 P.2d 512 (1975).

Palmateer v. *International Harvester Corporation*, 85 Ill. App. 2d 124 (1981).

Perry v. *Sinderman*, 408 U.S. 593 (1972).

Petermann v. *International Brotherhood of Teamsters*, 174 Cal. App. 2d 184, 344 P.2d 25 (Cal. App. 1959).

Pierce v. *Ortho Pharmaceutical Corporation*, 845 N.J. 58, 417 A.2d 505 (1980).

Pugh v. *See's Candies, Inc.*, 171 Ca. Rptr. 917 (1981).

Putnam v. *Producers' Live Stock Mktg. Ass'n*, 256 Ky. 196, 75 S.W.2d 1075, 100 A.L.R. 828 (1934).

Singh v. *City Serv. Oil Co.*, 554 P.2d 1367, 93 A.L.R.3d 654 (1976).

Tatterson v. *Suffolk Manufacturing Co.*, 106 Mass. 56 (1870).

The Hudson, (C.C.S.D.N.Y. 1846) (No. 6831).

Watson v. *Gugino*, 204 N.Y. 535, 98 N.E. 18 (1912).

Woolley v. *Hoffmann-La Roche, Inc.*, 491 A.2d 1257, *modified*, 499 A.2d 515 (1985).

Legislation

Age Discrimination in Employment Act (ADEA).

Americans with Disabilities Act (ADA).

Cal. Lab. Code § 1102.1.

Con. Gen Stat. Ann § 46a-81c.

Employee Retirement Income Security Act (ERISA).

Family and Medical Leave Act (FMLA).

Hawaii Rev. Stat. § 368–1.

Mass. Gen. L. ch. 151B § 4.

National Labor Relations Act of 1935 (NLRA).

Pregnancy Discrimination Act (PDA).

Racketeer Influenced and Corrupt Organizations Act (RICO).

Title VII of the Civil Rights Act of 1964.

chapter four

The Employee's Voice: Due Process, Whistleblowing, and Workplace Democracy

A weakening of the public/private distinction and the replacement of EAW as an acceptable norm together imply that an employee should have a voice in his or her employment. The employee's voice is relevant with regard to his or her work-related performance, the performance of his or her managers, and the performance of the firm in general. Due process, whistleblower protection, and workplace democracy serve as vehicles through which employees can have a voice in performance-related decisions. In this chapter we will explore and defend these options.

THE RIGHT TO DUE PROCESS

According to philosopher T. M. Scanlon, "The requirement of due process is one of the conditions of the moral acceptability of those institutions that give some people power to control or intervene in the lives of others" (Scanlon, 1977: 94). Due process provides the means through which a person can appeal a decision in order to get an explanation of that action and/or a disinterested, objective, or fair judgment of its rightness or wrongness. There are two components of due process: procedural and substantive. Procedural due process demands that people have access to channels through which they can challenge decisions. While procedural due process gives employees the right to some form of open grievance procedure in which the employer is required to give reasons for his action, it does not require that the employer have good reasons. Substantive due process, on the other hand, entails inquiry into the types of reasons that underlie decisions.

Procedural due process

Courts have traditionally recognized the rights of corporations in the private sector of the economy to procedural due process without requiring due process for employees within those companies. The justification put forward is that, since corporations act in the public interest, they, like individual citizens, should be afforded the right to due process. As we mentioned in chapter 2, due process is also guaranteed for permanent, full-time workers in the public sector of the economy, that is, for workers in local, state, and national government positions. The Constitution restricts governmental actions, even when the government is involved in employment relationships. The Constitutional provisions that protect liberty and property rights guarantee that any alleged violation or deprivation of those rights may be challenged by some form of due process, and public sector employment falls within the relevant categories of liberty and property rights. Federal and state courts have determined that state employees have protected property interests in their employment. As the Supreme Court held in *Cleveland Bd. of Education* v. *Loudermill*, 470 U.S. 532, 84 L. Ed. 2d 494, 105 S. Ct. 1487 (1985), while property interests are not created by the Constitution, they are protected by its provisions (*Cleveland* at 538). Persons in private employment, on the other hand, are not subject to or protected by the principles that govern the public domain.

Numerous statutes, for example, such as the Ohio statute in *Cleveland*, recognize property interests of employees, in particular, public employees. According to Ohio Rev. Code Ann. § 124.11 (1984), employees are entitled to their positions "during good behavior and efficient service," and they cannot be dismissed "except . . . for . . . misfeasance, malfeasance, or nonfeasance in office." The rationale underlying such prescriptives is that, as a result of the productivity they contribute to the place of their employment, employees acquire entitlements to their positions, absent a showing of good reasons to question their performance (e.g., poor work habits, habitual absences, and other abuses). While protection tends to be afforded only to employees in public workplaces, private employees nevertheless share similar interests. The difference between protection afforded public and private employees rests merely on the nature of employer, without regard for the actual proprietary interests of the particular employees.

Procedural due process in the workplace echoes the constitutional entitlement that every accused person has to a fair hearing and an objective evaluation of his or her guilt or innocence before being deprived of property or liberty. In workplace terms, "Every employee has a right to a public hearing, peer evaluation, outside arbitration or some other open and mutually agreed upon grievance procedure before being demoted, unwillingly transferred, or fired" (Werhane, 1985: 110). A person with a job at risk is like an accused criminal, in that both have at stake something that places their survival, liberty, or livelihood in serious jeopardy. Due process thus affords the accused, or the potentially fired, demoted, or transferred employee, an opportunity to hear an explanation, and to challenge that explanation if warranted.

Not everyone supports due process guarantees in private workplaces. Ian Maitland contends that there are grave consequences associated with providing for procedural due process in the workplace:

> [I]f employers were generally to heed business ethicists and institute workplace due process [for example] in cases of dismissals and take the increased costs or reduced efficiency out of workers' pay checks – then they would expose themselves to the pirating of their workers by other employers who would give workers what they wanted instead of respecting their rights in the workplace. . . . In short, there is good reason for concluding that the prevalence of EAW does accurately reflect workers' preferences for wages over contractually guaranteed protections against unfair dismissal. (Maitland, 1990: 34–5)

According to Maitland, due process procedures should not be implemented in the workplace because they undermine EAW, which, he indicates, already reflects "workers' preferences."

There are a number of weaknesses with Maitland's position. Such an argument assumes that (1) due process increases costs and reduces efficiency, a contention that is not documented by the many corporations that have grievance procedures; and (2) workers will generally give up some basic rights for other benefits, such as money. The latter is certainly sometimes true, but not always so, particularly when there are questions of unfair dismissals or job security. Maitland also assumes that an employee is on the same level and possesses the same power as his or her manager, and that the employee can design his or her own benefit package, through which grievance procedures, whistleblower protections, or other rights are guaranteed. Maitland implies that employers might include in that package of benefits their rights to practice the policy of unfair dismissals in return for increased pay. He also at least implicitly suggests that procedures such as due process preclude dismissals and layoffs. This is not true, however. Procedural due process demands a means of appeal, and substantive due process demands good reasons, both of which are requirements for other managerial decisions and judgments. Neither of these demands benevolence, requires guaranteeing lifetime employment, or prevents dismissals. In fact, having good reasons gives an employer a justification for getting rid of poor employees.

The problem with ignoring workplace due process lies in assumptions. If you assume that the employee to be fired deserves to be fired, then due process does not necessarily seem important at first blush. The employee who is habitually late, or who does not perform well, should not be surprised by the decision. But what about the satisfactory performer? What about the employee who is shocked not because he or she is negligent, but because there is no perceived work-related reason for his or her firing? What about the employee who is being fired because of fabricated allegations? Without due process, the true wrongdoing may never come to light and a solid employee, perhaps a valuable contributor, may be wrongfully accused or terminated.

Ironically, while many people consider due process a cost for the firm, it could actually be perceived as a cost-saver. Take, for example, the situation where false allegations have been made. Suppose they involve a key employee – an active contributor, someone who is on the "fast track" within the firm. It is not just the employee who is potentially harmed by the absence of due process; the firm will often suffer as well through the loss of a valuable human asset and the negative morale of remaining employees. It could be argued that the firm will suffer more in the long term, in that, if that employee is truly valuable, he or she will be unemployed for only a short period of time. In addition, not only will he or she be the loss of the firm, but also it is likely that the firm will suffer doubly if a savvy competitor then hires that person.

At a minimum, procedural due process affords an employee the right not to be demoted or fired without a hearing or some other grievance procedure. Due process falls squarely in line with the democratic ideal that guarantees the universal right to fair treatment, since, without due process, an employee does not receive fair treatment in the workplace. Notice that "fair treatment" is not equivalent to identical treatment. Just as murderers do not deserve the same treatment as non-murderers, so, too, weak employees do not deserve the same degree of job security as strong ones. Still, every person – murderer, drunk, sloth, or loyal employee – deserves a fair hearing to test his or her guilt or innocence in the workplace.

Establishing due process procedures in the workplace is often believed to contradict EAW, which allows employers and employees to change the terms of employment without cause. It is a mistake, though, to view EAW and procedural due process as inherently contradictory. EAW is a *default* rule, not a guiding principle. In other words, while EAW allows employers and employees to behave arbitrarily, it does not necessarily encourage it. The rationale for EAW encompasses values such as efficacy and simplicity, values aimed at enhancing firm performance. Firm performance is not enhanced by arbitrary firings for two reasons. First, arbitrary management behavior of any sort belies managerial best practices, and second, such behavior creates low employee morale and the loss of valuable employees. Procedural due process, as a mechanism for preventing such negative influences on firm performance, would be consistent with EAW and with consistent reasonable managerial behavior.

According to EAW, employers and employees are entitled to change the terms of employment for any reason or no reason, as long as the reason does not contradict public policy or the law. Procedural due process does not inherently impose upon employers or employees any additional obligations or responsibilities, in that it does not evaluate or judge the reasons employers choose to offer. All procedural due process does is to give employees the opportunity to hear the reasons for the changes made to their employment. Procedural due process does not enable employees to challenge those reasons, except where EAW would also provide for challenges, with regard to employment changes that contradict public policy or the law, such as those based on discrimination, sexual harassment, disability, or age.

Substantive due process

Procedural due process argues for giving employees the right to some form of grievance procedure. Substantive due process, on the other hand, requires that there are *good* reasons for employment decisions. Substantive due process, like procedural due process, does not preclude demotion or firing, but it questions the arbitrariness of employment decision-making. This second component grants substantive guarantees that an employee cannot be fired or demoted without good reasons. Respect for employees would seem to require that an employer provide reasons – sound reasons – for actions that affect employees. In particular, an action such as a firing or demotion, which radically changes the future of an employee, calls for an explanation. This is not to say that most employers do not have reasons, even good reasons, for their actions. It is to require that these be stated openly and objectively to an employee and that he or she have some way to appeal or to respond. Otherwise there is often a perception that an employer is assuming that an employee does not deserve or will not be able to comprehend the rationale for demotion or firing.

In addition, substantive due process ensures that the employer has to justify his or her action to the employee. This is valuable from an employer's perspective as well as from the point of view of an employee, for it makes public the poor judgments made by managers at all levels of employment, judgments that otherwise might not come to light.

Grievance and other due process procedures need not be lengthy or interfere with efficient productivity. Well-organized procedures that evaluate the issue in question quickly as well as objectively do not slow business activity. In fact, often, internal due process procedures can avoid lengthy and costly court battles. From a utilitarian perspective, arbitrary firing and demotion places employees at an unfair disadvantage vis-à-vis other employees or other persons seeking new employment. Such arbitrariness confers no benefit to productive organizations, save that it protects their alleged right to do as they please, a right surely restricted by whether or not exercising it harms other rights. The practice of due process in the workplace can protect an employer against arbitrary actions by employees, since these procedures can be used to evaluate questionable employee activities that conflict with the goals of the organization.

Critics argue that, even if it is true that EAW is to the advantage of the employer, the institution of due process in the workplace creates an imbalance of rights in favor of the employee, because it restricts the exercise of freedom of the employer without equally restricting the choices of the employee. They argue that it merely replaces one unjust principle with another. This objection is inaccurate. Due process neither alters employee–employer arrangements in place in an organization nor infringes on an employer's prima facie right to dispose of production or what happens to that production. Due process does not require that employers never dismiss workers. It merely restricts the employer's alleged right to control employment without having to state reasons for particular employment decisions. This restriction improves rather than disturbs employee–employer relationships, because it strengthens mutual trust.

An additional criticism of due process in the workplace is that employees are sometimes afraid to use it because of fear of retaliation by a superior. Due process procedures are only window-dressings that do not really protect employees. Any so-called "open door" policy also suffers in particular from such fears. This is a valid criticism, but it is scarcely a good reason for not instituting due process; rather, it suggests that there is a great need for comprehensive grievance policies in the workplace (Werhane, 1985; Werhane and Radin, 1996).

Finally, to be consistent, if employees have rights to procedural and substantive due process, then, by analogy, employers, too, should have correlative rights. This means that employers, like, employees, have the right to demand good reasons when an employee or manager asks to be transferred or quits without notice. In addition, employers have rights to their proprietary information, and they have rights to have policies enforced. Employees should not be able to disregard employer rights and avoid repercussions by quitting (Werhane, 1985).

Alternative dispute resolution

The right to due process in the workplace is an issue because American laws do not protect it consistently for public and private employees. Even where due process channels are provided, there is little scrutiny regarding their form or content. Alternative Dispute Resolution (ADR) has become an increasingly attractive option in a number of settings, as mediation and arbitration are encouraged as alternatives to the time-consuming and costly litigation process. In addition, the courts are overloaded. According to the Administrative Office of the US Courts, more than 20,000 employment discrimination claims are filed yearly (Gibeaut, 2001). Some employers have thus turned to arbitration as an alternative to the institution of internal due process mechanisms. Unfortunately, arbitration also provides a less than satisfactory solution in many situations. Even though ADR has not reached a large number of employees yet – the American Arbitration Association, the largest private dispute-resolution service, reported having run less than 2,000 employment-related mediations and arbitrations in 1999 – the rights of those employees have been endangered, and employer acceptance of the policy is growing (Gibeaut, 2001).

Arbitration is the process through which parties agree to submit to the resolution of their dispute by a person who is trained and certified to adjudicate disputes in the place of a judge and/or jury. When parties engage in arbitration, prior to the rendering of the decision, both sides agree to accept the decision of the arbitrator, regardless of what it is, and agree to forgo their right to take the matter to court. In other words, arbitration is a substitution for judicial adjudication.

While an acceptable alternative for many parties, it has become problematic where implicitly or explicitly required. In the employment context, for example, a number of employers have resorted to mandatory arbitration provisions as a condition for employment (Yatsco, 1998). While employees are not compelled to accept a particular resolution as a condition for employment, they are compelled to accept a particular form of adjudication. The rationale for mandatory arbitration provisions is that they do help to mitigate the costs associated with the resolution of disputes. "By agreeing to arbitrate a statutory claim, a party does not forgo the substantive rights afforded by the statute; it only submits their resolution in an arbitral, rather than a judicial, forum," wrote Justice Harry Blackmun, in *Mitsubishi Motors Corp.* v. *Soler Chrysler-Plymouth Inc.*, 473 U.S. 614 (1985). "[Mandatory dispute resolution] trades the procedures and opportunity for review of the courtroom for the simplicity, informality and expedition of arbitration."

In 1991, the United States Supreme Court held in *Gilmer* v. *Interstate/Johnson Lane Corp.*, 500 U.S. 20 (1991), that employers can bind employees through mandatory arbitration provisions, and thereby preclude employees from exercising their right "to institute a private judicial action." A number of courts have since echoed this ruling. In *Cole* v. *Burns Int'l Sec. Servs.*, 105 F.3d 1465, 1478 (D.C. Cir. 1997), for example, the court explained that "the Supreme Court now has made clear that, as a general rule, statutory claims are fully subject to binding arbitration. Similarly, in *Beauchamp* v. *Great W. Life Assurance Co.*, 918 F. Supp. 1091 (E.D. Mich. 1996), the court maintained that an arbitration cause is a reasonable precondition for employment. In addition, in *Cremlin* v. *Merrill Lynch Pierce Fenner & Smith, Inc.*, 957 F. Supp. 1460 (N.D. Ill. 1997), the court upheld mandatory arbitration, and maintained that it did not inherently translate into the deprivation of due process for employees.

What does this mean for employees? Unfortunately, the presence of *mandatory* arbitration clauses means that in many instances employee rights continue to be eroded. For Susan Brooks, it meant that she lost a lucrative job, in which she was performing well, without having an adequate voice to respond to what was happening to her. In 1997, Brooks was fired from her $90,000 job at Travelers Property Casualty Corporation when her position was allegedly eliminated. Although the Travelers employment manual indicated the presence of a mandatory arbitration policy, Brooks was never aware or informed of the policy. In addition, the policy was one-sided in favor of employers and extremely restrictive for employees: hearings had to occur on one day, and arbitrators could not award punitive damages or attorney fees to complainants.

This illustrates the primary problem with mandatory arbitration proceedings. Submission to an arbitrator is not inherently disadvantageous to one party or another, except when the proceedings themselves are couched within terms that favor one side over the other, and this is what tends to happen with mandatory arbitration provisions in employment arrangements. For this reason, the policy of conditioning employment on mandatory arbitration provisions has been met with criticism from employees, attorneys, and administrative agencies (Yatsco, 1998; Johnston, 2001). Brooks' situation is not an isolated example. In many situations, conditions are attached to the imposition of mandatory arbitration provisions that potentially bias the outcome of the proceedings. In Brooks' situation, restrictions on timing and damages placed her at a serious detriment. Mandatory arbitration procedures have thus become controversial when it is not clear that the rights of both parties are equally protected, particularly when employees do not find out about those clauses until after a problem arises (Gibeaut, 2001).

According to George Nicolau, a national arbitrator, "[A mandatory arbitration] policy is not fair to employees, does not afford adequate procedural or substantive protections and . . . does not afford employees rights to which they are entitled by law" (Gibeaut, 2001: 51). In addition, a policy of mandatory arbitration provisions works to the detriment of employers as well as employees (Yatsco, 1998). It creates a fundamental tension between employee rights and employers' interests in expediency not to spend excessive time or money on the resolution of employment disputes. This, in turn, causes potential tension in the workplace among employees, which can lead to losses in productivity. While indiscriminate adoption of such policies can limit short-term costs, it can cause severe harm to morale, as does the complete absence of due process, and long-term costs can increase as the policies themselves are taken to court, as has occurred in a number of instances. Even if the policies are upheld, the cost of getting to that decision seems to outweigh, or at least seriously challenge, any derived benefit.

The court's position with regard to the implementation of mandatory arbitration provisions in the workplace illustrates the lack of legally recognized and legally guaranteed employee rights. Mandatory arbitration provisions do not adequately replace this need.

WHISTLEBLOWER PROTECTION 

In the workplace, employees and managers usually have a voice with regard to others' actions. Employees are frequently positioned to observe one another's behavior, particularly as it influences firm activities. Organizations therefore often demand that employees comment upon the behavior of other employees through formal and informal feedback mechanisms. Supervisors, for example, are required to conduct periodic evaluations of their subordinates, and that information is often what employment-related decisions, such as terminations, are based on. In some firms employees are asked to evaluate their supervisors as well. When employees encounter unfavorable information regarding behavior that benefits the firm, however, they often confront a dilemma regarding what to do with that information. If they choose to exercise their voice, they can place their jobs in jeopardy.

Jeffrey S. Wigand is one among many who have confronted this very dilemma. As a vice-president in charge of research at Brown & Williamson, a leading cigarette manufacturer, Wigand stumbled upon information that other employees in his organization were defrauding customers. In addition, he became aware that Thomas Sandefur, former chief executive of Brown & Williamson, had lied to Congress (Dworkin and Callahan, 1998; Calvert, 1996). The situation for Wigand was complex: concealing this information would turn Wigand into an accessory to what he considered inappropriate behavior; revealing the information, however, would place him in professional jeopardy. Clearly, Brown & Williamson would not want to retain an employee who was a "snitch," particularly since the information he obtained was confidential. In addition, there were serious questions regarding who else might want to hire a whistleblower.

Wigand chose to divulge information regarding the business practices at Brown & Williamson. According to Wigand, Brown & Williamson knew that cigarettes were harmful to people's health, but they did not reveal this information to the public (Field, 1997). In addition, Wigand contended that Brown & Williamson intentionally manipulated nicotine levels to increase the addictiveness of cigarettes, in spite of knowledge of the presence of serious health hazards (Calvert, 1996).

The loss of his job was not the only consequence Wigand encountered, though. Not only did he lose his privacy by becoming a public figure, through media coverage as well as being featured in the movie, *The Insider*, but he also ended up being sued by his former employer for allegedly breaching a confidentiality agreement, fraud, and theft. While the suit was ultimately dismissed, Wigand nevertheless suffered from his decision to "blow the whistle" on the business practices being endorsed by high ranking executives at Brown & Williamson (Weinstein, 1997).

David Cray was also a whistleblower. Cray was a stockbroker for NationsSecurities, a joint venture between NationsBank (now Bank of America) and Dean Witter. Cray contended that "the bank was pressuring unsophisticated bank customers to buy securities without explaining the risks. He also reported that the bank was pushing high-commission proprietary products, even when they were not suitable, and failing to explain the fees" (Henderson, 1997: 18). Cray first complained to the Chief Operating Officer of NationsSecurities and, then, on June 17, 1994, he went public to the Tampa Bay Florida newspapers. That was also the day he was terminated. Eventually, after three years of arbitration, Cray won his suit against NationsBank. The court ordered that he be reinstated at the Bank, but with no compensation for three years of lost time. In the meantime, NationsBank has had to settle two class action suits for $60 million having to do with exactly Cray's accusations. Cray's personal and family life has suffered, and most of his friends and former associates shun him (Henderson, 1997).

"Whistleblowing" is the name given to the act of reporting apparent wrongdoing. Generally, whistleblowing occurs when an employee, or former employee, reports alleged wrongdoing either to a superior within the firm or leaks information to the media or reports it directly to administrative agencies. The term is derived from the English bobbies (policemen) blowing their whistles when they learned that a crime had been committed, in order to alert the public and other law enforcement officials within range (Corbo, 1994). Today the whistleblower is someone not regularly charged with law enforcement, who nevertheless elects to report corporate wrongdoing that he or she encounters:

> A whistleblower is an employee or officer of any institution, profit or nonprofit, private or public, who believes either that he/she has been ordered to perform some act or he/she has obtained knowledge that the institution is engaged in activities which (a) are believed to cause unnecessary harm to third parties, (b) are in violation of human rights or (c) run counter to the defined purpose of the institution, and who informs [a supervisor or] the public of this fact. (Bowie, 1982: 142)

Whistleblowing appears to be a way for employees to have a voice, a form of free speech, and we might justify it on that basis. Whistleblowing, though, is not merely a matter of a right to free speech. The whistleblower must have facts and grounds for his or her accusation. Merely "feeling" that there is wrongdoing, and making an accusation on that basis, is libelous, and unfair to the organization and to its employees. We thus would want to distinguish that sort of behavior from legitimate whistleblowing, where there is data to back up the contentions. Legitimate whistleblowing also appears to be justified on the basis of the virtue of truth-telling. In some cases, it is a detriment to the organization, or even the public interest, if a falsehood or wrongdoing is not made public. It is possible to argue, then, that whistleblowers have prima facie duties to blow the whistle in cases where the data supports a wrongdoing that, if not corrected, would continue to foster or abet harm.

Such arguments are too simplistic, however. Potential whistleblowers confront a panorama of moral conflicts. Whistleblowing often occurs in institutional settings where potential whistleblowers have developed loyalties in alliances with organizations and colleagues. Employees who gain access to potentially damaging information are often employees, like Wigand, who have a long and fruitful history with that organization. Accompanying company loyalty is a trust between employees that whistleblowing, even legitimate whistleblowing, threatens to unravel. Whistleblowers often seek discontinuation of the wrongdoing and punishment of the wrongdoers, but they ordinarily do not seek to cause undue harm to the organization and other employees, harm that will almost inevitably follow. Potential whistleblowers, particularly those who have been with the same company for a long time, are sometimes hesitant on the grounds of loyalty and good-faith employment relationships they might have enjoyed.

Whistleblowers are often reluctant to become branded as pariahs. While it might seem that other employees would be outraged by the wrongdoing, and would support the whistleblower, this is often not the case. Other employees frequently feel guilty, either for not seeing the wrongdoing themselves or for not reporting it, and they take this out on the person who exercised the courage to come forward. In addition, loyalty, even when misplaced, is often considered of the utmost importance. While the act of reporting wrongdoing serves the public good, no one wants to be associated with a "snitch." The whistleblower is often viewed as a "tattletale," and "telling tales," even when true, is still considered taboo in the workplace.

Whistleblowers often jeopardize their employment and future prospects. Those whistleblowers who do not lose their jobs still suffer in that their effectiveness is often hampered. In addition, they experience a notoriously difficult time finding positions elsewhere. According to Sissela Bok, "A government handbook issued during the Nixon era recommends reassigning 'undesirables' to places so remote that they would prefer to resign" (1980: 2). Whistleblowers are treated as "undesirables," by their firms and others, and this takes a toll on them and their families.

Whistleblowers are often attacked personally. Wigand, for example, was personally sued for revealing the wrongdoing. Even though the suit was eventually dismissed, it was not without consequences to him. Other whistleblowers suffer personal ostracism – not just by former co-workers. While the act of whistleblowing is arguably "heroic," whistleblowers are often treated as "troublemakers" (Lofgren, 1993).

Finally, whistleblowers are often reluctant to come forward when they are not convinced that their efforts will be productive. Not all whistleblowing is successful in remedying prior wrongs or countering future potential harms or violations of rights. It is not clear that NationsBank/Bank of America reformed its brokerage practices, or that Cray's activities have been adopted as a model for good brokerage practices.

Given these difficulties, Norman Bowie and Ronald Duska (1990) have proposed some conditions that whistleblowers should consider before choosing to report wrongdoing:

1 The intended whistleblowing is based on solid verified information of activities that have caused or will cause non-trivial harm.
2 The whistleblower has exhausted all alternative internal channels for dissent before informing the public.
3 The whistleblower has reasonable evidence to back up his or her accusation.
4 The activities in question are of a serious nature and threaten public interests, which cannot be ignored or addressed in another manner.
5 It is more likely than not that the concerns will be heard and that reform will take place.
6 There is no other person and no other means to make public the accusation. The whistleblower is the person of last resort.

If these preconditions are met, Bowie and Duska conclude, it is reasonable for someone with knowledge of wrongdoing to blow the whistle.

The employee's right to blow the whistle is significant. It is important for whistleblowers to be protected from retaliation because the concealment of wrongdoing can be harmful to employees, employers, and others. For example, in the recent Enron case, employees, stockholders, and the firm (among others) suffered permanent harm because no one within the company or in the external audit firm questioned what now appear to be unsavory accounting practices. As a result, the integrity of Arthur Andersen, the audit firm, was undermined, Enron was destroyed, and its shareholders, managers, and employees have suffered terrible financial losses.

It is also important to protect employers from false allegations. Because of the severity of the consequences, accuracy is key. It is difficult for an organization, or an individual, to recover the goodwill lost as a result of false allegations. In addition, particularly in the corporate setting, the spreading of untruths can set in motion events that are difficult to reverse, such as loss of trust or low morale. This is unfair to the organization and its employees. False allegations can, therefore, constitute prosecutable libel.

Some states have passed legislation that protects whistleblowers from retaliatory measures, and courts in other jurisdictions have enunciated the right to blow the whistle as an exception to EAW. The legal protection is useful, in that it can deter wrongdoing, and it serves to remove some of the impediments to whistleblowing. In addition, even though many whistleblowers are still shunned, it sends the symbolic message that whistleblowers are not wrongdoers.

Legal protection for whistleblowers is, nevertheless, far from guaranteed in every state. Whistleblowing involves the reporting of violations of law, harm to individuals, and infringements of basic rights. Reporting such occurrences, so that unjust practices can be remedied, is beneficial to society. Wrongdoing harms all those associated with it – the wrongdoers, their associations, and the organizations with which they are affiliated. It is thus advisable for organizations to have internal whistleblowing mechanisms, such as "hotlines," suggestion boxes, and ombudspersons, through which wrongdoing can be discovered and reported. When they operate properly, internal whistleblowing mechanisms can prevent public exposure and humiliation for both the whistleblower and the organization. In addition, providing internal reporting channels can contribute to the continual improvement of organizations. If organizations embed in their cultures acceptance of reporting wrongdoing, and respond to such information expeditiously and responsibly, everyone benefits. Then, whistleblower protection becomes irrelevant, because employees do not have to go outside their organizations to correct wrongs.

DEMOCRATIZATION OF THE WORKPLACE

Due process and internal channels for whistleblowing are ways in which employees can maintain a degree of control over their careers and the nature of their work. There are ways, though, in which organizations can be enhanced even further by tapping into employee expertise. It can be argued that employees, as those closest to the work being done, are in the best position to determine how that work can best be accomplished.

Examining the contemporary workplace through a democratization model opens up a number of possibilities. In *Authority and Democracy: A General Theory of Government and Management*, Christopher McMahon demonstrates how redefining employment can shed light on innovative solutions to workplace dilemmas (McMahon, 1994). McMahon suggests that the democratization of the American workplace could provide for healthier, more equitable employment relationships. He attempts to paint a picture of a democratized workplace that encourages mutually beneficial employment relationships through which legitimate authority is exercised without the sacrifice of individual autonomy. McMahon draws an innovative analogy between the state and the workplace, and he reconceptualizes the public/private distinction so as to bring government and non-government employment relationships together into the same public sphere. He is not concerned that employees do not all share the same interests, for he sees both political and labor theory as being about how successful institutions manage conflicting views. While McMahon's theory is not fully developed, the insights he offers open up interesting possibilities. He enables us to envision a workplace where employers and employees are assigned equal rights and responsibilities regardless of the political status of their corporations.

McMahon tells a story that he believes is both descriptive and normative. Although he refers to both the state and the corporation, he does not separate them according to the traditional understanding of the public/private distinction. McMahon instead redefines the distinction and brings the state and the corporation together into the same sphere. Whereas much criticism of the public/ private distinction tends to revolve around whether or not such a distinction exists, McMahon does not take issue with its existence. Rather, he suggests that the distinction is not embedded in property ownership, but in actual associations between people.

At the heart of McMahon's analysis lies a quest for a basis of authority that that is not merely legalistic. McMahon argues that traditional explanations of the public/private distinction are flawed in that they do not account properly for two separate spheres: ownership and management authority. He begins by attacking first the belief that property rights are the basis for the public/private distinction. If they were, then public actions would employ only publicly owned resources and private actions would employ only privately owned resources.

McMahon, though, parses out the distinction differently. Property rights have value only to the extent that property owners can exclude others from that property or from uses of that property. At the same time, McMahon asserts, "Property rights in productive resources cannot provide the moral basis for managerial authority, understood as the authority to tell employees what to do, as opposed to what to refrain from doing" (1994: 17). This is because ownership has to do with control of property, not control of people. Legitimate managerial authority cannot, therefore, be justified on the basis of property rights, and the public/private distinction that is based on property cannot serve as the basis for a distinction between public and private sectors of the workforce.

Without abandoning the public/private distinction entirely, McMahon redefines the spheres: "[W]e can define the public sphere of human life as the sphere of those social mechanisms that make it possible for people with conflicting aims, especially moral aims, to live together. . . . The private sphere then becomes the sphere of association among people with coincident aims" (1994: 17). It follows, then, according to McMahon, that the workplace is governed by the same rules, regardless of whether the state is involved in the employment relationship.

The employment relationship, as outlined by McMahon, does not detract from individual autonomy. Autonomy, in its broadest sense, is about self-determination. It is about voluntary personal decision-making linked to the achievement of certain ends. In the workplace envisioned by McMahon, autonomy translates into empowering employees to evaluate managers' decisions according to their own considered judgments. It is not that employees should refuse to obey all directives that conflict with their considered judgments, but they are expected to challenge those directives that appear clearly immoral. This distinction is significant, because McMahon anticipates a diverse workplace. He notices that various employees and employers who enter employment agreements will have a variety of concerns and interests. McMahon does not believe that the presence of diversity threatens workplace stability. Quite to the contrary, he indicates that the interplay between the concerns and interests can actually enable the workplace to thrive.

Legitimate authority should undergird every workplace agreement. "To have authority," he explains, "is to have a right to direct the actions of some other people" (1994: 27). In a democratized workplace, authority serves those governed. In other words, employees in a democratized workplace will accept their employers' authority autonomously if it is their considered judgment that this is in their best interests. "To the extent that employees are positively disposed to comply with directives and be good team players, they accord de facto authority to their bosses" (1994: 193).

McMahon then introduces a "contractarian" justification of authority, which he labels "C-authority." According to such a definition, authority exists not because of a legal or political system, but because of the agreements people make between one another to facilitate mutual cooperation. "People can often improve their situation by their own lights if they cooperate with others," McMahon states. "This is because by acting together the members of a group can produce an event or state of affairs that each values but that none of them could have produced alone. Authority can facilitate such cooperation" (1994: 102). According to McMahon, C-authority – authority generated from the mutual goal of cooperation – underlies a democratized corporation. He indicates that it is the only sort of legitimate authority through which employees can preserve their individual autonomy while still submitting to authority. Employers and employees work together because they recognize that cooperation is mutually beneficial. The role that managers take on is one of facilitating this cooperation. Employers and employees make decisions, not according to what lies in their personal best interests, but according to what lies in their collective best interests.

Cooperative democracy provides the vehicle through which McMahon envisions a renovated workplace. He envisions the democratized workplace as operating through joint efforts. Managers would continue to fill the primary decision-making roles, but employees would have avenues through which they would not only be allowed, but would also be encouraged to voice their criticism, concerns, and comments. For the workplace to be democratized it is not necessary that everyone participate in the decision, but, rather, that everyone's interests be reflected in the decision-making process and that everyone have the opportunity to be heard regarding the decisions made:

> The suggestions that representatives of such groups [as stakeholder constituencies] should participate are associated with a widely held, but I believe fundamentally mistaken, conception of democracy. This is the view that democracy requires that, or is more fully realized to the extent that, people have a say in what affects them. A little reflection shows that this is not a principle that we accept in the

> political sphere. Virtually everyone in the world is affected by the foreign policy decisions of the U.S. government, but we do not suppose that they therefore have a right to participate in making these decisions or in choosing those who make them. They have a right that their morally legitimate claims be taken into account by those who formulate the foreign policy of the United States, and this may imply a duty on the part of policy makers to give them a hearing, but they do not have a right to be among those who make the decisions by which this policy is formulated. Only the citizens of the United States have this right. (McMahon, 1994: 11)

In this way, McMahon explains how corporations take stakeholder interests into account, without having to incorporate actual stakeholders into all decision-making processes. Democracy does not relieve people of having to think about the ramifications of their actions upon other people just because not everyone is included in decision-making.

The democratization of the workplace adds an element of fairness that the EAW-dominated workplace does not recognize. McMahon asserts that, in dealing with employees or anyone else associated with the corporation, such as stakeholders, the guiding principle should be fairness:

> Replacing the view that managers should consider the interests of various 'stakeholders' with the view that they should avoid treating people unfairly would, I think, help to clarify the moral dimension of management. The stakeholder view provides no way of judging the relative importance of affected interests and leads to a strategy of trying to give everyone something. The concept of fairness, by contrast, enables us to judge some of the members of affected groups as having no valid claim to consideration, and others as having very strong claims. And when claims clash, the concept of fairness provides a basis other than the intensity of the associated desires for deciding which are more important. (1994: 173)

At the same time, McMahon emphasizes the participatory role of employees in the decision-making process through an analogy to political theory. "Citizens have the right to formulate foreign policy, or to choose who will formulate it, because the laws and policies of their country organize their collective actions – organize what they collectively do and allow," McMahon asserts. "The people who have a right, under democratic principles, to participate in a decision are not those who are affected by it but those whose actions are guided by it" (1994: 12). In the corporation, this translates into employees having the right to participate in decision-making because they are the ones expected to live by and carry out the decisions. In this way, McMahon nicely both narrows and widens the stakeholder list. He keeps out some of the extraneous parties who might like to participate, such as stakeholder interest groups (while still acknowledging their concerns), yet he is careful to include core stakeholders such as employees. McMahon thus argues that employees must be given the opportunity to participate (or, rather, to have their concerns incorporated into the decision-making process) as if they were citizens of a state (1994: 191).

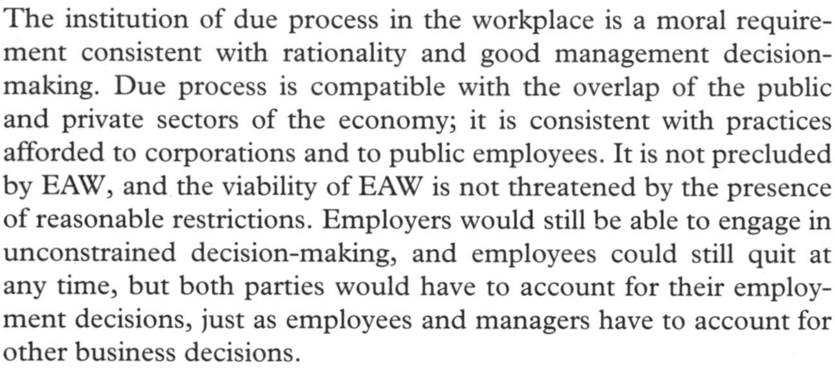

CONCLUSION

The institution of due process in the workplace is a moral requirement consistent with rationality and good management decision-making. Due process is compatible with the overlap of the public and private sectors of the economy; it is consistent with practices afforded to corporations and to public employees. It is not precluded by EAW, and the viability of EAW is not threatened by the presence of reasonable restrictions. Employers would still be able to engage in unconstrained decision-making, and employees could still quit at any time, but both parties would have to account for their employment decisions, just as employees and managers have to account for other business decisions.

Similarly, whistleblower protection, through either internal mechanisms or publicly available channels, benefits employees and employers by providing employees a voice. While organizations often object to the whistleblowing measures, they, along with the whistleblowers, eventually benefit from the elimination of the wrongdoing. Moreover, if organizations take the initiative to provide for internal reporting, they can prevent the publication of their mistakes.

This, coupled with McMahon's proposal, suggests that our efforts should be aimed at looking toward models of employment that emphasize the players (employers and employees) over the policies. McMahon redirects us away from traditional debates. Neither history nor law protects employees. The mistake, though, is in stopping there. The lack of formal protection does not indicate that protection is not warranted or desired.

By injecting democratic principles into employment relationships,

McMahon renders moot much of the criticism of EAW. In a democratized workplace, due process would not have to be mandated by law, for an appeals process most likely would be built into the corporate organizational structure. McMahon's arguments therefore imply that the EAW debate has been misdirected. It is not the rule that needs rewriting, it is the workplace that needs democratizing. Such democratizing does not entail the demise of free enterprise as we know it, and it does not eliminate managerial authority. In fact, in such a workplace, external whistleblowing has a different role, for a democratized workplace inherently contains internal channels for redress and reform. The democratization of the workplace simply reflects our morality intuition. It embodies the moral requirement of fair treatment; it is consistent with our political practices, and reflects new thinking about employee empowerment.

REFERENCES

Articles, books, and other similar publications

Bok, Sissela. 1980. "Whistleblowing and Professional Responsibility." *New York University Education Quarterly*, vol. 11: 2–7.

Bowie, Norman. 1982. *Business Ethics*. Englewood Cliffs, NJ: Prentice Hall.

Bowie, Norman and Ronald Duska. 1990. *Business Ethics*. Englewood Cliffs, NJ: Prentice Hall.

Calvert, Clay. 1996. "Stumbling Down Tobacco Road: Media Self-Censorship and Corporate Capitulation in the War on the Cigarette Industry." *Loyola of Los Angeles Law Review*, vol. 30: 139–75.

Corbo, Joan. 1994. "*Kraus* v. *New Rochelle Hosp. Medical Ctr.*: Are Whistleblowers Finally Getting the Protection They Need?" *Hofstra Labor Law Journal*, vol. 12: 141–62.

Duska, Ronald. 1996. "Whistleblowing and Employee Loyalty." In J. Des Jardins and John McCall, eds., *Contemporary Issues in Business Ethics*, 3rd edn. Belmont, CA: Wadsworth, 162–6.

Dworkin, Terry Morehead, and Callahan, Elletta Sangrey. 1998. "Buying Silence." *American Business Law Journal*, vol. 36: 151–91.

Field, Ingrid L. Dietsch. 1997. "No Ifs, Ands or Butts: Big Tobacco is Fighting for its Life Against a New Breed of Plaintiffs Armed with Mounting Evidence." *University of Baltimore Law Review*, vol. 27: 99–128.

Gibeaut, John. 2001. "Detoured to ADR: A New Round of Employment Issues is Coming to Court as Companies Look to Refine the Wording of Workers' Contracts." *American Bar Association Journal*, vol. 87: 50.

Henderson, Rex. 1997. "Whistleblowing Broke His Stride." *Tampa Tribune*, October 12: 18.

Johnston, Sarah. 2001. "Current Public Law and Policy Issues in ADR: ADR in the Employment Discrimination Context: Friend or Foe to Claimants." *Hamline Journal of Public Law and Policy*, vol. 22: 335–81.

Lofgren, Lois A. 1993. "Whistleblower Protection: Should Legislatures and the Courts Provide a Shelter to Public and Private Sector Employees Who Disclose the Wrongdoing of Employers?" *South Dakota Law Review*, vol. 38: 316–40.

Maitland, Ian. 1990. "Rights in the Workplace: A Nozickian Argument." In Lisa Newton and Maureen Ford, eds., *Taking Sides*. Guilford, CT: Dushkin Publishing Group, 33–7.

McMahon, Christopher. 1994. *Authority and Democracy: A General Theory of Government and Management*. New Jersey: Princeton University Press.

Radin, Tara J., and Werhane, Patricia H. 1996. "The Public/Private Distinction and the Political Status of Employment." *American Business Law Journal*, vol. 34, no. 2: 245–60.

Scanlon, T. M. 1977. "Due Process." In J. Roland Pennock and John W. Chapman, eds., *Nomos XVIII: Due Process*. New York: New York University Press, 93–125.

Weinstein, Brian Stryker. 1997. "In Defense of Jeffrey Wigand: A First Amendment Challenge to the Enforcement of Employee Confidentiality Agreements Against Whistleblowers." *South Carolina Law Review*, vol. 49: 129–65.

Werhane, Patricia H. 1985. *Persons, Rights, and Corporations*. Englewood Cliffs, NJ: Prentice Hall.

Werhane, Patricia H. and Radin, Tara J. 1996. "Employment at Will and Due Process." In T. Beauchamp and N. Bowie, eds., *Ethical Theory and Business*, 5th edn. Englewood Cliffs, NJ: Prentice-Hall. Reprinted in *Ethical Issues in Business*, 5th edn. Englewood Cliffs, NJ: Prentice Hall, 364–74.

Yatsco, Tanya A. 1998. "How about a Real Answer? Mandatory Arbitration as a Condition of Employment and the National Labor Relation Board's Stance." *Albany Law Review*, vol. 62: 257–91.

Cases

Beauchamp v. *Great W. Life Assurance Co.*, 918 F. Supp. 1091 (E.D. Mich. 1996).

Cleveland Bd. of Education v. *Loudermill*, 470 U.S. 532, 84 L. Ed. 2d 494, 105 S. Ct. 1487 (1985).

Cole v. *Burns Int'l Sec. Servs.*, 105 F.3d 1465, 1478 (D.C. Cir. 1997).

Cremlin v. *Merrill Lynch Pierce Fenner & Smith, Inc.*, 957 F. Supp. 1460 (N.D. Ill. 1997).

Gilmer v. *Interstate/Johnson Lane Corp.*, 500 U.S. 20 (1991).
Mitsubishi Motors Corp. v. *Soler Chrysler-Plymouth Inc.*, 473 U.S. 614 (1985).

Legislation

Ohio Rev. Code Ann. § 124.11.

part ii

New Models of Employment and Employment Relationships

In this section, we will explore the role of employment relationships and their contribution to the workplace and its productivity. In chapter 5, we explore role responsibilities. We contend that employee rights are not necessarily imposed on employment relationships. On the contrary, it can be argued that they emerge from within the relationships, as a result of people's interaction with one another. This is followed, in chapter 6, with a discussion of the meaning of work and meaningful work. Our primary argument is that it is important to pay attention to employees' perceptions of their work. This is particularly important, since employees engaging in what they perceive of as meaningful work tend to be more loyal and more productive than employees who are not similarly linked to their work. Chapter 7, written with Norman Bowie, argues that recognizing and protecting employees and employee rights in employment relationships not only coincides with our moral intuitions and legal obligations, but also can contribute to the economic value added to firm performance.

chapter five

Employee Accountability and the Limits of Role Responsibilities

One of the ways most political, social, and economic institutions organize themselves and their associates is through functional assignments, or *roles*. Nowhere is this more evident than in the workplace. That employees and managers have assigned roles and role responsibilities and are accountable to their employers is fairly obvious. What is not obvious is that these are limited responsibilities, which can be set aside by overriding moral concerns. Role responsibilities, and the accountability they entail, involve correlative and, indeed, reciprocal, obligations on the part of both employers and employees. Even absent formal democratization, for which McMahon calls, role definitions create the sorts of relationships that demand the recognition of employee rights. Examining these employer–employee relationships thus offers another way of deriving employee rights in the workplace.

ROLES AND ROLE RESPONSIBILITIES

A "role" is "a capacity in which someone acts in relation to others" (Emmet, 1966, 1996: 12). It defines a person's place or function in a social, economic, cultural, or political position, and "refer[s] to constellations of institutionally specified rights and duties organized around an institutionally specified social function" (Hardimon, 1994: 334). Roles, then, are socially-constructed titles – offices and/or positions that correspond to sets of responsibilities, norms, and expectations in a particular context or set of contexts or in an institution. An institution, then, is the public system or social arrangement that "define[s] offices and positions which can be occupied by different individuals at different times" (Hardimon, 1994: 335). Families, professional associations, trades and trade unions, corporations, churches, and states are all examples of institutions. In this context, the term "role" can refer also to an ideal, a role model, that is, a set of rules or norms indicating how one *should* function or behave in a particular social context. Or "role" can describe how persons *actually* behave in such relationships.

People in society play a number of roles, all of which help to define the various relationships that exist between individuals, between individuals and institutions, and between individuals, institutions, and the state. We each have an array of interacting and overlapping cultural, professional, religious, and social roles, and these roles change over time. For example, a woman who is of Irish background can have many roles such as a child, a mother, a student, a professor, an author, a consultant, an employee, an employer, a Protestant, an American, a member of the world community, an environmentalist, a liberal, a humanist, and so on. Because one person is all of these things, as most of us "wear a variety of hats," so to speak, we as a society are comprised of a multitude of intricate social relationships. It is therefore said that we play a variety of "roles." Interpretations of roles vary. In an organization, for example, role responsibilities are generally conceived of in a variety of ways: as the normal demands of the job, as the expectations of the position, as the individual's conception of his or her part in the organization, or as the way in which a person satisfies or violates the expectations of the organization's leaders.

Role responsibilities are derived from a number of sources and often depend upon how others in the organization perceive of their relationship to the individual in his or her role. Demands might be imposed by the job description or by the actions and expectations of other members of the organization. Take, for instance, the traditional view that secretaries were supposed to make coffee. Although this was generally not enunciated in the formal job description, for many years it was a responsibility assumed by secretaries, expected by their supervisors. Role responsibilities also derive from personal conceptions of positions and from the actions taken that help to define positions. Similarly, actions can enable people to break out of traditional roles as well. Secretaries revolted against their image as coffee-makers and have refused to perform that task. Many saw it as demeaning, in that it seemed to perpetuate their roles as permanently placed assistants. They saw their roles and their role responsibilities differently from the way in which the organization perceived them, and acted according to their own view of their roles. In doing so, they have, in essence, created new roles for themselves in many organizations – roles with room for upward mobility.

Roles and role responsibilities have two other important characteristics. First, roles have an impersonal quality. Although a person's behavior in his or her role is personal, the expectations and perceptions of that role are impersonal. When a person defines a role, such as that of a mother, she gives a generalizable description that could apply to any number of mothers. Second, roles are defined by implicit or explicit rules, standards, or norms. These rules range in specificity, and may be as explicit as civil service regulations or as vague and implicit as the duties society expects of a father. In the workplace, rules are often fairly clear. Expectations, for the most part, tend to be spelled out in job descriptions, organization handbooks, job hierarchies, organizational cultures, and institutional structures. In addition, job-related roles are influenced by the expectations of subordinates, co-workers, and supervisors, as well as by personal career demands, and even societal mores.

The "rules" associated with roles often paint the picture of the ideal. While the rules assign pertinent rights and responsibilities, they may also prescribe the model of the ideal in that position, such as the ideal father, for example, or the perfect manager. The rules for roles, then, are both descriptions and directives for correctness of behavior that give rise to legitimate expectations on the part of others. There thus emerges a set of impersonal, socially-defined collections of expectations and demands associated with each role. When we take on roles, we inherently assume certain rights and duties as we "play the roles" (Downie, 1971; Emmet, 1966; Hardimon, 1994; Luben, 1988; Werhane, 1985).

According to David Luben, each role we play places different moral demands upon us. Luben indicates that, when moral decisions vary according to our roles, this results in "role morality" (1988: ch. 6). Each of us is enmeshed in a collection of overlapping social, professional, cultural, and religious roles, each of which makes moral demands. This becomes problematic when the demands of the roles we play become confused or seem to conflict with one another. Additional complications occur when the demands of our roles clash with what we might call "common morality," or society's "moral rules." For example, the lawyer who protects a known repeated murderer, the psychologist or priest who honors the confidentiality of a criminal's confession, and the reporter who witnesses his or her spouse committing a crime all confront role conflicts as a result of the conflicting demands of their professional responsibilities, personal ties, and socially-based moral norms.

A number of years ago, Alan Goldman distinguished two models for describing role responsibilities in business and in the professions: weakly differentiated role responsibilities and strongly differentiated role responsibilities. A role is considered "weakly" differentiated if role-related conflicts can be resolved by applying regularly accepted principles of common sense morality, those standards commonly accepted as moral principles in most societies. For example, a clerk would regard him- or herself as having a weakly differentiated role if, when asked to forge a check, he or she were to apply ordinary moral judgments in making the decision. In contrast, a "strongly" differentiated role is one in which certain professional obligations, as defined by professional codes of ethics, outweigh, or are thought to override, ordinary moral considerations. An example of a strongly differentiated role would be the psychiatrist who claims confidentiality for his or her patient being accused of child abuse in a court of law.

Goldman argued that, although many professionals have strongly differentiated roles, businesspeople do not. According to Goldman, it is significant that many professionals, such as engineers, healthcare professionals, accountants, and lawyers, have independent professional moral codes. Since business managers and employees do not have independent professional moral codes, they have only weakly differentiated roles. The result is that, when conflicts arise with regard to business obligations, common sense morality overrides employee role responsibilities. This differs from professionals who have strongly differentiated obligations to their professional codes, for the codes offer an independent set of obligations that govern their decisions and behavior. A priest who violates the confidentiality of the confessional or a lawyer who violates the confidentiality of his or her client, even when life is at stake, violates strongly differentiated professional obligations (Goldman, 1980).

To illustrate, in the 1986 *Challenger* explosion, engineers and managers at Morton Thiokol, the maker of the o-rings, now traced to be the cause of the explosion, were pitted against one other as a result of what turned out to be conflicting roles. On the night before the fated launch, a number of engineers working on the project at Thiokol protested against the launch because of the impending bad weather predicted for the next morning. The engineers cited three factors in their protest: first, they believed that there would be considerable difficulty retrieving the shuttle boosters after the launch in choppy sea waters; second, they feared that the ice in the booster support troughs might affect the shuttle orbiter; and, third, they were concerned that they could not predict the behavior of the o-rings that sealed the booster joints, because the o-rings had not been tested at temperatures below 50 degrees (Fahrenheit) while the weather prediction was for about 30 degrees for scheduled launch.

The engineers in this case operated according to two important roles. Obviously, the men were employees of Thiokol. At the same time, however, they were members of a profession. As members of the engineering profession, these men saw their first responsibility as being to safety, for that is the first priority for all professional engineers. In addition, as engineers, they held the scientific conviction that if a phenomenon has not been tested, it is not appropriate to presume it will work. Indeed, the engineering assumption is generally that, without proof of safety, it is not possible to conclude that the mechanism will not fail.

In contradistinction, the managers at Thiokol seemed to have seen themselves in different roles and thus evaluated the data differently. Their first priority was to execute the launch. Since there had been 24 previous successful launches, their conclusion was that this one had a great chance of success. Moreover, because the engineers could not prove that the o rings and shuttle orbiters would *not* function at temperatures below 50 degrees given such short notice, and since the engineers could not verify that the boosters could not be recovered in high seas, and since none of these had been tested, the managers at Thiokol assumed that all would go well. In other words, the managerial assumption in this case was that if failure cannot be proven, it is appropriate to assume that a product will work. Thiokol's managers failed to acknowledge the engineers' point of view, one of the senior managers overrode their protest, and Thiokol signed off on the launch.

Interestingly, too, the engineers at Thiokol who protested against the launch did not blow the whistle before the launch took place, perhaps because, as engineers and not managers, they saw their roles as providers of data, not as managerial decision-makers. As professionals, according to Goldman's distinction, they had strongly differentiated role responsibilities to the code of their profession, and the safety of the launch was their first priority (Werhane, 1991).

Another interesting role phenomenon also emerges. It is frequently the case that people adopt contradictory roles without perceiving possible conflicts of interest. An obvious example is found with members of the American crime syndicate who are known to be exemplary church members and good family people. It is ironic, because such people employ a decision model in business dealings that comes into direct opposition with the values of church, family, and society. "Mafia mentality," as we might crudely label this phenomenon, is the ability to function in such contradictory roles simultaneously.

This phenomenon is not limited to criminals, however, as was evidenced by the notorious Salomon Brothers bond trading scandal in 1991. Paul Mozer, the head of Treasury Bond trading at Salomon Brothers was caught purchasing more Treasury Bonds than was legally allowed for three consecutive trading quarters, often using client funds without their permission. Mozer's reasoning might have been that he had strongly differentiated role responsibilities to Salomon that superseded obeying Treasury Department regulations (Bartlett, 1991: 1).

ROLE ACCOUNTABILITY AND RECIPROCITY

Employment role responsibilities provide a source of accountability in the workplace. When a person has a job, he or she makes a commitment to exchange work for remuneration. It is sometimes considered just or fair to dismiss an employee for failure to perform his or her job functions, even if the employer pays poorly and sometimes even if the employer does not respect other employee rights.

Accountability can be narrowed by role definitions. "When one is accountable for an action one is held liable to answer for responsibilities acquired by one's role, one's office, one's associations, station or situation. Role accountability defines a narrower range of obligations than role responsibility – only those responsibilities for which one is held liable" (Werhane, 1991: 98). In other words, the presence of roles both assigns liability under certain circumstances, and insulates a person from liability under other circumstances.

Role accountability might also take the form of a collegial obligation – an obligation a person acquires by belonging to a group, club, or association. For example, union members have certain obligations to the unions of which they are members. Such obligations are similar to role duties in that they stem from socially-defined positions; the difference is that the binding force of such liabilities is sometimes weaker than in job role accountability, since membership is more voluntary in nature and one's duties are not so seriously considered.

Role accountability and collegial obligation are usually described only as duties of persons to other persons or to organizations such as employees to employers or to the institutions where they are employed. Such a description is incomplete, however. There are, in addition to these, duties on the part of the person, group or institution to which a person is accountable, such as the responsibilities of employers to employees. These obligations arise in part from the role responsibilities of the party to whom one is answerable, in part from the definition of one's own role, and in part because of the nature of the relationship. These duties are taken for granted or even forgotten except when circumstances challenge their existence. Often neglected in an analysis of accountability, they are reciprocal or correlative obligations implied by role responsibility. This notion of reciprocity is crucial to an understanding of the notion of role accountability.

"Reciprocity," according to Gould, "may be defined as a social relation among agents in which each recognizes the other as an agent, that is, as equally free, and each acts with respect to the other on the basis of a shared understanding and a free agreement to the effect that the actions of each with respect to the other are equivalent" (Gould, 1985: 213–14). Reciprocity in accountability relationships operates in part, as follows. If I am to justify my actions to a certain group or institution because of my role in that group or institution, this accountability implicitly assumes a reciprocal accountability to me on the part of the institution to whom I am answerable. If no such reciprocal obligations exist, or if they are not respected, my accountability to that individual, group, or institution becomes weakened.

It is useful to examine a distinction that may exist between two kinds of accountability: legal accountability and moral accountability. As an American citizen, a person is expected to pay income tax on earnings, and he or she is held accountable for his or her income tax return, which justifies these payments. This answerability is a legally enforced obligation, that is, a legal liability. Let us suppose that the person is also an engineer. As a tax-paying engineer and a member of the American Society of Mechanical Engineers (ASME), he or she is accountable for honesty and competence, and for upholding certain ethical principles spelled out in the ASME code of ethics. Both paying taxes and adhering to a particular code of ethics are role liabilities, but the latter is a collegial obligation because people voluntarily join, and can resign from, the ASME. Unlike taxing bodies, professional societies can only punish members in ethical, rather than legally enforceable, manners. For example the ASME can recommend, but not enforce, the firing of one of its members from a job if the member is not performing in an ethically acceptable manner. If a person is tired of paying American taxes, he or she can, of course, become an expatriate, but, as long as the person resides in the United States, he or she can be forced to pay taxes or suffer the consequences (i.e., jail time and/or financial penalties). Because of the enforcement factor, it is important to distinguish legal accountability from moral accountability.

While differences exist between moral and legal answerability, these two forms of accountability exhibit one common characteristic: both involve reciprocal first- and second-party obligatory relationships. Both entail moral responsibilities on the part of each party to the other. This sort of relationship is evident in the foregoing examples. In legal accountability, the reciprocal obligations of taxing bodies to taxpayers are obvious. A person's accountability to the taxing body is based on the assumptions that taxes are necessary, that everybody will receive equal treatment from the federal taxing agents, and that revenues will not be misused. When one side of this two-party answerability breaks down the strength of the relationship, trust, and political as well as legal commitment is often weakened as well.

Turning to moral accountability, the ASME's right to hold their members accountable is based on the collegial obligations of members to that association. It is also the case, though, that the ASME is, and should be, held accountable to its members. Part of this reciprocal accountability of the ASME to its members is to uphold the ASME standards by reprimanding offenders. These actions should be taken not merely to enforce the accountability of offenders to the ASME code of ethics, for the ASME is more than a police force. Rather, the organization has a collegial obligation to all members, part of which is to defend their rights. Perhaps it is in part because some professional associations have failed in their reciprocal collegial obligations that many members have not taken their own role obligations to associations seriously.

Can all role accountability be described in terms of reciprocal or correlative relationships? It has sometimes been argued that moral accountability cannot be merely thought of as a reciprocal relationship because the notion of correlative responsibility is defined only in contractual relationships such as those that may exist between employees and employers. A contract implies that all aspects of the relationship are, or can be, definite. Often, however, role liabilities are more open-ended. Most hierarchical relationships, such as parent–child relationships, for example, are not contractual. It is the reciprocal relationship implied in accountability that is evidenced in hierarchical accountability relationships. When parents mistreat children (who did not choose to be children), the children are justified in complaining; and when a child misbehaves the parents have similar rights.

The specific basis for such protests is different in each case, and sometimes the particular rights and obligations are not well-defined. In the case of children, the child's right to complain is clearly justified even though that child might not actually understand the warrant for the complaint. In general, though, such protests are justified because they are social relationships. What we are suggesting, then, is that reciprocal obligation is an important element in a variety of accountability relationships: legal, moral, hierarchical, and collegial. Although the obligations are not necessarily contractual, the strength of first-party role liabilities or collegial obligations depends at least in part on the equally strong, though obviously not identical, role obligations of the second party to the first.

The argument justifying the existence of reciprocity in role accountability might be stated this way. The role expressed in a collegial obligation defines not only the place of the accountable person in a group, but also it spells out the place of the group in the life of that person. In being held answerable, people must justify their actions within certain contexts. These contexts include certain implicit benefits derived from the role, benefits that translate into second-party obligations of the groups to whom they are answerable. Reciprocity is, therefore, an assumed part of role accountability.

Assuming that role accountability is important, and that accountability involves not only first-party collegial or role obligation enforced by the group to whom one is answerable, but also reciprocal obligations of groups to their members or of employers to employees, the problems occasioned by accountability are then not only caused by failures of collegial obligation or lack of group enforcement of these obligations, but also in part by the fact that groups do not always uphold their role responsibilities to their members. In addition, this latter failure has the effect of weakening the collegial or role obligation by diminishing the loyalties of those being held accountable.

What this analysis of role accountability means for the workplace is that, in taking jobs, employees assume responsibilities connected with that job, responsibilities often only implicitly stated in a verbal contract with the employer. The employee is liable for the terms of the agreement and for exchanging a certain quantity and quality of work. At the same time, accountability is not limited to these obligations, and it also requires reciprocal obligations on the part of the party to whom one is accountable. The justification for reciprocal accountability is that employee–employer relationships are social relationships between persons and groups of persons, as well as contractual ones, voluntarily entered into and freely dissolvable by both parties. If employees are accountable to their employers, then the employer, in our society usually a corporation, is also accountable for upholding its part of the agreement by being accountable in return, albeit in a different way, to its person-employees (Gould, 1985).

 RECIPROCITY AND EMPLOYEE RIGHTS 

The reciprocal nature of employee–employer relationships in the workplace entails some important employee rights, in particular, rights to fair treatment and respect. If an employee is expected to "act solely for the benefit of the principal . . . and not to act or speak disloyally. . . ." as spelled out in legal language in the Restatement (Second) on Agency (1958: 385(1)), the employer has a duty to treat the employee with similar respect.

What constitutes fair treatment and respect? Obviously, fair[1] pay in exchange for work is essential. This exchange is commonly recognized. Since, in addition to working, employees are expected to respect and be fair to their employer, employers have reciprocal obligations that go beyond fair pay. Employer "loyalty" includes respect for employee privacy, for worker safety, for employee information, and for due process in the workplace.

Specifically, if an employee is to respect his or her employer and the decisions of that employer, the employer needs to honor the privacy of employee records. The employer thus needs to treat personnel information with confidentiality and to respect the privacy of the employee's activities outside the workplace. Since employment agreements are reciprocal, employers cannot expect respect for their privacy, that is, respect for corporate secrets, unless they, in turn, respect the privacy of their employees. Unfortunately in today's information age one's privacy, whether it be of an individual, a company, or even of national secrets, is virtually public knowledge. The most companies can do is to try to keep employee and company proprietary information out of the hands of those who might misuse or take advantage of it.

Respect for the employee also entails minimizing workplace safety dangers and providing information about unavoidable hazards in the workplace. Expectations of loyalty and obedience are unjustified if one does not protect workers' physical well-being.

Keeping the employee informed about his or her job, the quality of his or her work, and the stability of the company is also part of respect for the employee. Such information is required for employees to be able to retain control of their lives. Only with accurate and timely information about the place of employment can an employee make informed decisions about his or her future. It is illogical to expect a person to remain committed to an employer if the employer is not forthcoming with information, such as that which pertains to the person's job, the status of his or her position, or the economic situation of the employer. This is not to suggest that an employer is a welfare agency responsible for every aspect of his or her employees' lives, but since work is so central to our lives, information about the future of employment is critical to maintain control over that future.

Interestingly, a number of employers find that information and transparency increases loyalty, even when that information is negative. For example, with the recent economic downturn, an increasing number of companies are going out of business or attempting mergers. Firms are often afraid of sharing information with employees, for fear that they will "jump ship." Having to replace employees under such conditions, or handle the work without adequate support, only threatens to make a bad situation worse. Many companies are nevertheless finding that, even in the face of "bad news," such as pending layoffs, key personnel are more likely to stay if they are kept informed.

Due process in the workplace refers to any procedure, usually a grievance procedure, by which an employee *or* an employer can appeal a decision in order to get an impartial evaluation of that decision. An employer has the right to dismiss any employee who does not meet work expectations, and in times of economic downturn. Because the employer has demanded loyalty and respect, though, the reciprocal nature of employment warrants the employee's demand for equal respect. If he or she feels unfairly treated or dismissed, he or she has the right to demand due process. As we have argued in chapter 3, due process does not specify that employees are never dismissed, but, rather, that employer actions meet impartial standards of reasonableness – the same sort of reasonableness expected of employees.

The employee rights we have just enumerated – the rights to privacy, worker safety, employee information, and due process – are rights that result from role accountability in the workplace. Another way to think about employee rights is thus to realize that they can be derived from institutionally defined roles, role responsibilities, and correlative accountability. Employee rights are a logical extension of role accountability and the theory that one can morally justify the demands of role responsibilities *only* by honoring these rights as well. In the United States, employers in the private sector are not legally obliged to respect employee rights, but, in not doing so, an employer undermines the moral justification for employee accountability.

LIMITS OF ROLES AND ROLE RESPONSIBILITIES

While role responsibilities account for a great deal of what we do, not all moral responsibility can be reduced to role responsibility or described merely in terms of conflicting responsibilities. This was evidenced by the *Challenger* incident, in which each manager acted within the ordinary guidelines of his or her role, where the consequences were dreadful.

Because each of us plays a variety of roles and role responsibilities, no one role completely defines the self. Moreover, no person is mired in one role such that he or she cannot get at a distance from its demands even though, in many instances we fail to do so. That this is possible is evidenced by the fact that even as children we learn to play and play-act various roles. We learn early on about distancing ourselves from identifying completely with any one particular role. Each of us can compare and contrast various roles and role responsibilities simply because no one role is complete and because we have so many of them (Goffman, 1961: 92–5).

We tend to judge people in their roles not merely by the demands of that role, e.g., motherhood, but also by the demands of common morality. Our evaluation of the famous Second World War Nazi clerk, Adolph Eichmann, offers a very dramatic example. Eichmann was an exemplary clerk and a law-abiding citizen. That is not enough, in itself, though, to excuse his behavior, for he was also responsible for mass genocide. We do not want to let him off the "moral hook," so to speak, despite his "proper" behavior, his efficiency, and patriotic commitment, for, in filling up freight cars with human beings and sending them to concentration camps – even when he kept impeccable records and made sure his trains ran exactly on schedule – he was wrong and evil *because* he so completely identified with his role, his station, and its duties, and because of the terrible consequences of his role actions (Arendt, 1963).

How do we account for such moral blameworthiness? In this context, it is tempting to conclude that the object of the moral judgment is the self apart from its roles – the self as an independent moral agent, not merely the self as it is engaged in its roles – a self that is both free from identification with any particular role and is ultimately, because of its autonomy, morally responsible. It is that self we are holding morally responsible when we condemn Eichmann for following his role responsibilities. When a person attempts to separate his or her "self" from his or her "roles," there is a further difficulty – the difficulty of getting at that "self." What happens when we eliminate all of a person's roles? Who is the woman, if not professor, mother, daughter, sister, writer, citizen, environmentalist, humanist, democrat, and so on?

As Michael Sandel and others argue, the "self" cannot be purely autonomous from *all* its social relationships without being "radically disembodied" and indeed, altogether empty. In that case the notion of autonomy makes no sense since, as a purely autonomous self, the individual is left without psychological resources to form choices, accept or reject alternatives, or make moral judgments. It can be neither responsible nor irresponsible, because it has no resources with which to make judgments at all (Sandel, 1983; Luben, 1988). Without roles, we are left with the quandary of how to relate agency to roles and role morality so that moral judgments about role behavior are not merely confined to role morality, i.e., whether or not the agent is fulfilling his or her role.

On the other hand, if the self is merely a product of, and determined by, its various socially-defined roles and social relationships, it is "radically situated," such that what it does is merely an outcome of the complex interrelationships between the roles in which it is continually engaged. As a result, it is not easy to explain how it is that we are self-reflective, self-critical, creative, makers of history, and authors of change, and that description cannot account fully for moral blame. As a result, we would have to conclude that Eichmann was simply a product of the Third Reich, and thus exempt from further moral condemnation.

Trying to account for moral agency that avoids both the difficulties of proposing a radically situated social self and the problems of postulating a purely autonomous self, in his book *Thick and Thin* (1994), Michael Walzer distinguishes a "thick" and a "thin" self. Walzer accepts the position that all our experiences are socially-derived and constructed. In addition, he argues, who we are as subjects is a late development from our socialization process. In that socialization process we develop a number of interests, roles, memberships, commitments, and values, such that each individual is a historical, cultural, and social product, a pluralistic bundle of overlapping spheres of foci, a "thick" self or selves.

Self-reflection and self-criticism, what Walzer calls a "thin" self, does develop, but only, later, out of the thick socialized self or bundle of selves. Self-reflection arises when there are inconsistencies, disagreements, or clashes between personal interests, commitments, and spheres of value, clashes that jar one into taking another point of view, a "meta"-point of view that is still one's own. This meta-point of view where one judges and redirects one's interests and commitments is what Walzer calls the "thin" self. The thin self accounts for the unity and continuity of overlapping, changing thick selves. To borrow a term from Lionel Trilling, as Walzer does, the thin self "perdures" though time and change, in that it "persists" and "endures" (Trilling, 1972: 99; Walzer, 1994: 101).

Even though the self perdures, and thereby accounts for self-identity, the self is no more than the unity of a bundle of social selves – the self-reflective locus of this vast array of experiences. The thin self, then, is socially-derived but not merely socially-determined. It accounts for our ability to choose, manipulate, and even change events, and it explains our ability to get perspective on our situation and its positive and negative features. The self that is the role-evaluator, and that same self we hold morally responsible for role behavior, could best be thought of as a thin self – that which is the locus of the thick self, the self engaged in, defined by, and changed by and changing its various roles. The moral agent we attempt to hold responsible for his or her role behavior is always an engaged agent, not an abstract transcendental entity, but he or she is not merely determined by social relationships and roles – he or she is something more than his or her engagements (Walzer, 1994: ch. 5).

Luben attempts to solve this problem by arguing that, in making moral judgments about role responsibilities, we acknowledge each other as persons subject to precepts of common morality. At the same time we cannot get at the self within us that is an utterly independent autonomous agent *except* as a nexus of roles:

> Ultimately, we reserve our autonomy from our stations and their duties so that we have the freedom to respond to persons *qua* persons – to obey what one may call the *morality of acknowledgment*. The situation is curiously asymmetrical: we are bound to extend to others a courtesy we are bound to refuse to ourselves. It is a delusion to think of *myself* as just a person *qua* person, a "me" outside of my social station[s]; but when the chips are down, it is immoral to think of you as anything less. (Luben, 1988: 127)

There are two problems with Luben's conclusion. First, Luben tends to assume that a human being, the thick self, is *merely* the sum of his or her roles, or at least, that all human relationships are role relationships. There is more to be said, though, about the person who is the self. While it is true that we cannot divorce ourselves from the thick self and its relationships, the fact that we can get at a distance from particular roles implies that that act is an act of an autonomous self, despite the fact that we cannot get at that self. Moreover, because we recognize and treat others as persons and because we expect and, indeed, demand, reciprocal respect, those exchanges between persons give us understanding of ourselves as moral agents, despite the fact that we can never isolate that phenomenon. It is in those exchanges, where we treat others as persons, and where we recognize other persons' considerations and judgments of ourselves as persons, that we recognize ourselves as moral agents in the sense that we realize that we are more than our roles, despite that fact that we cannot get at the "more" without a loss of the sense of self altogether (Werhane, 1999).

Returning to the question of role morality and moral responsibility, what we may conclude from this discussion is that roles, role responsibilities, and role morality do not explain all moral or immoral behavior nor do they offer avenues for resolving conflicts of interest between conflicting role obligations. Because we are not exhaustively defined by our roles, though, each of us can get at a distance from and evaluate our roles and role responsibilities. Tools for evaluation include appeals to the precepts of common morality, those rules or precepts that most of us, in the mode of disinterested spectators, would regard as rules for how we ought to behave, such as equal respect for persons, avoidance of harm, respect for rights and fairness, honoring contracts, and respect for property, however particularly or socially defined.

Role responsibility is an important, though limited, concept useful for describing social, employment, and institutional obligations, but not useful as an absolute criterion for making ethical judgments. As applied to the workplace, it defines reciprocal responsibilities. In the broader scheme, though, individuals and institutions are accountable for more than their role responsibilities. They must answer to one another, and to basic moral minimums, regardless of whether or not those minimums are enunciated in their roles.

What does the conclusion that role responsibility and role accountability are limited concepts have to do with employee rights? One difficulty with the assignment or acceptance of role responsibilities in the workplace is that these are sometimes perceived as strongly differentiated, or, even, as ethically neutral. Such perceptions may lead people to act in the workplace against their own ethical standards, and, sometimes, in violation of commonly espoused human rights. The justification for strongly differentiated role responsibilities neglects the broader accountability to which every individual is subject. A strongly differentiated position asserts that professional or business demands are themselves overriding moral demands, demands that may and should, in crucial cases, take precedence over other moral claims. As we saw in the *Challenger* disaster, though, strongly differentiated roles, even professional roles, have their limitations.

An ethically neutral interpretation of role responsibilities is an even less tenable position. This position assumes that moral principles can be bracketed out, or do not count in the workplace at all. If this were the case, there would be no basis for demanding employee adherence to role responsibilities, for no moral obligations can logically be justified in a situation where ethical principles do not operate. Since an ethically neutral position undermines the basis for demanding employee loyalty and obedience, to expect employees to adopt such a stance is inconsistent with other employer expectations.

Roles are socially-assigned positions that create boundary conditions for certain behaviors. If this is the case, then even professionals have only weakly differentiated role responsibilities, constrained by common sense morality, just as employees have. If, in a more general way, every person were accountable within his or her capabilities to meet societal moral obligations and not to cause societal harm, then employees would have obligations to act in ethically responsible ways in the workplace. From these obligations, employees derive the rights to object to participating in, and to protest against, morally or legally irresponsible activities when they occur in the workplace. Such rights include a number of commonly assumed or desired practices: conscientious objection, the right not to be harassed or "punished" for speaking out or blowing the whistle, and even the right to strike when asked to perform illegal, immoral, and/or socially dangerous jobs, or when such practices occur in the workplace. These employee rights are part of the accountability of every person to society, and they need to be safeguarded in the workplace in order for employees to be able to meet these broader societal obligations.

CONCLUSION

Employee rights logically evolve from demands for employee responsibility, loyalty, and respect. People involved in relationships with one another naturally acquire inherently reciprocal interpersonal obligations and responsibilities. If employees have role responsibilities with employers to whom they are accountable, this role accountability is a correlative notion, which entails the recognition of employee rights to respect and fair treatment in the workplace. Examples of these rights include employee rights to due process, privacy, safety, and information in the workplace.

The reality that emerges is that the interpersonal relationships that underlie specific roles people play serve to define reciprocal rights and responsibilities that are not necessarily spelled out in codes or agreements. Because a person is involved with someone else, regardless of whether that relationship is personal or professional, certain feelings emerge, such as of care, empathy, loyalty, and trust. Those feelings that accompany the continuity of the reciprocal relationship thus create the correlative rights and responsibilities.

This is the case with employment. Even where specific rights are not embedded in law or contract, they nevertheless exist and should be acknowledged and protected, as a result of the relationship out of which they emerge. In addition, if the continuity of the relationship is desired, it becomes imperative that reciprocal rights and responsibilities are recognized and protected, or the relationship itself is jeopardized. In fact, both employers and employees benefit from guarantees for employee rights in the workplace. As we explain in chapter 7, there are a number of benefits that accompany protecting employee rights, not the least of which is the economic value added for employers.

NOTE

1. What is meant by "fair" is complicated and often difficult to assess from a moral point of view. Fair pay at a minimum would be a living wage, one that competed with comparable positions both within the company and in the political economy, met and probably exceeded legal minimums, and one that was related to the difficulty and risks of the job in question. Whether or not there are, in fact, any wages that meet these and other specifications is certainly a matter of debate. Minimally, we can specify what would be unfair, e.g., below a minimum legal or living wage, not competitive or comparable either within the company or in the economy, discriminatory in some other way, not taking into account difficulty, responsibility or overtime involved in the job, and so on.

REFERENCES

Articles, books, and other similar publications

Arendt, Hannah. 1963. *Eichmann in Jerusalem.* New York: Viking Press.

Bartlett, Sarah. 1991. "Salomon's Errant Cowboy." *New York Times.* August 25: C1.

Downie, R. S. 1971. *Roles and Values.* London: Methuen.

Emmet, Dorothy. 1966; 1996. *Rules, Roles and Relation.* New York: St. Martin's Press.

Goffman, Erving. 1961. *Encounters: Two Studies in the Sociology of Interaction.* Indianapolis, IN: Bobs-Merrill.

Goldman, Alan. 1980. *The Moral Foundations of Professional Ethics.* Totowa, NJ: Rowan and Littlefield.

Gould Carol. 1985. "Economic Justice, Self-Management and the Principle of Reciprocity." In Kenneth Kipnis and Diana T. Meyers, eds., *Economic Justice*. Totowa, NJ: Rowman and Allanheld, 210–22.

Hardimon, Michael. 1994. "Role Obligations." *Journal of Philosophy*, 91: 333–63.

Luben, David. 1988. *Lawyers and Justice*. Princeton: Princeton University Press.

"Restatement (Second) on Agency." 1958.

Sandel, Michael J. 1983. *Liberalism and the Limits of Justice*. Cambridge: Cambridge University Press.

Trilling, Lionel. 1972. *Sincerity and Authenticity*. Cambridge, MA: Harvard University Press.

Walzer, Michael. 1994. *Thick and Thin*. Notre Dame, IN: Notre Dame University Press.

Werhane, Patricia H. 1985. *Persons, Rights, and Corporations*. Englewood Cliffs, NJ: Prentice-Hall, Inc.

Werhane, Patricia H. 1991. "Engineers and Management: The Challenge of the Challenger Incident." *Journal of Business Ethics*, vol. 10: 605–16.

Werhane, Patricia H. 1999. "Justice and Trust." *Journal of Business Ethics*, vol. 21: 237–49.

chapter six

Meaningful Work and the Development of Employment Relationships

In the United States today, many people are spending a growing number of hours at work. While the emergence of the Internet and e-commerce has in some cases changed where work takes place, it has also caused people to spend more time working. The "nine to five" job is no longer the norm. The typical work day now starts much earlier than 9 a.m., and ends much later than 5 p.m. Even businesses that "close" at night often use night hours for other activities, such as restocking and inventory control. In addition, office workers are increasingly taking work home with them.

Technology has also drastically altered the work that takes place. As the Industrial Revolution transformed the workplace of the nineteenth century, technology has similarly revolutionized the workplace of the late twentieth/early twenty-first century. Widespread access to and use of the Internet and e-business services has given rise to a global marketplace and an e-marketplace. Time and geography no longer carry the same sort of significance for business undertakings, because they do not represent the same sort of obstacles or hindrances as in the past. Businesses can achieve an international presence, for example, without any physical travel having to take place.

The nature of the work being done by employees has also been affected. Employees have had to become acquainted with technology, regardless of their job functions. In addition, many employees have had to learn to be flexible in order to accommodate the changing work environment. At the same time, the range of available job functions has changed. People are able to tailor their work to their interests in new and exciting ways.

All of this has created a new dynamic in the American workplace, or at least one not formerly recognized: a view that work is something positive – not necessarily something akin to an obligation or responsibility to be dreaded. While it is true that people work to earn a livelihood and to fill time, it is also true that work is, or can be, something that people like to do, through which they attain self-fulfillment. In other words, people often find meaning in their lives through their work.

The recognition of the significance of people's relationships with their work – at all levels, not just for professionals – has kindled conversation, both scholarly and otherwise, regarding the meaning of work and the creation of meaningful work. It is important that people find satisfaction in their work, particularly considering that they are spending 30 to 60 percent (if not more) of their waking hours working (or in transit to and from their workplaces). It is also important for employers, because happy, fulfilled employees more effectively contribute to realizing corporate goals.

In this chapter we will analyze views of meaningful work. We will first discuss meaningful work from the employee perspective, then from the perspectives of employers. Although we will conclude that it is impossible to fulfill a promise of meaningful work for every manager and employee and during every aspect of his or her job and career, there are nevertheless ways to create worthwhile work and employee satisfaction. While it is not the sole responsibility of the employer to create meaningful work, it is important for employers to provide channels through which employees can develop meaning in their work. Later in the chapter we will examine two employer alternatives to the demand for meaningful work: the concept of employability, a late twentieth-century notion that allegedly replaces the outdated notion of lifetime employment, and outplacement services.

THE MEANING OF WORK: ITS HISTORICAL ROOTS

To begin thinking about the meaning of work and meaningful work, it is useful to go back to its modern Western origins in the eighteenth-century work of Adam Smith and the nineteenth-century writings of Karl Marx. As Smith, and later Marx, argued, the Industrial Revolution provided the opportunity for workers to become independent of landholder serfdom and free from those to whom they had been previously apprenticed or chatteled. It will turn out, however, that each thinker had a different view of the outcome of industrialization for worker freedoms. Adam Smith, who is often called the "philosophical father" of the Industrial Revolution, recognized the importance of worker liberties in the new age of free enterprise that was just emerging at the time he wrote. The Industrial Revolution provided workers opportunities to choose and change jobs, and to be paid for their productivity; thus people were able to trade their labor without indenturing themselves.

Smith's unique contribution to the analysis of labor, as we saw in chapter 1, is his thesis that the distinction between the laborer and his or her labor, created by wage-earning, means that the *productivity* of labor – not the *laborer* – is treated as an exchangeable value, and, therefore, as a commodity (Smith, 1776, 1976: iii; Werhane, 1991a, 1991b), thus freeing the laborer from slavery or serfdom.

At the same time, Smith recognized that repetitive assembly-line work was deadly to both personal autonomy and well-being. While the specialization of labor is critical for economic growth, Smith acknowledged its limitations. According to Smith,

> The man whose whole life is spent in performing a few simple operations, of which the effects too, are perhaps always the same, or very nearly the same, has no occasion to exert his understanding, or to exercise his invention in finding out expedients for removing difficulties which never occur. He naturally loses, therefore, the habit of such exertion, and generally becomes as stupid and ignorant as it is possible for a human creature to become. . . . His dexterity at his own particular trade seems, in this manner, to be acquired at the expence of his intellectual, social, and martial virtues. (Smith, 1776, 1976: v.i.f. 50)

Smith considered worker malaise a serious problem. Indeed, as Smith predicted, contemporary studies demonstrate that those who do repetitive jobs, with little variation, lack of input into the process or its shortcomings, and no outlet for control over the task, tend to be equally docile, obedient, and dull outside the workplace as well (Gini, 2000). Smith's answer was to advocate universal, publicly-funded education of all males, so that men from all classes, including assembly-line workers, would be intellectually able to distance themselves from the torpor of their work. Although Smith does not mention "meaning" in work specifically, an underlying theme is evidenced in his thinking. While he recognized the individual's quest for meaning, he saw people as working for wages, and finding meaning in leisure activities, not at work.

Marx, having read Smith, worried about the dehumanization of industrialized labor and concluded that people should not have to seek alternatives to work-related activities to find meaning in their lives. He agreed with Smith that the Industrial Revolution provided opportunities for free wage labor that were previously unimaginable, but he concluded that the promise of free labor was not realized (Marx, 1844, 1963). According to Marx, people define themselves in terms of their work. It thus follows that, for there to be meaning in work, it must encompass the sorts of activities with which individuals identify, what they would choose to do, would enjoy doing, and would be proud to consider theirs. Marx departs from Smith in his criticism of distinguishing individuals from their productivity. According to Marx, since worker productivity is impossible without workers, working and its productivity are and should be treated as inseparable parts of the person. His contention is that, in attempting to separate the productivity from the person, the individual is separated, thus alienated, not just from his or her labor, but also from an integral part of his or her self. Thus alienation entails a loss of meaning.

Wage labor causes an array of problems. While people are paid for their work, they are never paid the full value of what their labor is worth, but, instead, merely what the market will bear (Marx, 1844, 1963).[1] The individual is thus often left out of the equation. Employers talk about productivity, often without regard for the human producers of that productivity. An entrepreneur noted this sort of distinction in Max Frisch's play, *The Firebugs*, when he said, "I hired workers but people came instead" (Frisch, 1959).

According to Marx, since the alienation of labor is something to be resisted, society should reject those elements that contribute to it. He proposed a worker-owned, moneyless, communal society, where, as long as basic needs were met, every individual would choose his or her own contribution of work. Such a proposal has never met with practical success over any sustained period of time and will not be thought of as viable, given the success of free enterprise.

The themes that underlie Marxist thinking nevertheless underscore some essential points about work and its relationship with the worker. Since the ability to choose and change one's job or occupation, in theory always an option, is not easy, questions concerning the alienation of labor and the alleged concomitant loss of meaning for workers is an important consideration. It is important that people's work be structured satisfactorily – even in today's mobile society. And it is hard to imagine that Smith's solution – studying Shakespeare – would actually enable a worker to divorce himself from assembly line doldrums. At the same time, vibrant employees, who are provided a voice in their workplace, tend to be strong contributors at work and in their communities, all of which benefit (Hampden-Turner, 1974).

MEANING AND MEANINGFUL WORK

There is a common understanding, certainly explicit in the thinking of Smith and Marx, that it is important for people to find meaning in their lives, but there are different views regarding where that meaning should be derived: in work-related activities or in leisure activities, or in both. Smith's conclusion that meaning should be found outside of working is echoed in some contemporary thinkers such as Joanne Ciulla:

> Organizations do not have a moral obligation to provide meaningful work; however they do have an obligation to provide work and compensation that leave employees with the energy, autonomy, will, and income to pursue meaning at work and a meaningful life outside of work. (Ciulla, 2000: 226)

Others, echoing some of Marx's concerns, focus on the notion of meaningful work and the importance of making work worthwhile for employees. But what "meaningful work" means is ordinarily both socially constructed and personal. Various societies define both "meaningful" and 'work" differently, and what is valued as work varies from culture to culture (Ciulla, 1997: 402). Meaningful work has personal dimensions as well. What is meaningful to one person may not satisfy another, even for people with the same skill sets working in similar jobs in the same company. Despite the fact that it is difficult to define, however, some have argued that employees have a right to meaningful work, to a job, vocation, or career that is self-satisfying and respectful of human dignity, autonomy, and self worth (Marx, 1844, 1963; Schwartz, 1982).

A number of recent scholars have contributed to the development of a workable definition of meaningful work. While it is difficult to arrive at a single definition, such proposals help reveal certain underlying elements. Meaningful work is "work that is worthwhile, significant, satisfying, and conducive to personal growth, worth, and well-being" (Ciulla, 1998: 402). Similarly, it is "worthy work," or work that "carries with it the hope of pleasure in rest and the hope of pleasure in our daily creative skill (Morris, 1885: 21, quoted in Ciulla, 2000: 66). In addition, it "is useful, challenging and respectful of individual autonomy" (Bowie, 1990: 107). Work must have some sort of personal value. At a minimum, work should not be demeaning or degrading, if not enjoyable.

Meaningful work is sometimes identified with a profession or vocation. According to Mike Martin, meaningful work is the sort of labor carried out intelligently and is based on professionally trained expertise with specific goals – usually those concerning professional excellence, and often to help others:

> A profession [or position of employment] can be a job, career, vocation, or all three . . . Viewed as a job, work is a means to earning money that facilitates the pursuit of meaningful activities and relationships during leisure. Viewed as a career, work is a pathway to achievement, power, and social recognition. And viewed as a vocation, work is a value-laden activity directed toward public goods, those shared by members of a community. (Martin, 2000: 28)

We would suggest, however, that the connection of meaningful work to profession or vocation is merely a starting point. While some meaningful work may be linked to vocation, that is not a necessary precondition. And a person's vocation, or "calling," does not necessarily provide an explicit link to public goods. For example, golf professionals ordinarily find a great deal of meaning, or satisfaction, in the work itself – even those who are not big money winning players. It is debatable, though as to whether golf professionals actually contribute to the public good, except peripherally. Martin's conflation of meaningful work with vocation implies that only value-laden work connected with a public good is meaningful. This ignores the intrinsic rewards of working, irrespective of external or public contributions.

Ciulla, like Martin, links work with some extrinsic moral worth:

> Meaningful work, like a meaningful life, is morally worthy work undertaken in morally worthy organizations. Work has meaning

> *because* there is some good in it. . . . The most meaningful jobs are those in which people directly help others or create products that make life better for people. (Ciulla, 2000: 225)

While there is often extrinsic moral worth to working, meaningful work does not have to stand up to external validation, and not all "good works" are meaningful or rewarding to those who engage in them. Martin claims that "[b]y definition, vocations have a moral dimension linking one's identity to social practices and communities" (2000: 28). This is surely an exaggeration. Martin's identification of work with vocation and his further connection of all vocations/work with public good or social practices are questionable conclusions. Michael Jordan, for instance, has a vocation with which he identifies, but it is a stretch, at best, to say he sees playing as contributing to some social good.

Martin, however, may be making another point. He may be asserting that all work *should* be framed under the rubric of profession in the following sense. The development of an expertise allows workers to be more independent and able more easily to change jobs or find new positions. It is then the expertise that makes the work meaningful, not its location in a particular company. We will return to this idea in chapter 9.

Meaningful employment is often identified with participation in the decision-making processes in the workplace. This participation could be as slight as choosing work hours, or it could include taking responsibility as part of a team for the manufacture of a certain product. Participation might also extend to full participation in the management and the decisions of the business, a position Christopher McMahon defends, as we illustrated in chapter 4. In its most radical interpretation, meaningful work is equated with worker control and/or ownership of the means of production, as Marx proposed.

Since every person perceives what is important and meaningful at work from a different perspective, however, the concept of meaningful work cannot be defined merely as participation or participatory management. Despite the fact that repetitive or menial tasks are usually thought of as dull and degrading, some persons – though probably very few – are not dissatisfied with such work. There are even those, working to their capacities, for which so-called menial tasks are neither dull nor degrading. Other persons identify meaningful work with a certain position, a title, or with remuneration. Still others, such as researchers, define a meaningful job as one where they are left alone to work. Taking any part in management or participatory decision-making is, for these persons, contrary to their notion of work satisfaction.

A. R. Gini proposes an alternative definition of meaningful work, a definition that takes participation into account as part, but not all, of what is important in work: "[A] meaningful job is one that the employee enjoys and excels in, often feeling in control of the work activity. It is a job that fits the individual worker's talents and personality" (Gini, 2000: 53). The personal fulfillment, as indicated by the "feeling in control of the work activity," emerges as an important operative notion. Although it could be something as small as being in control of choosing how to wash windows, or as important as being in charge of a research lab, the key is that it is left to the worker to determine for him- or herself what is meaningful.

Common elements in most definitions of meaningful work are notions of dignity, self-control, self-respect, and autonomy. Adina Schwartz, who has written extensively on meaningful work, argues that "people achieve autonomy to the extent that they lead lives of intelligence and initiative" (Schwartz, 1982: 635). Part of autonomy includes being able to form some idea of personal interests and interest satisfaction, and the ability to plan, evaluate, and revise choices and decisions. Since so much of our time is ordinarily spent at work, Schwartz addresses the difficulties with industrial employment or with any form of working that is over-repetitive. Many jobs even today are repetitive, demeaning, or degrading and are overburdened with rules that seem to restrict liberty, she contends. Interestingly, too, as we will see in chapter 7, some contemporary studies show that flexible job arrangements, rotating jobs and responsibilities, restructuring hierarchies, team decision-making, and self-management are likely to produce better quality products and services and higher productivity, and indeed, more satisfied employees (Pfeffer, 1998).

Schwartz's conclusion is that "a just society [is one that] respects all its members as autonomous agents, [so, that] society must grant extensive liberties in order to respect its members as autonomous agents" (Schwartz, 1982: 635). If we accept her definition of autonomy as leading a life of "intelligence and initiative," and if we find that central to leading a life as a moral agent the edict that a just society must respect that autonomy for all its citizens, we are led to the following conclusion. A just society must grant as much liberty as possible, equally, to all its citizens. Part of this entails ensuring work and working conditions that are not degrading and that allow autonomy in choice in the range of existing employment contexts. Schwartz concludes that governments should intervene, both to eliminate over-repetitive or degrading work situations and to provide new forms of industrial employment. While Schwartz' conclusion might seem harsh, her findings parallel others'. Such findings have sparked interest in the private sector to voluntarily create new kinds of work environments, because of the evidence that suggests that a positive work environment not only makes workers happy but also promotes organizational success.

In summary, while no single definition of meaningful work exists, we propose as a stipulative definition that meaningful work is work that workers enjoy and excel in where they can exercise a degree of control in one way or another. Definitions of meaningful work should also encompass the need for a sense of satisfaction (albeit different from person to person and from culture to culture) and identification with the work as "my job," or as "good" or "rewarding." Most importantly, meaningful work should be linked to autonomy – the notion that the employee can freely choose or be offered job alternatives and/or the opportunity, but not the obligation, to participation in ways that are meaningful to him or her (Bowie, 1990). Without some identity or satisfaction with a job, profession, or vocation, people do not feel loyalty or commitment – the work seems of no consequence (Werhane, 1985: 50–1).

Work satisfaction is realized over time. It is not necessarily the case that a person has a great day every day. In fact, people often vary in their levels of satisfaction and contentment. That is why autonomy is so significant. As long as employees have the opportunity to exercise choice and make changes, that sort of freedom makes the work meaningful, even when there are spells of boredom or frustration.

MEANINGFUL WORKPLACES – THE EMPLOYER PERSPECTIVE

Ask five . . . people what makes their work meaningful and you'll get five different answers, including creativity, the ability to learn, a high salary, and being able to influence others. That's because meaning is as unique as our fingerprints. Given that, how can companies be expected to light a fire under all employees when the fuel is different for everyone?

(John Meeker quoted in Caudron, 1997: 5)

If defining meaningful work is difficult, and if creating and encouraging some form of meaningful work is important for employee satisfaction and economic value added, the challenge for organizations is imposing. Companies cannot be expected to create positions such that every employed person loves his or her work all the time, can always choose his or her tasks, constantly finds every aspect stimulating, and looks forward to coming to work every day. In addition, the fact is that some jobs are just more interesting than others, and that not even the same job is the same from day to day. In truth, no job is intrinsically stimulating all the time. Still, the initiatives that organizations implement and the environment that they create play a significant role in the development of meaningful work. Through good morale and productivity incentives, and by recognizing the connection between such things and employee satisfaction, employers can produce and maintain employee satisfaction and increased productivity.

Many organizational theorists argue that the most successful way to create an atmosphere of meaningful work is through employee motivation techniques. In turn, it is tempting to argue that the best way to motivate employees and managers is through salary increases or decreases, depending on the quality and quantity of the work produced. This "carrot/stick" approach is standard management thinking in many companies. Other forms of motivation now generally include reduced work weeks, flextime, fringe benefits, total quality management training, team development, employee counseling, and even job participation. All of these are motivating to some extent, but each is extrinsic to the work itself.

Frederick Herzberg, in a classic *Harvard Business Review* article, actually dismisses all such approaches. Herzberg argues that each of these so-called motivators trains employees to perform for the rewards. It is like the dog that trains his or her master by misbehaving (Herzberg, 1968, 1981: 113). When the master asks the dog to behave, he or she does so for the reward of a treat. The master thinks he or she has accomplished something, because the dog obeyed in the end. Why did the dog misbehave in the first place?

Lasting motivation in the workplace, according to Herzberg, is thus not the result of transient "tools," but of a restructuring of the workplace itself. For example, reduced work weeks and flextime motivate – they motivate people to work less. Total Quality Management initiatives, team development, counseling, sensitivity training, and the like, usually focus on relationships between employees and employers. Participatory management schemes too, are usually failures because employees are usually not really participating in the decision processes, and often managers are reluctant to give up their own decision power. Negative incentives such as reduced pay, longer working hours, and threats of dismissal are not only discouraging, they also create illusory temporary compliance, subsequently decoupled from commitment and interest in the work itself (Kohn, 1993b).

Motivation, according to Herzberg, should be thought of as intrinsic job satisfaction, that is, employee identification with, and responsibility for, his or her work. "Motivation is a function of growth from getting intrinsic rewards out of interesting and challenging work" (1968, 1987: 118). Herzberg continues that the factors that create a kind of motivation or job satisfaction defined as satisfaction with what one does (not the rewards one receives), are "achievement, recognition for achievement, the work itself, responsibility, and growth or advancement" (1968, 1987: 113). In other words, "If you want people motivated to do a good job, give them a good job to do" (1968: 1987, 115). To motivate employees, we should give people worthwhile tasks, or reorganize the workplace so that the work is worthwhile, train for achievement, praise employees for good work, and give them responsibility for that work and opportunities for advancement. Advancement here does not mean necessarily huge bonuses, but rather, more robust job assignments and responsibility enhancement or enrichment (Kohn, 1993a).

According to Herzberg there is one more essential aspect connected with motivation and the creation of meaningful work, that is, the simple matter of fairness. Employees should be well informed about each other, about pay, assignments, promotions and demotions. While achieving perfectly fair and transparent treatment for every employee is impossible, that goal is well worthwhile. Perceived inequalities in pay for comparable work, favoritism in job or travel assignments, political promotions, perks, and other targeted rewards will be demotivating factors creating a loss of morale that will translate into poor performance (Herzberg, 1968, 1987; Nelson, 1996; Herman and Gioia, 1998; Harkness and Mai, 2001).

To see how Herzberg's principles work in practice, let us consider two examples: Marriott's program to motivate and retain low-wage workers and Unilever's encouragement of a middle manager to take on a company-wide audacious project. The Marriott hotel chain recently reorganized its workforce. Hotels rely on low-wage hourly workers, and the turnover among most workers in this sector is alarmingly high, up to 400 percent per year. Many of the workers are unskilled, often have little education, and some are new immigrants without English language skills. Given this situation, and considering that the company relied on a workforce that numbered nearly 150,000, Marriott saw a need to improve the quality of the work so as to reduce turnover. At the same time, the view was that tight profit margins prevented the organization from raising the wages significantly for this class of workers. Marriott thus confronted head on the challenge of motivating a large number of $7–10/hour workers with undeveloped skill sets.

Marriott began by instituting a set of reforms including day care, welfare-to-work training (called "Pathway to Independence"), social services, referral networks, clearly stated benefits, and "English as a second language" classes. These, Herzberg would argue, are important to attract and train this particular group of workers. They are not intrinsic motivators, though, that will improve retention dramatically in the long run. Marriott recognized this. The next steps thus involved revamping employee training and mentoring programs in order to tailor them to this workforce and focus expressly on making low-wage employees proud of their work. Marriott's philosophy was to improve their best asset – their human asset – by developing employee pride in good work, without dwelling on the low wages. It matters, Marriott preaches, matters deeply, if beds are clean and well made in hotels, just as it matters that automobiles have the fewest possible quality defects or that pharmaceuticals are pure and safe for internal use. To convey that, along with respect for individual workers, helps give even the lowest-paid worker a sense of importance and dignity, and in the process Marriott has reduced turnover by over 200 percent (Yang et al., 1996: 108–16).

Unilever is a multibillion dollar Dutch/British agricultural, food, and home products company with operations in more than 100 countries. During the early 1990s, one of its middle managers, Jan-Kees Vis, began to realize that, as a large company with so many products in so many countries, it needed to begin to take more seriously its commitment to the social environments in which the organization operated. In particular, Vis believed that Unilever needed to measure its social responsibilities and environmental impact as seriously as it measured its financial outcomes. He thus adopted a "Triple Bottom Line" approach.

At a social function one evening Vis approached his boss, a senior executive in the company, with this idea. The executive responded: "You are Unilever and I am Unilever. If you think more should be done, then do something about it" (Standish, 2000: 147). Vis took this as a mandate, and, since 1993, he has been engaged in extending the Triple Bottom Line approach to every division of Unilever for which he takes full responsibility. Vis describes the Triple Bottom Line approach, the aim of which is to measure environmental sustainability, social responsibility and economic outcomes quantitatively and equally, as follows:

> Each type of asset represents a source of value to the company and its shareholders. The sustained development of each of these sources of value ensures that the overall value accruing to shareholders is built up over the long term. This is in essence the significance of sustainable development to a company that aims at sustainable profit growth and long-term value creation for its shareholders, [customers], and employees. (Vis, 1997: 3, quoted in Standish, 2000: 168)

While this project is far from complete, Vis has made a visible impact throughout the company, and he has created meaning for his own work and for the company's goals. Vis is still a middle manager, and his salary has not increased dramatically. He has not been promoted to a senior position; he is, though, respected (and sometimes feared) throughout the organization. He has been given full autonomy for this project, and he has a lifetime commitment to the Triple Bottom Line philosophy and to the company. Vis's story demonstrates how employees can create their own meaningful work when their employers do not thwart their efforts.

THE NEW WORKPLACE

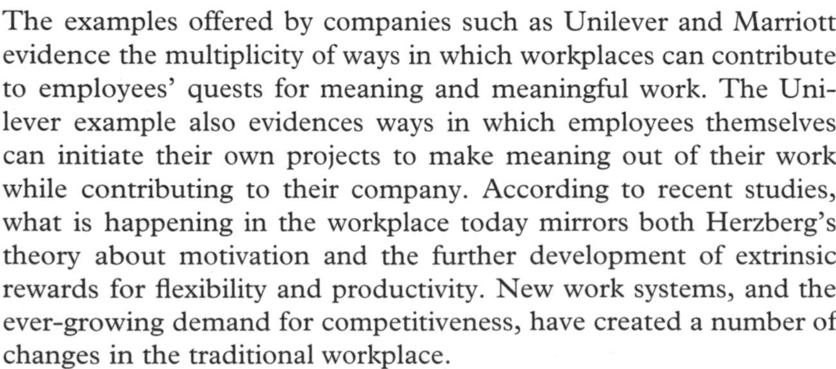

The examples offered by companies such as Unilever and Marriott evidence the multiplicity of ways in which workplaces can contribute to employees' quests for meaning and meaningful work. The Unilever example also evidences ways in which employees themselves can initiate their own projects to make meaning out of their work while contributing to their company. According to recent studies, what is happening in the workplace today mirrors both Herzberg's theory about motivation and the further development of extrinsic rewards for flexibility and productivity. New work systems, and the ever-growing demand for competitiveness, have created a number of changes in the traditional workplace.

While the ideal probably never existed, the traditional workplace before the 1980s in this country was allegedly a place where low-skilled workers could get entry-level jobs, receive on-site job training, and eventually work their way up to more permanent and skilled positions. There were few part-time or contract workers in most sectors of the economy. Wages increased with longevity and skill development, and the wage differences between the lowest-paid worker and top management were not strikingly disproportional. Downsizing was less common except during periods of economic exigency. Organizational structures were, by and large, hierarchical systems of management control. The result in most companies was a less flexible workforce, less prepared for change and restructuring, but a workforce that was loyal and hardworking. Job security was part of expectations, and there was an implied psychological contract between employees and management that employees would be trained, promoted, rewarded, and retained in compensation for good work and loyalty (Cappelli et al., 1997: 200–1).

All of this changed dramatically during the last decade of the twentieth century. With global pressures of competition for low wages and cheap products, with the demand that companies be more change-oriented, flexible, and ready to produce "just-in-time" products and services, and with market pressures for strong quarterly earnings, many companies across this country have restructured their work organizations. Downsizing has become a way to gain economic advantage, and, as "rightsizing," has become a way to reorganize work. In 2000 alone, more than 1.4 million people were laid off or downsized ("Snip, Snip, Oops," 2001: 60). There are both positive and negative results for employees and middle managers. Downsizing usually results in a flatter organization. This creates greater demands on employees and managers who are expected to take on more responsibilities, to be less supervised (and act as self-supervisors), to have opportunities to be more innovative and creative, and to develop interpersonal skills in team-building and networking throughout the organization. Coupled with greater autonomy and responsibility, all positive motivating attributes, according to Herzberg, is less job security. Downsizing, or rightsizing, can eliminate jobs or whole divisions at any time, and employees and managers know that. In addition to massive downsizing and layoffs, in 1997 alone "two thirds of all employee turnover [was] voluntary quits" (Cappelli et al., 1997: 211).

The negative consequences are expensive both for companies and for employees. First, companies are becoming less eager to develop new massive training and retraining programs, both because of the changing workforce within the company, and because of external pressures of global competition and changing market conditions. There is, then, increased "poaching" of skilled employees from other companies. Second, with less focus on employee development opportunities unskilled workers are less likely to be hired and, if they do get jobs, less likely to have opportunities to improve their skill sets on the job.[2] Third, companies are increasingly replacing permanent workers and managers with part-time, contract, contingent employees who usually earn lower wages and receive few, if any, benefits (Brockner and Wiesenfeld, 1992). Fourth, morale and loyalty are at an all-time low among full-time employees who are not laid off or downsized, particularly among middle managers who recognize that, if laid off, they will have difficulty finding new jobs. They perceive themselves as expendable. According to one study, fully 86 percent of companies that had laid off employees reported a decline in employee morale – a decline that translated into lowered productivity, initiative, and bottom-line dollars (Cappelli et. al, 1997: 201). This is partly because "displaced workers have seven times the unemployment rate of others as long as two years after their job loss" (Cappelli et. al, 1997: 70). Indeed, it is speculated that one of the reasons that productivity rates have been increasing is that workers and managers want to demonstrate that their skills are worthy of retention.[3] The result is that while work has, in many sectors, become more meaningful in the sense of increased autonomy and responsibilities, there is a perception that employees and managers have little job security, and employee development and training is constantly being reduced. It is fear or compulsion, or the perception of the fragility of one's position, that, for many employees, creates negative extrinsic barriers to job satisfaction.

How do these economic and workplace changing dynamics affect employee claims to rights to meaningful work and employer attempts to address those claims? Implicit in many definitions of meaningful work is the assumption that most employees will remain in the same occupation and even at the same place of employment for most of their careers. But with increased geographical and professional mobility coupled with massive layoffs that create further incentives to this mobility, the connection between meaningful work, employee motivation, and job stability, however fragile theoretically, is virtually broken. Entrepreneurial employees respond to this by seeking new employment opportunities whenever possible, and while the best employees and managers contribute substantively to the workplace, the notion of loyalty to one's employer is becoming an extinct virtue (Hirsch, 1987). Employers have addressed this issue with two alternatives: employability mechanisms and outplacement services.

EMPLOYER ALTERNATIVES TO MEANINGFUL WORK: EMPLOYABILITY AND OUTPLACEMENT

Changing economic conditions make it incumbent upon organizations to provide workplaces through which employees can not only find meaningful work, but which will also lead them to find meaningful alternatives if their current opportunities disappear. It cannot be said that employers are obligated to retain employees indefinitely, particularly when there is not work to be done. This hurts both the organization and the individual, who is able to earn an income, but who is deprived of meaning. The responsibility is thus for organizations to keep the door open, so to speak, for employees to be trained for and find meaningful work opportunities both within and outside a particular organization.

Employability

Despite the problems with meaningful work, there are some refreshing new trends in our modern political economy. According to Ghoshal, Bartlett, and Moran, in an article in the *Sloan Management Review* (1999), many companies are reacting to the "lean and mean" approach to employment. Avoiding paternalistic and hierarchical structures evident in companies of the past, competitive firms are engaged in "continuous innovation" in order to create long-term value and are rethinking employment arrangements. These firms exhibit an understanding of the contemporary employment relationship:

- The growth of firms and, therefore, economics is primarily dependent on the quality of their management. [Therefore,]
- The foundation of a firm's activity is a new "moral contract" with employees and society, replacing paternalistic exploitation and value appropriation with employability and value

> creation in a relationship of shared destiny. (Ghoshal et al., 1999: 10)

Employees and managers today in progressive companies are expected to internalize the goals of the company and take responsibility for its progress. In return, employees are not offered lifetime employment, but something perhaps more valuable – training, education, empowerment, and experience that keeps them abreast with the company direction and makes these employees and managers employable in changing market and technological conditions.

Rosebeth Moss Kanter argues that it is valuable, in terms of both economics and respect for workers, to have a workforce that is comprised of highly skilled and employable people who would be desirable assets in a number of employment settings, both within a particular company and among industries. Thus it lies in the firm's interest for companies to give their employees what she calls "employability security": abilities and skills that are transferable to other jobs and other situations in that company or elsewhere so that employees are adaptable in a world of technological and economic change. Today, while some companies engage in layoffs to change employee skills, many managers and companies are training and retraining old workers, giving them new skills to become adaptable in a changing work environment (Kanter, 1993).

According to Ghoshal, Bartlett, and Moran, this new employability contract is successful only in companies where it is not the "plan of the week" nor the latest of many new human resource programs. On the contrary, employability has to be built into the philosophy of the company. The mission of employability is not a mission of altruism – it is a means to get, train, motivate, and retain the best, most adaptable, creative, responsible employees and managers. In doing so, the motivating aim is to create employees and managers who have flexible talents that make them employable in a number of venues. Such a program forms the basis for corporate and employee growth, employee loyalty even when laid off, and economic value as well. From a rights perspective, a philosophy of employability circumvents EAW, although it does not repudiate it. This is because, when administered appropriately, it creates a workplace atmosphere that promotes respect for individual employee talents and for their future in the workplace. It demands employee autonomy and creates avenues of empowerment by providing opportunities to find or develop job skills that can be transferable to other settings. For some employees, who identify meaning with their professional or job skills rather than within a particular workplace environment, such skills can become intrinsically meaningful.

Outplacement

Rather than directly address the question of layoffs, meaningful work or employability, some companies have turned to outplacement. Outplacement services in the United States are mechanisms companies use as a benefit for middle and upper managers who are dismissed, laid off, or, more commonly, become redundant due to a merger or acquisition. They are ordinarily thought of as part of a severance benefit and have become more prevalent as companies increasingly change the size and focus of their workforce. Outplacement services range from advice, résumé writing, consulting, and, sometimes, even, placement in new positions.

Outplacement seems to be an important benefit, indeed, allegedly one owed to those managers who lost their jobs for economic or redundancy reasons. This so-called benefit, though, masks some deep underlying problems. That these services are available only to a select group of managers and executives raises obvious questions of fairness. Interestingly, even union members, who make up 10 percent of the present workforce in the United States, have little access to professional outplacement services. Union officials focus primarily on rights and benefits of their members, but seldom on replacing them in other similar positions in different organizations. Indeed, while outplacement services help managers and executives, there are few within companies that focus on lower managers, white-collar or blue-collar workers. These folks must seek new jobs through outplacement services not provided by the company: employment agencies, word of mouth, or advertisements.

While the unfairness issue is a critical one, we want to focus on another aspect of outplacement, that is, its importance, its moral importance, in thinking about employment and employee rights. The problems include the following:

- First, outplacement distracts from attention to more important issues in employment, such as unemployment, overhiring, and employability.
- Second, outplacement is "the tail wagging the dog." In other words, it ranks very low in priority of employee rights.

- Third, and most importantly, outplacement encourages paternalistic behavior in an age of what is becoming entrepreneurial or "free labor."

In times of prosperity, many companies in the United States tend to over-hire, and redundancy therefore exists, even without the merger phenomenon. Because of EAW, companies are allowed to reduce their employees "at will" with few legal or contractual sanctions. Many companies, such as IBM, lay off some employees while they simultaneously hire others with different skill sets. Senior managers are often let go to be replaced by lower-paid younger folks with the same skills. Outplacement is a cheap way to allow companies to feel good about themselves and retain some modicum of loyalty from managers who go to competing companies, while at the same time reducing wage and benefit costs. At least in the United States, outplacement masks excessive over-hiring, lack of retraining of otherwise skilled employees, questionable treatment of senior employees, and other abuses of employee rights. Moreover, if wages are costs, the cost of outplacement might be more expensive than monies invested in careful hiring and employability training.

At the same time, it is important to ask if outplacement is truly a "right". A "benefit"? Surely rights to organize and strike, due process, freedom of speech, safety, company information, decent wages, job security, meaningful work, and employability training are much more important issues. Outplacement should be near the end of this list. Moreover, it is not a very good benefit at that. Outplacement encourages what we find to be endemic in most employment situations all over the world (historically, culturally, socially): dependence – the dependence of employees and managers on their employers, their bosses, or their companies. This perpetuation of employer dependence is hardly a long-term benefit to self-respect and autonomy, and if I am an at-will employee, why should I *expect* to be dependent on company outplacement services to find a new job?

In response to this critique, in Europe there is a new movement to connect employability and outplacement. The SOCOSE project is an inter-European initiative proposing, given high unemployment rates throughout Europe, that companies team with governments to provide retraining and outplacement services for laid off employees, thus creating an employable and more mobile workforce. This is an interesting proposal. It requires, however, government as well as corporate cooperation, (a definite overlap of the public and private sectors), and it does not rid employees of their dependence on firms and the social system for their careers (Kieselbach and Mader, forthcoming).

CONCLUSION

It would be difficult to maintain a consistent argument that employees have absolute rights to meaningful work and that employers have absolute responsibilities to provide it. What is clearer, however, is that for most employees finding meaning at work is linked positively to morale, loyalty, and long-term performance. As Marriott illustrates, it is important to note that meaning is not synonymous with sophistication. People can find meaning in simple work, and in work that others might find dull or unfulfilling. Employees who find meaning at work and an amenable workplace culture can contribute to successful organizational performance. Those organizations that stand as role models are companies that offer meaningful workplaces, which contribute to employee satisfaction with their jobs. In chapter 7 we will support this contention with a plethora of examples.

The burden to create meaningful work and worker satisfaction is not, though, merely the employer's responsibility. If worker autonomy and dignity are of value and are part of what we mean by meaningful work, responsibility rests, too, on employees. In the United States we have failed and probably will continue to fail to adapt new metaphors that challenge EAW. Outplacement services do nothing to abate that failure, but merely reinforce the paternalism (or maternalism) to which we have become accustomed. The model of the worker, the employee, the manager, or the executive as a responsible agent, responsible for seeking or creating meaning at work and in his or her career, offers another paradigm – a paradigm of the worker or employee as an independent professional. We will develop this theme in chapter 9.

NOTES

1. It is interesting to note that we still use the term "human resource management," as if employees represented a quantifiable resource.
2. According to some data, "[t]he biggest factor contributing to poverty in

the United States appears to be low wage rates, not unemployment or involuntary part-time employment (Gardner and Herz, 1992.).

3. In fact, despite the rhetoric about mobility, it turns out that even in 2000 less than one third of the total workforce in the United States changed their occupations or moved geographically.

REFERENCES

Articles, books, and other similar publications

Bowie, Norman. 1990. "Empowering People as an End to Business." In G. Enderle, B. Almond, and A. Argandona, eds., *People in Corporations*. Dordrecht, The Netherlands: Kluwer Academic Publishers, 105–12.

Brockner, J. and B. M. Wiesenfeld. 1992. "Living on the Edge (of Social and Organizational Psychology): The Effects of Job Layoffs on Those Who Remain." In J. Keith Murnighan, ed., *Social Psychology in Organizations: Advances in Theory and Research*. Englewood, NJ: Prentice Hall, 195–215.

Cappelli, Peter, Bassi, Laurie, Katz, Harry, Knoke, David, Osterman, Paul, and Useem, Michael. 1997. *Change at Work*. New York: Oxford University Press.

Caudron, Shari. 1997. "The Search for Meaning at Work." *Training and Development*, vol. 51: 24–7.

Ciulla, Joanne. 1997. "Meaningful Work." In Patricia H. Werhane and R. Edward Freeman. eds., *The Encyclopedic Dictionary of Business Ethics*. Oxford: Blackwell, 402–3.

Ciulla, Joanne. 2000. *The Working Life*. New York: Random House Times Books.

Frisch, Max. 1959. *The Firebugs*. New York: Hill and Wang.

Gardner, Jennifer M. and Herz, Diane E. 1992. "Working and Poor in 1990." *Monthly Labor Review*. December: 20–8.

Ghoshal, Sumantra, Bartlett, Christopher A., and Moran, Peter. 1999. "A New Manifesto for Management." *Sloan Management Review*, Spring: 9–20.

Gini, A. R. 2000. *My Job My Self*. New York: Routledge.

Hampden-Turner, Charles. 1974. *From Poverty to Dignity: A Strategy for Poor Americans*. Garden City, NY: Anchor Press.

Harkness, James and Mai, Lea. 2001. "'Getting it': The Making of a Dot-Comer." *Communication World*, February–March: 7–9.

Herman, Roger E. and Gioia, Joyce L. 1998. "Making Work Meaningful: Secrets of the Future-Focused Corporation." *The Futurist*, vol. 32: 24–6, 35–8.

Herzberg, F. B. 1959. *The Motivation to Work*. New York: Wiley.

Herzberg, F. B. 1968, 1987. "One More Time: How Do You Motivate Employees?" *Harvard Business Review*,vol. 65: September–October, 109–20.

Hirsch, Paul. 1987. *Pack Your Own Parachute.* Reading, MA: Addison-Wesley Publishing.

Kanter, Rosebeth Moss (1993) "Employability Security." *Business and Society Review*: 11–14.

Kieselbach, Thomas and Mader, Sabine. Forthcoming. "Social Convoy and Sustainable Employability – Innovative Strategies of Outplacement/Replacement: A European Research Project" (SOCOSE).

Kohn, Alfie. 1993a. "Rethinking Rewards." *Harvard Business Review*, vol. 71: 37–4-9.

Kohn, Alfie. 1993b. "Why Incentive Plans Cannot Work." *Harvard Business Review*, vol. 71: 54–63.

Martin, Mike. 2000. *Meaningful Work.* New York: Oxford University Press.

Marx, Karl. 1844, 1963. *The Economic and Philosophic Manuscripts of 1844*, trans. T. B. Bottomore. New York: McGraw-Hill Book Company.

McMahon, Christopher. 1994. *Authority and Democracy: A General Theory of Government and Management.* New Jersey: Princeton University Press.

Morris, William. 1885. *Useful Work versus Useless Toil.* London: Socialist League Office, Socialist Platform, no. 2.

Nelson, Bob 1996. "Dump the Cash, Load on the Praise." *Personnel Journal*, vol. 75: 65–9.

Pfeffer, Jeffrey. 1998. *The Human Equation.* Boston: Harvard Business School Press.

Schwartz, Adina. 1982. "Meaningful Work." *Ethics*, vol. 92. 634–46.

Smith, Adam. 1776, 1976. *The Wealth of Nations*, ed. R. H. Campbell and A. S. Skinner. Oxford: Oxford University Press.

"Snip, Snip, Oops." 2001. *The Economist*, October 13: 59–60.

Standish, Myles. 2000. "Unilever." In Michael Gorman, Matthew Mehalik, and Patricia H. Werhane, eds., *Ethical and Environmental Challenges to Business.* Upper Saddle River NJ: Prentice-Hall, 146–83. Originaly published 1998 by the University of Virginia Darden School Foundation.

Vis, Jan-Kees. 1997. *Unilever: Putting Corporate Purpose Into Action.* Unilever Publication.

Werhane, Patricia H., 1985. *Persons, Rights, and Corporations.* Englewood Cliffs, NJ: Prentice-Hall.

Werhane, Patricia H. 1991a. *Adam Smith and his Legacy for Modern Capitalism.* New York: Oxford University Press.

Werhane, Patricia H. 1991b. "Freedom, Commodification, and the Alienation of Labor in Adam Smith's *Wealth of Nations*." *Philosophical Forum*, vol. 22: 383–98.

Yang, Catherine, Palmer, Ann Therese, Browder, Seanna, and Cunio, Alice. 1996. "Low-Wage Lessons." *Business Week*, November 11: 108.

chapter seven

Employment Practices as Economic Value Added

Written with Norman Bowie

In chapter 1 we spelled out a theory of moral rights and argued that one of the reasons employee concerns do not reflect Constitutional rights is the existence of a managerial mindset that depicts employees as economic costs. That depiction, however, describes only one set of views. In this chapter we will describe another set of views – the mindset that employees and managers are essential to firm performance, and that productive well-trained, involved long-term employees and managers create economic value added for the firm.

Despite conventional wisdom on the costly nature of employment, an increasing number of scholars and firms are identifying ways in which businesses can improve firm financial performance by recognizing and celebrating employee rights. The leading scholar in this area is Jeffrey Pfeffer. Pfeffer has argued in a recent series of books that many of the most financially successful firms are those that engage in innovative employment practices designed to create a highly committed, highly motivated, highly involved, high performance work force.

Pfeffer defends the position that the more successful firms share people-oriented systems that exhibit seven common characteristics:

1 Employment security.
2 Selective hiring of new personnel.
3 Self-managed teams and decentralization of decision making as the basic principles of organizational design [self-determination].
4 Comparatively high compensation contingent on organizational performance [equitable competitive pay].
5 Extensive [and lifelong] training [employability training].

6 Reduced status distinctions and barriers, including dress, language, office arrangements, and wage differences across levels.
7 Extensive sharing of financial and performance information throughout the organization [transparency]. (Pfeffer, 1998: 64–5)

According to Pfeffer, these are key employee-oriented values that contribute to firms' success. Each translates into an employee right. Employment security and high, performance based pay are the most obvious. Selective hiring is a means to create a cohesive more job-secure workforce of mutual respect. Employability, as we argued in chapter 6, extends the notion of meaningful work. Reduced status barriers is part of the argument for diversity, an issue we will take up in the next chapter. Transparency is part of an employee right to information, which in turn contributes to self-determination, as do all forms of self-management. In other chapters, we have touched upon the significance of organizational transparency, information sharing, workplace democratization, and employability training. In this chapter, we make the *business* case, from the perspective of employers, for protection and recognition of employees' rights to reasonable job security, to reasonable self-determination on the job, and to fair compensation. Following Pfeffer, our argument in this chapter is that protecting and recognizing such values or rights are not only for the benefit of employees – there is also an argument from the perspective of the firm that operationalizing these rights creates economic value added for the company and its shareholders.

EMPLOYMENT SECURITY

Job security has become an increasing concern in the United States, particularly in light of mergers, acquisitions, global competition, and other economic changes in the American marketplace. According to a recent survey, nearly 50 percent of workers anticipate a job change within the next five years (Humphrey Taylor, 2000). Layoffs, as well as individual terminations, occur with seeming regularity, and not always by the decision of the employee. In 2001 alone, according to the *Economist*, more than 1.5 million employees will be displaced in the United States labor market ("Snip, Snip, Oops," 2001: 60).

In the current labor market, what most employees appear to want is merely the right to a reasonable amount of job security. This often translates primarily into reasonable notice prior to employment changes, just terminations, and due process. People tend to understand that business circumstances change and cause layoffs. They also understand that managers make decisions, either in the course of business or to correct prior mistakes, that result in individual and group firings. Employees do not, though, expect to have to bear all the costs of business decisions personally. They expect that, as long as they perform properly and adequately, that they will retain their jobs or be employable in other markets.

Employment security is most frequently violated during downsizing, or what some, through a misuse of language, describe as "rightsizing." Although layoffs during times of economic stress are sometimes justifiable, this is not always the case. While, through layoffs, an organization might be able to reduce expenses by trimming itself to the "right" size – to a size more in line with the scale of its business – this does not mean that the layoffs are necessarily "right."

Firms tend to approach downsizing as a "quick fix" – a speedy way to improve their financial outlook. The underlying mental model is that employees are expensive and expendable. Some layoffs that take place, therefore, result not from economic necessity, but from the mere desire to cut costs and put more money in the pockets of stockholders and the managers who make those very downsizing decisions.

Underlying this sort of thinking is a misplaced management mantra that cost-cutting leads to greater efficiency. When managers look at employees, they often see *costs*. What they see are the salaries, benefits, and office space associated with those employees. When the bottom line is in danger, a seemingly logical solution – and certainly a quick one – is to eliminate those costs so that the financial numbers and ratios, at least in the short term, will reflect seemingly greater productivity and higher profits. Indeed one writer argues the "cost-asset" language is misapplied. Workers and employees can and do create economic value, but the metaphor of "employees are our most important assets" repeats the mistake of thinking of workers as costs (Davenport, 2000: 31). According to Eric Flamholtz, "To treat people as an asset is to confuse the agent that provides services [the employee] with the asset itself (the expected [goods] or services)" (Davenport, 2000: 32).

It is understood that in many circumstances certain costs must be cut in order for long-term improvements in financial and general firm performance to result. Many firms, though, have found useful ways of cutting costs through negotiating deals with suppliers, distributors, and other business partners, and by "rightsizing" executive pay. While trimming an organization of the people who make it work might reduce short-term costs, it does not pave the way for long-term performance and profits.

Putting employees on notice that their jobs are not secure destroys any notion of employee loyalty – such feelings would be misguided, and arguably foolhardy, under the umbrella of "the new social contract." As a result, whenever a company experiences any sort of difficulties, employees are quick to explore their options. Ironically, it is often the best employees – the ones most needed to carry the firm through the rough times – who "jump ship" first.

Interestingly, it is not even clear that layoffs achieve the purpose for which they are intended. An increasing number of people are now arguing that layoffs are not guaranteed to enhance even the short-term outlook. As Pfeffer points out, "[D]ownsizing is not a sure way of increasing the stock price over the medium- to long-term horizon, nor does it necessarily provide higher profits or create organizational efficiency or productivity" (Pfeffer, 1998: 174). While often, in the short term, just after a down-sizing announcement is made, the stock of a company involved in downsizing rises, this does not always happen. A study cited in the *Wall Street Journal* shows that, after two years, the stock prices of two thirds of the companies who downsized lagged behind the stock prices of comparable firms by 5% to 45%. In addition, the stock prices of 50% of the companies who downsized lagged behind the stock prices of the general market by 17% to 48% (Dorfman, 1991).

Stock price is not the only performance measure that indicates the costs of layoffs to firm performance. Overall productivity, too, can be harmed by layoffs. Pfeffer cites a study that reveals that, for companies operating during 1977–87, a third of those companies who downsized experienced significant correlative decreases in productivity. At the same time, ironically, of those companies who increased employment, 52 percent experienced significant increases in productivity as well (Pfeffer, 1998).

In terms of costs associated with fluctuations in employment, training represents a cost that is often overlooked, but one that can account for meaningful changes in firms' financial performance. This is true particularly in sectors of the economy that involve high levels of training of new employees. Training costs are especially high in the high tech industry, for example, where there is a shortage of skilled workers. This cost is a sunk cost, and when that training is expensive and technical, it is often worth carrying trained employees through a short-term downturn, in order that firms can avoid having to pay that cost again later for a new set of employees. Firms nevertheless tend to lay off large numbers of people when they experience temporary setbacks. When the economy turns around, they are compelled to rehire and again cover the expense of new training.

When these firms lay people off, the labor pool usually increases, and labor is relatively inexpensive. When conditions change, it often happens simultaneously for many firms, and this causes the labor market to boom and the cost of labor to be higher. Firms that have engaged in extensive layoffs, now not only bear the cost of retraining their workforce, but they also have to pay more for their labor. It is likely that such costs, coupled with loss of productivity and other intangibles such as the costs to loyalty and morale, call into question the prudence of many layoffs. Such firms would be better served to explore from the start employment strategies that take into account the cyclicality of their hiring needs and thus enable them to avoid mass layoffs and rehiring.

Apple Computer serves as a poignant example of the irreparable harm that can be caused by layoffs. In its early days, under the leadership of Steve Jobs and Stephen Wozniak, Apple brought to the market what many people considered the best technology available. At the same time, Apple exhibited a unique culture that boasted high employee morale. Even the employee handbook celebrated the importance of people to firm success. Apple was known for employee accessibility to management, recognition of employee milestones, and bagels and cream cheese on Fridays. The devotion of employees was even considered "cult-like."

Apple found a tough competitor in Microsoft, though. John Scully replaced Steve Jobs, and, with the transition, came a new management style. Unlike Jobs, Scully adhered to traditional management philosophy. He was in touch with sound management principles, but he was not in touch with his people. He saw employees as costs, and, in order to compete with Microsoft, Scully was convinced that costs had to be eliminated. Apple began a series of layoffs in 1985, followed by more rounds in 1991, which cost Apple nearly 10 percent of its work force. Then Scully was fired. More layoffs took place in 1993, when another 14 percent of the workforce was lost, followed by even more layoffs in 1997, which left Apple with less than half of its original workforce. The loss of people was accompanied by loss of technical skills and morale. Not only did the numbers decrease, but also, according to Pfeffer, the people were treated without respect and without regard to their dignity as human beings:

> The dismissal process occurred on a single day. Each employee was told to be at their desk at 9:00 a.m. in the morning. Those who received early calls into their managers' office were laid off. They were given pink slips, final checks, and severance information. They were then escorted to the door. The remaining employees were gathered into a room at around 11:00 a.m. to discuss their new jobs, since restructuring followed immediately. (Pfeffer, 1998: 25)

Amenities disappeared as well: no more bagels and cream cheese on Friday mornings. Cost-cutting managers could quantify the cost of the cream cheese and bagels, but they could not quantify the benefits of having people get together periodically to discuss and resolve issues. Lip service continued to be paid to the importance of people, but there was little perceivable evidence that any person was more than an expendable liability.

Not surprisingly, these were the first steps of Apple's continuing downward spiral. It was not until Jobs was persuaded to return that Apple showed signs of possible recovery. Jobs was greeted as a hero. He immediately got rid of the cost-cutting mentality, and Apple's stock price began to improve. The damage had been done, though, and the future of Apple remains in doubt (Pfeffer, 1998).

Unfortunately, Apple is not an isolated example. Many companies today continue to suffer from serious financial ramifications of unwise employment decisions relating to hiring cycles. According to an American Management Association survey of 720 companies, 30 percent of companies that downsized brought back the laid off employees either by rehiring them outright or by engaging in contracts with them for consulting services (Pfeffer, 1998: 183–4).

The replacement costs of lost employees can be significant. Many of the people let go, particularly in the advertising industry, are hired back as consultants – but at a higher cost. In other words, firms are willing to pay more for the same people, in order to avoid having to commit to those people. What happens, though, is that firms also lose their long-term claim on those people, and can lose their investment as well. As firms avoid commitment to their talent, now considered "consultants" instead of "employees," they increase their risk of losing them too, or having to share them with competitors.

This situation is arguably less common than the situation where a firm needs to rehire former employees, but is precluded from doing so. Many severance packages are accompanied by agreements that the employees who accept such packages will not work for that firm again. In such cases, even if the firm does need to rehire employees, it must absorb costs of finding, training, and, possibly, relocating new employees.

Losses associated with downsizing can constitute more than numbers. In many instances, fired, or laid off, employees take with them client accounts. Where trust develops between clients and firm representatives, clients often feel allied to those representatives, not to the firm itself. This can be true with professionals such as accountants, lawyers, and financial analysts. When the people in such positions are fired or let go, and then the positions are filled again, many original clients might be lost, and there is down time during which the new professionals must develop relationships with new clients.

Additional evidence that downsizing is ultimately harmful comes from Frederick F. Reichheld's studies published in *The Loyalty Effect*. Among the studies Reichheld cites are the following: an American Management Association study that shows that after five years less than half of the companies that have downsized have increased their profits and that only a third have increased their productivity. Also cited was a Wall Street Journal study that indicated that, three years after restructuring, the restructured companies suffered a negative 24 percent growth compared to the S & P 500. All of this comes as no surprise to Reichheld. As he says, "Companies forced to jettison their human assets should be worth less – in the same way that a ship that jettisons part of its cargo will be worth less when it finally arrives in port" (1996: 95). (Note, again, the "asset" language, which likens employees to cargo.)

In his studies Reichheld is able to show a high inverse correlation between employee turnover and productivity. When one chain ranked its stores "it found that the top third in employee retention was also the top third in productivity with 22% higher sales per employee than the bottom third" (1996: 98). The most profitable of the national brokerage houses, A. G. Edwards, also had the highest retention rates. Reichheld reported that the total cost of hiring a new broker was $100,000. New brokers will not earn any real profit for their firm until their third year. More than half the new brokers will not last more than three years, however, which pushes the real investment of the surviving new brokers to $300,000. In other words, an increase in broker retention from 80 to 90 percent will increase the value of a new broker by 155 percent (1996: 105).

Happily, an increasing number of firms are recognizing the wide array of benefits that accrue from successful people management. Thinking of employees as creating added value can translate into firm value. In the service sector, for example, competent, courteous, and attentive employees are key to success – employees deal with the public head on. Visionary leaders such as Herb Kelleher, former CEO and current Chairman of Southwest Airlines, recognized this, and thus emphasized careful and parsimonious hiring decisions early on.

What Pfeffer, among others, has shown is that treating employees as adding economic value even pays dividends in more traditional business sectors. A study of 192 banks revealed a positive correlation between job security and financial performance (Delery and Doty, 1996; Pfeffer, 1998). In another study, Pfeffer cites a doctoral dissertation that compared the responses by American and German banks to increased competition from other financial service industries. While, in the United States, banks resorted to cost-cutting measures such as layoffs and the curtailing of services, German banks invested in training, updated services, and enhanced their competitive positions (Pfeffer, 1998: 20, 22).

The results demonstrate that investments in people pay off. After a decade, demand deposits in the United States had fallen from 32% to 22% of household assets, and, in Germany, they had fallen from 60% to 48%. In the investment market, though, while American banks held only 17% of the American mutual fund market, German banks controlled the investment market with 66% of bond sales to private individuals. While American banks stayed out of the insurance industry, German banks captured market share from the German life insurance industry. Also, while American banks watched as their share in the credit card market dropped from 80% to 60%, German banks drove their share from 25% to 80%. Banks in the United Sates lost a quarter of the market for consumer loans to retailers and finance companies, while German banks became virtually the sole provider of consumer loans.

Experiences of firms in the United States and around the world thus illustrate the importance of recognizing the value of people for firm performance. Such a mentality often leads to increased firm loyalty and high employee morale. It can also lead to greater camaraderie among employees, and employees joining such firms are likely to stay longer, both because they are welcome to stay and because they want to stay. In addition, firms committed to people, firms that do not consider layoffs an appropriate business answer, often take better care in making initial hiring decisions, both in terms of how many to hire and whom to hire. This sort of selective hiring, as exhibited by companies such as Southwest Airlines, Hewlett Packard, and Peoplesoft, enhances employee productivity as well as general firm performance. The benefits of providing job security are almost too many to count. It is not just about treating people with respect and dignity, but also about doing what benefits the firm in intangible and tangible ways.

The provision of employment security is not without limitations. It is never good business to tolerate poor or inadequate job performance. In addition, there are unforeseen conditions that can warrant the legitimate need for layoffs. For example, in the wake of the terrorist attacks on September 11, 2001, a number of businesses have had to reduce their workforce dramatically in light of changing economic conditions. Several airlines were among the first to announce layoffs. While changes were probably inevitable, it is interesting to note that Southwest Airlines remained committed to its "no layoff" policy. It was the only airline that neither reduced employees nor reduced its schedule, and it was the only airline that remained profitable in 2001.

"Employment security" encompasses the notion that employment decisions will be linked to sound business practices, and that they will be carried out with respect for the dignity of the people involved. This requires that information be given in order to provide employees with reasonable notice, and that employees be afforded due process with regard to decisions made about their careers. While many managers tend to dread the term "employment security," it coincides with good business judgment and holds the potential for actually improving firm performance.

SELF-DETERMINATION 

Self-determination is an extremely controversial right. To build a business case for self-determination we first need to articulate some of the management practices that, together, add up to employee self-determination. Then we will make the business case for these practices. It will turn out that there is no one list of practices that will create self-determination and profitability. On the other hand, a number of management employment practices do go together in creating economic value added.

Although Pfeffer does not use the language of rights, he has made the abstract business case for a right to reasonable self-determination (Pfeffer, 1998: 33). He shows how managers can turn employees into value creators that turn into profits by giving those people a meaningful voice. His argument is as follows:

1 People work harder because of the increased involvement and commitment that comes from having more control over and say in their work.
2 People work smarter – high performance management practices encourage the building of skills and competence and, as importantly, facilitate the efforts of people in actually applying their wisdom and energy to performance.
3 High commitment management practices, by placing more responsibility in the hands of people farther down in the organization, save on administrative overheads as well as other costs associated with having an alienated workforce in an adversarial relationship with management.

How large is the gain from applying these management practices? Most studies show that it is in the neighborhood of 40 percent (Pfeffer, 1998: 32). Pfeffer refers to a study that shows an increase of $18,000 per employee in the value of firm stock as a result of people-centered management. There is another study, according to Pfeffer, which indicates that one standard deviation improvement in high commitment management practices is associated with an increase of shareholder wealth of $41,000 per employee. An analysis of five-year survival ratings of initial public offerings (IPOs) demonstrates a 42 percent survival probability between those in the upper and lower tail of the distribution of firms regarding human resource value.

One of the best-known studies in this area involves a General Motors (GM) plant in Freemont California. When it was governed according to GM's low commitment human resource philosophy, the plant was well known in the industry as a productivity disaster. GM closed the plant in 1982, but reopened it after it entered into a joint venture with Toyota. The plant was then managed according to Toyota's high commitment human resource plan called Toyota Production System. The acronym for the joint venture was NUMMI (New United Motor Manufacturing, Inc.). Adopting the Toyota system enabled the Freemont plant to produce an automobile with half the labor hours. Elements of this system were instituted in the Saturn Program – another of the rare GM success stories. The beneficial results of the Saturn and Freemont programs were not implemented system-wide, though. Today, GM retains a reputation for a less-than-enlightened human resource policy.

There are a number of management practices that, when properly implemented, could be said to enhance an employee's right to self-determination. Such a list would include participative management, employee teams, empowerment, open book management, 360 degree supervisor–employee evaluation, and total quality management. Although all of these practices represent a departure from traditional hierarchical management and from what is called the "scientific" management of Taylorism,[1] they also have enjoyed proven success in a number of ongoing enterprises.

To get at the difference between these practices and traditional management, it is useful to consider two different views concerning the nature of work and the employment relationship. These views are often referred to as theory X and theory Y (McGregor, 1960). One view, called theory X (or Taylorism), assumes that employees do not want to work, that they find work unpleasant, and that they will shirk whenever they can. Given this attitude, workers are not considered creative, and it is assumed that they will not make good decisions in the interest of management. It thus follows, according to theory X thinking, that workers need to be given orders and monitored to make sure that they carry out those orders. According to theory Y, though, in the appropriate organizational context, workers find meaning in their work and are, therefore, creative and capable of independent thought. Workers operating according to theory Y need far less in the way of monitoring.

Empirical research shows that some employees behave as predicted by theory X and some behave according to theory Y. Most, though, fluctuate between the two types of behavior. This research also indicates that organizational forms and structures influence how employees behave. Management style therefore serves as a sort of self-fulfilling prophecy. If a person manages as if all employees behave in accordance with theory X, behavior in conformity with theory X increases. On the other hand, if a person manages as if employees behave in accordance with theory Y, behavior according to theory Y increases (McGregor, 1960; Bowie, 1991).

Employee teams, empowerment, and participatory management

"Employee Teams" is one of the new managerial buzzwords aimed at increasing productivity and efficiency. In fact, well-managed work teams can do exactly that. Why, then, do not all companies develop that management style? According to Douglas McGregor, those who think that employees are more likely to behave according to theory X will adopt hierarchical management with a command and control focus. On the other hand those who think employees can behave according to theory Y will adopt the types of management practices that will increase employee determination in the workplace, including the use of employee teams.

When properly carried out, the use of teams shifts decision-making from the manager to the team itself. The assumption is that those working in teams are closest to the assembly line as in manufacturing industries or closest to the customer in service industries. By delegating decision-making to the teams, better (ultimately more profitable) decisions are made. Teams also run against the Taylorist assumption of specialization. Rather than having an individual do one simple task over and over, employees working in teams learn all the steps in a given process. Teamwork therefore eliminates layers of hierarchy and substitutes process knowledge for specialization. In addition, allowing teams to make decisions empowers employees. The total quality management movement now argues, in part, that the best quality is achieved when tasks are team-governed, when the layers of management are reduced, and when employees can make decisions on the spot. Teamwork, empowerment, and total quality management are thus linked. This set of practices can be called *participative management.*

In chapter 4 we presented McMahon's defense of workplace democracy. Pfeffer's version, what he calls participative management, is somewhat differently structured but with the same ends in mind. According to Pfeffer, participative management involves, at least in part, the removal of status differentials in the workplace. Pfeffer and others argue that teamwork reaps even greater rewards when differences of status are removed. When the entire organization is seen as a team then there is no need for an officers' dining room, reserved parking places for managers, differences in dress, or stock options or gain sharing plans not open to all employees. If these status differences were eliminated, the implications for pay and benefits would be enormous.

What are the economic advantages? First, teams displace layers of management in the traditional hierarchical structure. If teams make decisions, employees do not need to "go to" the boss to ask permission. Being a member of a team puts tremendous pressure on absenteeism. Pfeffer cites AES Corporation, a developer and operator worldwide of electric and steam generating plants, and Vancom Zuid-Limburg, a Dutch public bus company, as examples of organizations whose commitment to teamwork has had bottom-line payoff. Pfeffer notes how AES achieved benefits from teams:

> The company developed a $400 million plant in Cumberland, Maryland, with a team of just ten people who obtained more than thirty-six separate permit approvals and negotiated the complex financing, including tax exempt bonds and ten lenders. Normally, projects of this size require hundreds of workers, each with small specific tasks to perform within large corporations. (Pfeffer, 1998)

A person who thinks people behave in accordance with theory X will point out that this claim that teamwork lessens absenteeism is counterintuitive. Teams, they would argue, are subject to prisoner dilemma problems. There is a tendency to slack off when others are equally responsible. Since each team member reasons this way, productivity of the team as a whole is less than it would be if each person worked and was evaluated independently. This abstract argument based on a theory of human nature gets only partial empirical support. As one author studying the phenomenon has put it, "Economists Free-Ride, Does Anybody Else?" (Marwell and Ames, 1981). The empirical data also shows that as people come to know each other and form a coherent group, there is little free-riding. Productivity in that sort of team is actually higher. That was the case at NUMMI and at Saturn. One of the more profitable grocery chains, Whole Market Foods, credits its superior financial performance to the use of teams (Pfeffer, 1998: 75–6).

Open book management or transparency

Open book management is an extension of participative management. It operates on the philosophy that everyone in the business should know the financials that make a business run. Everyone should know how the work of their team affects the bottom line. Armed with that knowledge, the bottom line serves as a monitor of performance for all employees – not just for the managers. With full disclosure of financial information, organized in teams, and authorized to make decisions, these employees have a significant amount of self-determination in the workplace. According to John Case, an open book management consultant, open book management gives people a chance to act and a reason to accept responsibility for those actions:

> How does open book management do what it does? The simplest answer is this. People get a chance to act, to take responsibility, rather than just doing a job. . . . No supervisor or department head can anticipate or handle . . . all situations. A company that hired enough managers to do so would go broke from the overhead. Open book management gets people on the job doing things right. And it teaches them to make smart decisions . . . because they can see the impact of their decisions on the relevant numbers. (Case, 1995: 45–6)

These sorts of management practices implement self-determination. Moreover, such practices – when implemented as a set – contribute directly and positively to the bottom line. The empirical evidence supports the contention that the implementation of such practices is more profitable than traditional management techniques. Research documenting the adverse effects of hierarchical organizations stretches back over a 50-year period (Likert, 1967).

Renis Likert, of the University of Michigan, distinguished four types of organizations: the exploitative authoritarian, the benevolent authoritarian, the consultative, and the participative group. The participative group form of organization is the one that most closely represents an organization compatible with a recognition of employee rights. The participative organization is highly democratic, with group involvement in setting the goals of the organization and in meeting them. Compensation plans are decided by group participation. Communication is initiated at all points in the organization and the flow of communication is multidirectional. There is a high level of teamwork in this type of organization. Surely this is an organization that recognizes the employee's right to a reasonable amount of self-determination in the workplace. But how does it compare with the other types of organization in terms of profitability? Likert cited evidence that the participative group is most productive. It has lower absenteeism, less waste, and a more accurate sharing of information among members of the organization (Likert, 1967).

A Pratt and Whitney Plant in Maine was about to be closed because of inefficiency and quality problems. The new plant manager, Robert Ponchak, adopted a profit-sharing plan and extensive worker retraining actions consistent with a right to fair compensation. Those actions, however, were simply announced and despite the fact that they would benefit employees, there was worker resistance. When one of Ponchak's decisions regarding a new production scheme could not be implemented, Ponchak attempted to implement a heavy dose of representative democracy. He appointed 22 representatives from both the factory floor and the clerical office to leave their regular jobs and come up with a new pay and job classification scheme to link pay to learning the new techniques. They accomplished this, and they ended up saving the plant from closure (White, 1996: A1–2).

Trust

All of these practices: employee teams, corporate transparency, and participative management, relate to providing respect in the work place. One way to show respect in the workplace is to eliminate unnecessary differences in status. A growing list of companies abide by a policy of universal first name, that is, everyone in the company is on a first name basis: Mars, Corning, Walt Disney, General Electric, UPS, Electronic Data Systems, Hewlett-Packard, and Xerox (Pfeffer, 1998). A number of companies have dropped the term "employee" because of its hierarchical implications. They have substituted terms like "associate" that have a more egalitarian connotation. Of course, simply changing terms is not enough. Behavior must be consistent with the rhetoric.

The strategy and organizational studies literature is virtually unanimous in arguing for the importance of building trust in organizations. "The essence of high performance work arrangements is reliance on *all* organizational members for their ideas, intelligence, and commitment to making the organization successful. Such efforts will not be successful in the absence of trust" (Pfeffer, 1998: 124). What set of management practices is most likely to instill trust? The evidence is overwhelming. It is that set of practices that we have associated with implementing the employee's right to self-determination on the job. How can you build trust if you do not meet with employees to explain and to seek advice? How can you build trust if you keep information secret? How can you build trust if by word and deed a manager reflects that he or she is of a higher status and therefore a "better" person? The answer is that you cannot. To build trust, business practices such as participative management, open book management, and teamwork are required. These practices are the very same ones that allow managers to implement the right to a reasonable amount of self-determination in the workplace.

Again, the business case, from the employer's perspective, in favor of practices that constitute the implementation of self-determination in the workplace are overwhelming. A study of the steel industry, which ranked steel plants on a 1 to 4 scale with 4 being the most progressive and 1 being the most traditional (organized on Taylor's principles of "scientific management"), demonstrated that a 1 percent increase in the time the line operated resulted in an increase of income of $360,000 per year. Lines in a system 1 plant operated 87 percent of the time, while lines in a system 4 plant operated 98 percent of the time (Ichniowski, Shaw, and Prennushi, 1995).

Another study ranked performance in the semiconductor industry on the basis of a participation scale. In terms of our system of employee rights, two of the measures implemented the right to reasonable participation and two of the measures implemented the right we will discuss next – equitable compensation. The power dimension measured the extent to which decision-making was decentralized. The information dimension measured the extent to which performance data was systematically collected and widely shared. The knowledge dimension measured the extensiveness and effectiveness of training. Finally, the reward dimension measured the use of gain sharing and other forms of group-based contingent compensation. The highest performers in the semiconductor industry were those who scored highest on the four dimensions (Brown,

1994). A similar study of oil rigs indicated similar results (Ricketts, 1994; Salpukas, 1995).

EQUITABLE COMPENSATION

Of all the alleged employee rights, compensation or pay is perhaps the most controversial. Right or wrong, most of us who are employed measure ourselves and our accomplishments according to the magnitude of our pay. We also often compare ourselves to our peers according to their pay, and we measure the importance of our work as relative to our compensation. What is most difficult is to determine what is meant by a fair wage. Is that to be measured in terms of contribution? Should it differ depending on age, gender, responsibilities or experience? What about economic differences depending on the region or country in which one works? Economists argue that wages are set by the market and are pretty much out of the control of individual managers. If managers pay more that the market-driven going wage, their products or services will be at a competitive disadvantage and thus they will be driven to lower their wages back to the market level. The only "fair" wage is the wage that is set by a competitive market.

Perhaps the most heated controversy today involves executive compensation. People have become increasingly cognizant of the vast discrepancies between employee and executive pay. Productivity has been rising in the United States since the early 1990s. While this is attributable largely to technological innovation and a more skilled workforce, the evidence shows that financial benefits are being enjoyed primarily by executives and owners of capital. In fact, executive salaries are still on the rise. Executive pay climbed 571% between 1990 and 2000, and grew even in 2000, a year in which the Standard & Poor's 500 stocks suffered a 10% decline. For the same period of time, employee pay increased only 37%, which barely outpaced the inflation of 32% (Anderson et al., 2001).

Given all these difficulties, we will focus in this section on what we will call "equitable compensation." Equitable compensation is pay that takes into account market demands for the labor skill with the proviso that no wage is acceptable that is below a living wage. What constitutes a "living wage" is also subject to extensive debate. We will assume, for the sake of the argument, that a living wage is a wage that allows someone (and his or her family) to live adequately above the poverty level and to be a property-owner. Equity also demands that people are paid comparably for their skill sets (including education and experience) and the worth of the job or position. Thus gender, age, or ethnic background, for instance, ordinarily would not be acceptable criteria for wage differentials.

While trying to create equitable compensation packages places huge demands on employers, it also provides benefits. It is possible to argue, as we suggested in the last chapter, that workers who perceive that they are fairly compensated are more productive (Herzberg, 1968, 1987). Part of fair compensation, Herzberg argues, is comparable pay for comparable work without biased favoritism. In addition, Pfeffer argues, compensation should be above the market norm and pay differentials should be based on productivity. When productivity is increasing, high compensation employers are not at a competitive disadvantage. Indeed, such firms have a competitive edge. Ironically, if this argument is factually sound, it should be easy for other firms to change their compensation policy. Given the way that traditional management views employees, though, many managers will not accept the empirical findings. The unconventional firm will thus, all other things being equal, have and maintain its competitive advantage.

Competitive compensation is not simply a matter of wages. The organizational behavior literature illustrates that the most successful organizations are those that "provide comparatively high compensation contingent on organizational performance" (Pfeffer, 1994: 64). In other words, employees tend to respond well to contingent pay – pay based upon firm performance, as well as equitable compensation. Saturn, for example, based a variable percentage of pay (12 percent in the late 1990s) on performance (Bohl, 1997), and this compensation system proved tremendously successful. In 1997, Saturn was the only small car in the GM roster to turn a profit.

Employee stock ownership is another device through which employee compensation can be enhanced in the eyes of the employees. Management has long recognized the value of these devices for increasing the profitability of the firm, but relatively few firms have extended this sort of compensation to all employees. Firms who have extended employee stock ownership to all employees have found it a successful initiative. Publix, a large supermarket chain in the Southeast, outpaced the industry average of net sales by nearly 2 percent in 1995. Publix attributes its success to its stock ownership plan for which all employees are eligible after a year of service and one thousand hours (Pfeffer, 1998: 81).

Satisfied employees can translate into tangible firm savings. Starbucks, for example, enjoys tremendous savings as a result of employee retention. Starbucks provides all employees – even part-timers – with stock options and health insurance, and invests substantially in training. Starbucks has also implemented a "bean option plan," open to all employees, which allows them to secure options to buy shares of Starbucks stock in the future at today's price. This can translate into significant profits for individual employees. An employee with ten years of service at Starbucks receives stock options worth three times his or her salary (Bollier, 1996: 218). Not surprisingly, the turnover rate at Starbucks is 60 percent, in an industry where the average usually climbs above 300 percent. Chevy's, a Mexican restaurant chain, has also contained its turnover rate to 91 percent, seemingly through generous benefits, including financial rewards linked to tenure of service and participative management (Pfeffer, 1998: 179).

A growing number of firms are realizing the importance of treating employees equitably with regard to compensation. Intel also offers a stock option plan and profit-sharing that is available to all employees. Such plans are not inexpensive. In 1996, Intel paid $820 million in profit-sharing and retirement benefits to 48,500 employees worldwide (Takahashi, 1997: B6). The $214 million in profit-sharing was equivalent to 27 days of pay for every employee. Even junior employees enjoyed significant benefits. An entry-level person earning $25,000 a year would have received a bonus of approximately $8,000. While expensive, this, according to Craig Barrett, CEO, was how Intel showed its appreciation to its employees, and secured their future cooperation: "This outstanding year would not have been possible without the remarkable efforts of Intel employees. Our bonus and profit-sharing plan are one way we can recognize their significant achievement" (Takahashi, 1997: B6).

Other companies with stock option plans for all employees as listed in the 1998 *Fortune* survey of the best companies to work for include Amgen, Cisco Systems, First Tennessee Bank, General Mills, W. L. Gore, Great Plains Software, McCormick, Merck, Proctor and Gamble, and Microsoft in addition to Intel. These are highly successful companies, and there is a positive correlation between companies that have profit-sharing or gain-sharing plans and productivity – especially when they are combined with a high degree of worker participation.

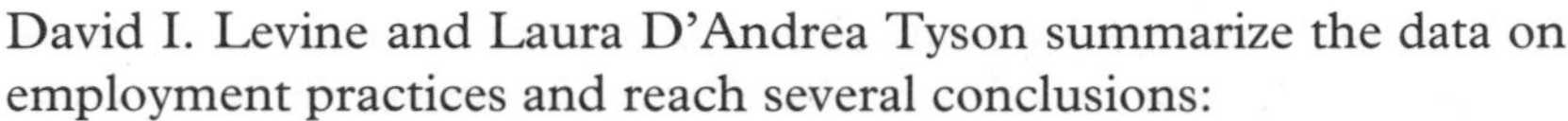

BEST PRACTICES

David I. Levine and Laura D'Andrea Tyson summarize the data on employment practices and reach several conclusions:

> Participation is more likely to have a long term effect on productivity when it involves decisions related to shop floor daily life, when it involves substantive decision-making rights rather than purely consultative arrangements (for example, quality circles), and when it occurs in an environment characterized by a high degree of employee commitment and employee-management trust. . . . On the basis of several participatory arrangements . . . we identify four features of a firm's industrial relations system needed to maintain employee support for participation. These include gain sharing, long term employment relations, measures to build group cohesiveness, and guaranteed individual rights for employees. (1990: 205)

Levine and Tyson remind us of a very important point: the business argument in favor of employee rights and the management practices to implement them is a set, a "package." As a set of sound management practices is implemented, it must be done with consistency if financial gains are to be reaped. This is clearly illustrated in team-organized firms. It makes little sense to organize one factory as a team but not others. It makes no sense to have a team on the factory floor – even on all factory floors – without having teams elsewhere in the organization. As Pfeffer reports, Whole Foods is a corporation that implemented teams throughout the organization: "Senior management is a team, regional managers are a team, each department in the store is a team, and so forth" (Pfeffer, 1998: 76). Similar remarks apply to the relationship between compensation and teamwork. Many companies institute teams but still reward people on the grounds of individual merit. That approach is inconsistent with sound management practice. If decisions are made by a team, the rewards should be team-based as well.

Assuming the data assembled here is correct, it is interesting to question why there has not been a more widespread adoption of such management practices, especially since, on the surface, they seem so easy to copy. The answer lies most probably in the integration of the practices. While the individual practices are relatively simply to emulate, a complete integrated program of practices is more difficult to copy. As a set, the practices reflect underlying management philosophy or culture, and culture is a very difficult thing to copy. In the language of transaction cost economics, corporate culture has high asset specificity.

A high commitment human resource strategy is especially difficult to copy in the United States, where the broader culture reflects values that are so inconsistent with it. Individual achievement is of great value in the United States. A person exhibits individual achievement by standing out from others, by having more income, a larger office, or managing more employees. Our "individual achievement" or "winner takes all" mental models thus blind us to the benefits of adopting practices that would improve profitability, even when these measures of achievement do not fit well with employee rights or with sound management practices that lead to the best financial results (Frank and Cook, 1995).

CONCLUSION

Economic value can be added from implementing the rights to reasonable job security, reasonable self-determination on the job, and reasonably equitable and competitive compensation. In order to achieve this value added, however, firms must be committed to implementing all three rights, along with the set of sound business practices that are conditions for successful implementation of those rights. Not all managers or the firms they manage have the wisdom and imagination to do so. This is a moral and economic pity.

NOTE

1. Taylorism is the view that workers should be managed in a maximally efficient way. F. W. Taylor undertook extensive time and motion studies that enabled him to break up tasks into discrete pieces. Employers could then organize an assembly line so as to get maximum productivity from the combination of machines and people.

REFERENCES

Articles, books, and other similar publications

Anderson, Sarah, Cavanagh, John, Hartman, Chris, and Leondar-Wright, Betsy. 2001. "Executive Excess 2001." *Pension Benefits*, vol. 10, no. 10: 11–12.

Bohl, Don L. 1997. "Case Study: Saturn Corp. – A Different Kind of Pay." *Compensation and Benefits Review*, vol. 29, no. 6: 51–6.

Bollier, David. 1996. *Aiming Higher.* New York: American Management Association.

Bowie, Norman. 1991. "Challenging the Egoistic Paradigm." *Business Ethics Quarterly*, vol. 1: 1–22.

Brown, Clair. 1994. "Executive Summary." *The Competitive Semiconductor Manufacturing Human Resources Project: First Interim Report.* Berkeley, CA: Institute of Industrial Relations.

Case, John. 1995. *Open Book Management.* New York: Harper Collins Publishers.

Davenport, Thomas O. 2000. "Workers are *Not* Assets. " *Across the Board.* June: 30–4.

Delery, John E. and Doty, D. Harold. 1996. "Modes of Theorizing in Strategic Human Resource Management: Tests of Universalistic, Contingency, and Configurational Performance Predictions." *Academy of Management Journal*, vol. 39, no. 4: 802–35.

Dorfman, J. R. 1991. "Stocks of Companies Announcing Layoffs Fire Up Investors, But Prices Often Wilt." *Wall Street Journal*, December 10: C1, C2.

Frank, Robert. H. and Cook, Philip J. 1995. *The Winner-Take-All Society.* New York: Free Press.

Herzberg, F. B. 1968, 1987. "One More Time: How Do You Motivate Employees?" *Harvard Business Review*, vol. 65: September–October, 109–20.

Ichniowski, Casey, Shaw, Kathryn, and Prennushi, Giovanna. 1995. "The Effect of Human Resource Management Practices on Productivity." Working Paper, Graduate School of Business, Columbia University. 16.

Levine, David I. and Tyson, Laura D'Andrea. 1990. "Participation, Productivity, and the Firm's Environment." In Alan S. Blinder, ed., *Paying for Productivity*. Washington, D.C.: Brookings Institute, 183–244.

Likert, Renis. 1967. *The Human Organization.* New York: McGraw Hill.

Marwell, Gerald and Ames, Ruth E. 1981. "Economists Free-Ride, Does Anyone Else?" *Journal of Public Economics:* 15: 295–310.

McGregor, Douglas. 1960. *The Human Side of Enterprise.* New York: McGraw Hill.

Pfeffer, Jeffrey. 1994. *The Competitive Advantage Through People.* Boston: Harvard Business School Press.

Pfeffer, Jeffrey. 1998. *The Human Equation.* Boston: Harvard Business School Press.

Reichheld, Frederick F. 1996. *The Loyalty Effect.* Boston: Harvard Business School Press.

Ricketts, Richard. 1994. "Survey Points to Practices that Reduce Refinery Maintenance Spending." *Oil and Gas Journal*, vol. 92, no. 27: 37–41.

Salpukas, Agis. 1995. "Uncapping New Ideas for U.S. Oil." *New York Times Current Events Edition*, November 16: D1.

"Snip, Snip, Oops." 2001. *The Economist.* October 13: 59–60.

Takahashi, Dean. 1997. "Hey Big Spender: Intel Shares Wealth With Its Employees." *Wall Street Journal*, February 12: B6.

Taylor, F. W. 1911. *The Principles of Scientific Management.* New York: Harper & Row.

Taylor, Humphrey. 2000. "The Mood of American Workers." *The Harris Poll*, no. 4, January 19: http:/www.harrisinteractive.com/harris_poll/index.asp?PID=5.

White, Joseph P. 1996. "Dodging Doom: How a Creaky Factory Got Off the Hit List, Won Respect at Last." *Wall Street Journal*, December 26: A1–2.

part iii

The Evolving Workplace

The final section of this book explores the workplace of the twenty-first century. In chapter 8, we examine workplace diversity, both as morally required from a rights perspective and as adding economic value added to firms. In chapter 9, the concluding chapter, we take a more pessimistic position. In truth, defenses of employee rights and the empirical data that supports their protection have not dramatically succeeded in changing the mindset of EAW or employment practices in many American workplaces. As American-style free enterprise expands and is emulated globally, such failures could be exacerbated.

Given this conclusion, in this last chapter, we postulate three new models for employment: the citizenship metaphor, the depiction of employment as part of a political-economic system, and, finally, a model of the employee as a professional. These three models represent possible ways of re-envisioning employment so as to advance employee interests, even in the absence of legal protection or moral agreement.

The model of the employee as a professional incorporates elements of the other models as well. It proposes that employees and managers at all levels in all positions take charge of their jobs, their talents, and their careers, in order to establish themselves as independent agents or professionals with professional standards and bargaining powers with which to balance employer prerogatives and enhance self-worth. While this proposal might seem difficult to attain, we will suggest some practical ways in which it could be achieved.

chapter eight

Diversity, Affirmative Action, and Equity in Employment Practices

In the words of Henry David Thoreau, "The world is wider than our view of it." This is the reality that businesses are now confronting. Recent decades have witnessed the emergence of a host of initiatives aimed at promoting employee diversity in the workplace. There is increasing recognition that traditionally accepted practices of hiring and promotion did not always entail equal opportunities for all qualified applicants and employees, and such practices often failed to reflect the diversity or the talent of our present population. Enlightened management now acknowledges prospective employees' talents and rights to equal opportunities, and a number of legislative agendas focus on assuring non-discrimination in the workplace. Firms are now realizing that they are better positioned if the diversity of their employees mirrors, or at least in some sense parallels, the diversity of the community they serve. In addition, they have calculated the bottom-line benefits of diversity that result from the exchange of ideas between people with different perspectives.

DIVERSITY

The first step toward understanding diversity involves arriving at a suitable definition. This can be somewhat problematic, in that what we call "diversity" encompasses a wide array of attributes and qualities, and its particular meaning can vary according to the setting. According to *Webster's Dictionary*, diversity is defined as "difference or variety." In many settings, diversity is construed as difference defined by factors such as gender, sexual orientation, race, ethnicity, religion, or national origin. These are important elements in creating a diverse community, but diversity in the workplace also includes diversity of opportunities, ideas, intellectual and professional challenges, and leadership.

Sharon Davie has offered a definition that aims to capture the broad implications of "diversity":

> [D]iversity refers to 1) an array of characteristics of human beings which significantly mark their own and/or others' perceptions of their individual and group identities, especially characteristics of race, gender, ethnicity, age, national origin, sexual orientation, religion, physical ability, and class; and 2) the heterogeneity of a group or organization based on the inclusion of individuals of different backgrounds or experiences, especially in the areas listed above. (Davie, 1997: 173)

Heterogeneity could reflect the surface characteristics of the local, national, or global population (e.g., race, gender, ethnicity, national origin), it could take into account surface characteristics of the population of professional or managerial qualified personnel suitable for positions within the firm, and/or it could include a diversity of nationalities if the firm operates in more than one country or has a strong emphasis on international business. Heterogeneity could also refer to other, "deep" characteristics, such as functional and socioeconomic background, educational experience, and even tenure in the field or in the company.

There are a number of arguments defending a racial, ethnic, and gender-mixed diverse workplace: first, as a matter of employee rights and institutional fairness, any organization that does not base its hiring, retention, and promotion on equal opportunity and job qualifications, rather than characteristics related to the position or positions in that organization, is violating the moral rights of those against whom it discriminates. Second, companies must meet legal requirements that increasingly demand the creation of programs and policies that do not discriminate. Third, without offering equal opportunities for everyone in our diverse society, companies overlook valuable talent. Fourth, a diverse workforce is critical as companies do business in increasingly pluralistic communities – nationally and internationally. Associating surface diversity with differences in perspectives, a fifth set of arguments contends that, in our rapidly changing economic environment, creativity – the input of new ideas

– is essential to survive and remain competitive. Another set of studies makes the same claims for deep workforce heterogeneity – that economically, culturally, educationally, and professionally diverse personnel will be more creative. A diverse workplace can thus create economic value added for a firm.

EQUAL OPPORTUNITY AND FAIRNESS

Reflecting on our arguments in chapter 1 in support of employee rights, we argued that any theory of rights is a theory about *equal* rights. Rights claims are valid, therefore, only if they apply equally to everyone. One of these is the right to equal consideration, that is, if rights talk makes sense, each of us has the right to be considered as an equal with every other person. Equal consideration or, as it is called in the workplace, "equal opportunity," is rooted in a deeply held moral belief that, while people are different, each should have the freedom and equal opportunity to develop his or her talents with opportunities and positions open to everyone. As we argued in chapter 1, freedom is not merely the right to be left alone, but it also includes the right to an equal starting place, and the right to develop talents and capabilities – whatever they may be.

This right to equal consideration or equal opportunity is not the same as the right to equal treatment because each is applicable in different contexts. For example, as an adult citizen, each of us has the right to vote, and equally so – a right to the same treatment as every other adult citizen (who has not been convicted of a crime), despite personal characteristics, office, financial ability, or other qualifications. As an athlete, student, candidate for public office, job-seeker, or employee, on the other hand, each of us has the right to equal consideration – to receive the same consideration or opportunities as others with similar talents applicable to the relevant sport, political office, academic institution, or business.

In sports, politics, education, or business we do not, and, we shall suggest, should not, enjoy the right to receive equal treatment: to play, hold political office, earn good grades, or obtain jobs. This is because, in these arenas, other criteria dominate the selection process: talent, qualifications, merit, and scarcity. While everyone should have the equal right to be considered for a position, the criteria for serious further consideration are related to the position in question and the qualifications of candidates. Even with a pool of qualified applicants there are usually not enough teams, political offices, spaces in the best schools, or employment opportunities for all those who are qualified for these positions.

To put this another way, the requirement of fairness in these cases demands that (1) everyone has a right to be considered equally with every other person in the applicant pool, (2) out of that pool, every qualified person has the right to be considered equally with every other, but (3) when there is scarcity in society, not everyone or every qualified person will receive equal treatment. There are exceptions, of course. In a full employment economy, it is possible to argue that every person has a right to a job. When there is a scarcity of talent for a particular position, a scarcity that sometimes occurs in high tech positions, for example, every qualified person has claims to those positions. Usually, though, there are not enough employment positions or places on sports teams for all the talented people who are available.

Equal opportunity begins with hiring. Every job candidate should be considered for employment irrespective of personal characteristics that do not affect their abilities to fulfill job responsibilities. There are, though, many characteristics that do affect job performance. For example, it could be considered difficult for a deaf person to serve as a receptionist. The difficulty lies in distinguishing between those characteristics that are acceptable as job criteria, and those that are not. In addition, technology has created mechanisms through which we can compensate for many characteristics. Advances in telephone technology, for example, enable the hearing impaired to communicate with hearing callers. Does this mean that an employer is morally obligated to hire a hearing-impaired applicant as a receptionist?

Laws offer guidance in many situations, but there are no clear answers. It is, therefore, incumbent upon managers to consider the specifics of their hiring decisions so as not to ignore qualifications of diverse job candidates. While no employer is expected to restructure his or her workplace to accommodate idiosyncrasies, it is important that employers nevertheless keep in mind that there are accommodations that can be made for many types of diverse employees.

BARRIERS TO EQUAL OPPORTUNITY

Getting hired is merely the beginning. In the workplace, equal opportunities should continue in transfers, promotions, and rewards. This translates into equal pay for equal work, comparable pay for similar positions, and equal opportunities for promotion and employment security. While all these arguments supporting the right to equal consideration and equal opportunity may seem simplistic and blatantly obvious, American workplace practices, even in 2002, do not reflect this obviousness, particularly at the managerial and executive levels. While 47 percent of the workforce is comprised of women, (and this number has remained fairly steady for some years), only 12 percent hold managerial jobs. Out of the *Fortune* 1000 companies, in 2001, only seven were led by women, and 26 percent have no women on their boards. Arguably worse, in a survey of ten dominant industries in the United States conducted by the General Accounting Office (GAO) between 1995 and 2000, the wage gap between female and male managers increased during that period. "The GAO study found that in 1995 a full-time female manager . . . earned 86 cents for every dollar earned by her male counterpart. By 2000, however, a female manager in the same industry took home only 73 cents for every dollar earned by a male manager" (Lewis, 2002: E1; General Accounting Office, 2002).

The data for minorities is no better. While Asian Americans are almost twice as likely to graduate from college and business schools than Caucasians, only 1.5 percent of all top executives in the *Fortune* 1000 are Asian American ("Is the Glass Ceiling Cracking? 2001a). Black, or African-American, managers comprise less than 10 percent of all management positions, even though there are now five African American CEOs heading *Fortune* 500 companies (Hutchinson, 2001). All of them are men (Graves, 2002).

Such numbers are often considered to reflect what has become known as the "glass ceiling" phenomenon. "Glass ceiling" is the name given to situations where barriers – often invisible – exist that prevent traditionally underrepresented employees (e.g., women and minorities) from achieving positions of authority in the firms where they work. In other words, there is a limit, or "ceiling," to what they are able to accomplish. Glass ceilings are caused by a variety of circumstances. Sometimes, in the past, there were conscious efforts to prevent diverse employees from taking on controlling positions.

For example, when Ruth Bader Ginsburg, now an associate justice on the Supreme Court of the United States, graduated at the top of her law class at Columbia in 1959, she received no job offers. "As she recalled, her status as 'a woman, a Jew, and a mother to boot' was 'a bit much' for prospective employers in those days" (*Ruth Bader Ginsburg*, 2001b). Ginsburg finally received a clerkship with a district judge and eventually a professorship at Columbia Law School. That path, too, though, was fraught with barriers to entry at each stage of her career, and she is only the second female ever to be appointed to the Supreme Court.

More often in today's climate, diverse employees who hit up against glass ceilings are likely to be victims of the past prejudices that placed the people at the top who are there today. Let us think about it this way: people tend to associate socially with people with whom they identify. While this can result from geography and socioeconomic class, it also tends to be influenced by arbitrary visual traits, such as gender and race. This does not have to be intentional or malicious in any way. The simple fact is that people evaluate others through their cultural lenses, and within the context of the types of concerns they understand. This sort of thinking appears in the workplace as well. You hire, and, more importantly, promote people whom you trust. Often, you trust people based on being able to identify with them. And with whom do we identify? It tends to be the case that most people with whom we identify are people who look, think, and act like ourselves. Since most people at the top of companies in the United States are traditionally Caucasian males, intentionally or not, they tend to identify with, and trust, other Caucasian males who are also often former schoolmates or work colleagues.

Glass ceilings are particularly insidious because of their invisibility. In fact, they are often only discovered after a person has invested in a career at a particular company. While it is possible to see how certain attributes, such as gender, are reflected among a company's ranks, it is not always possible to determine the cause for possible disparities. In addition, potential employees may pay more attention to promises made and assurances given than to the visible makeup of the firm at which they are seeking employment.

This was true for Kim Miller, a long-time and devoted Wal-Mart employee (Cox, 2001). She joined the company as a cashier when she was 24 years old, with the expectation that Wal-Mart would provide a suitable environment for her to pursue a career. The company boasted forward thinking and a caring workplace, under the umbrella of their "Our People Make The Difference" motto. The company publicized regular staff pep rallies, assurances of training and advancement, and an "open-door" policy for airing complaints and grievances. When she joined the Wal-Mart team, Miller looked forward to a fast-moving, engaging career.

Nine years later, Miller recognized that something was askew. During her time at Wal-Mart, "Miller's career had stagnated while she watched men with less experience advance. Formal announcements about job openings were erratic. When she complained that a boss called her a 'bitch,' and that male coworkers watched a porn video during work hours, she was told that the problem was a 'personality conflict,' and no action was taken" (Cox, 2001). She then began to realize what was going on at Wal-Mart. Women comprised 72 percent of the company's hourly workers, but less than 40 percent of Wal-Mart's managers were women. While numbers alone do not prove that a Wal-Mart is discriminatory, such numbers, coupled with the practices that Miller herself experienced, served as strong indicators.

Wal-Mart Stores, Inc., the country's largest private sector employer, now confronts the biggest employment discrimination lawsuit ever filed in this country. An estimated 700,000 current and former female Wal-Mart employees are seeking class action status in their demand for back pay and damages for Wal-Mart's "pervasive and conscious pattern of discriminating against women" (Cox, 2001).

A second, connected, phenomenon is the "revolving door." "Revolving doors," like glass ceilings, serve as barriers to diversity in the workplace. Unlike glass ceilings, which stand as barriers to movement and promotion, revolving doors operate where the employees self-select themselves out of particular companies. A "revolving door," then, is a metaphor for the phenomenon where diverse employees are hired, but do not stay, because of lack of institutional and infrastructural support and understanding of differences in perspective. For example, Corning Glass discovered that, although they were hiring an increasing number of Asian employees and engaged in extensive training of these new people, Asians were leaving the company in droves. Interviews with former employees helped Corning to discover that their well-meaning employment practices did not match the communication style their Asian employees anticipated. In addition to negative ramifications on equal opportunity and rights, the revolving door syndrome also creates increased costs for workplaces. Simply put, turnover is expensive, as Corning discovered, regardless of the cause of that turnover. After dramatic changes in their approach, training, and communication facilitation, today Corning is considered one of the best places for women and minorities to work (Perry, 2001).

DEFENDING EQUAL OPPORTUNITY, AFFIRMATIVE ACTION, AND DIVERSITY

Many initiatives aimed at promoting diversity in the workplace are voluntary, while others reflect firms' efforts to comply with legal mandates. American jurisprudence is increasingly protecting the voice of diverse individuals. There is growing recognition that traditional practices often fail to coincide with our moral intuitions. In addition, firms are realizing that they are better positioned if the diversity of their employees mirrors, or at least in some sense parallels, the diversity of the community they serve. They are beginning to acknowledge the bottom-line benefits of diversity that result from the exchange of ideas between people with different perspectives.

Legal mandates

Although rights talk has been prevalent in the United States at least since the founding of the country and the drafting of the Bill of Rights, little attention was paid to the rights of those who fell outside the norm until fairly recently. In fact, equal opportunity in this country was not initially apparent or accepted. It took roughly 200 years for slavery to be abolished, and 70 years for women to earn the right to vote (Paltrow, 1999; O'Connor, 1996). Indeed, the road to legal recognition and protection of women, minorities, and non-citizens has been slow and agonizing (Dumond, 1966).

Legal protection for workplace opportunities is thus a relatively recent phenomenon, for it was only after equality of all races and genders began to be accepted in the community that it was even considered in the workplace. Although legislation began regulating labor standards in the 1930s, protective measures on behalf of race and gender equal opportunities were not triggered until the 1954 Supreme Court decision in *Brown* v. *Board of Education*, which held that public schools had to be desegregated.

The 1960s was the start of an explosion of federal and state legislation (most of which mirrors comparable federal legislation) that has targeted workplaces issues, and much of this legislation has been aimed at equal opportunity (McLennan, 2001). In the early 1960s, the *Equal Pay Act* of 1963 was passed, which prohibited discrimination on the basis of gender in the payment of wages. This was followed by Title VII of the *Civil Rights Act of 1964*, which created a more substantial foundation for protecting the rights of all individuals.

According to Title VII of the *Civil Rights Act of 1964*,

> It shall be an unlawful employment practice for an employer—
>
> (1) to fail or refuse to hire or to discharge any individual, or otherwise to discriminate against any individual with respect to his compensation, terms, conditions, or privileges of employment, because of such individual's race, color, religious, sex, or national origin; or
>
> (2) to limit, segregate, or classify his employees or applicants for employment in any way, which would deprive or tend to deprive any individual of employment opportunities or otherwise adversely affect his status as an employee, because of such individual's race, color, religion, sex, or national origin. (§ 20002–2 (§ 7–3), 1964)

Title VII thus demands both equal opportunity and equal treatment in the workplace.

Title VII serves a somewhat narrowly defined role. For example, it does not offer general protection to diversity, but serves identified categories of diverse individuals, as characterized by "race, color, religion, sex, or national origin." In addition, the only people within these protected categories are those considered previously disadvantaged (i.e., color refers to non-Caucasian individuals, "sex" refers to females, and so on). Interestingly, Title VII is built on the understanding that there are disadvantaged classes of people, and its established purpose is to correct these prior wrongs. In other words, the legislation was not intended to promote equality by protecting it for all, but to approach equality by tipping the balance in favor of those whose rights had been previously trampled.

In addition to its literal directives, Title VII has been interpreted as a demand for proactive steps to be taken by companies and government agencies. Title VII thus gave rise to "affirmative" action, the requirement that companies and government agencies take positive "affirmative" actions to change their employment practices by targeting traditionally underrepresented classes of job applicants, typically women and minorities.

Diversity is no longer just about the traditional categories of people, such as those defined by gender, race, religion, and so on, but about a much larger array of characteristics. Diversity, as the term is presently used to refer to employment practices, encompasses the entire spectrum of attributes that distinguish people from one another. While the early legislation focused on race, color, religion, gender, or national origin, subsequent legislation has expanded legal protection of diversity to include circumstances such as age, disabilities, and family status. The *Age Discrimination in Employment Act* (ADEA), for example, passed in 1967, protects employees over 39 years old from discrimination in the workplace. The *Pregnancy Discrimination Act*, passed in 1978, protects women in the workplace from discrimination as a result of their pregnancy, childbirth, or related medical conditions. The *Family and Medical Leave Act* (FMLA) was passed in 1993. It expands "diversity" to cover caregivers, in providing that they are able to take up to 12 weeks of unpaid leave, with their jobs being protected, to care for a sick child, spouse, or parent, for the birth or adoption of a child, or for the employee's own serious health condition.

The *Americans with Disabilities Act* (ADA) represents one of the more significant strides in the promotion of diversity in the workplace. The ADA was passed unanimously by Congress in 1990. Originally intended to protect people with certain disabilities, such as physical, hearing, and sight impairments, the ADA has been interpreted expansively to cover broader conditions than those contemplated by the legislation, such as bad backs, diabetes, and heart conditions.

Affirmative action and defenses of diversity initiatives

Under pressure from the *Civil Rights Act of 1964*, firms began adapting affirmative action policies and procedures targeted toward attracting and hiring underrepresented classes of job applicants such as blacks, females, Hispanics, Asians, and others. Affirmative action programs were designed to increase the representation of qualified underrepresented populations in the workplace and to break up habitual patterns of discrimination. Toward that end, such programs deliberately focused on underrepresented populations.

Affirmative action programs initially concentrated on hiring practices, and typical affirmative action programs generally fell within three categories: First, some firms interpreted affirmative action as a mandate to fill quotas – usually numbers that reflected population distribution of the underrepresented class in question. Since, for example, approximately 50 percent of the population in most areas in the United States are women, a quota system would require that a firm seek to hire 50 percent women. Quota systems were often based on a questionable principle of equal treatment – merely to fill slots with available women or minorities in order to respond to the Civil Rights mandate. These practices led to many mishires of underqualified people. Worse, it has contributed to the perception that most of those hired on the basis of race or gender are not qualified – or at least not as qualified to fulfill the job demands in question.

The idea that affirmative action was to be interpreted as a mandate for quotas misrepresented the spirit of affirmative action and the *Civil Rights Act*, which were to provide racially-, gender-, and ethnicity-blind equal opportunities. Even when firms interpreted the mandate as a requirement to hire representative numbers of qualified applicants, the idea persisted that firms had to fill a certain number of slots with women and minorities. This quota mindset was not in keeping with the intent or the spirit of affirmative action.

A second approach to affirmative action encompassed the view that firms were supposed to set goals to hire representative numbers of those classes of people formerly discriminated against. The belief was that firms were not required to hire just anyone or to fill quotas, but that they should aim to hire qualified people of a representative population. While such programs were more successful, some were thought to result in forms of reverse discrimination, which arguably perpetuated the very practices they were created to change by discriminating against the dominant employed class, usually (but not always) Caucasian males.[1] The basis for this argument was that it was perceived that firms could hire *only* the underrepresented. In these cases, therefore, the result was that preferential treatment was given to the underrepresented and discrimination took place against Caucasian males. Out of these practices again rose the fear that firms were hiring *less* qualified people if they belonged to the discriminated class, and a second form of reverse discrimination was reinforced (Taylor, 1995; 2002).

A third interpretation of affirmative action programs, now called "diversity initiatives," argues that firms should target underrepresented classes, but (1) it is not required nor does it make sense to hire unqualified people, and (2) a firm should consider and continue to hire and promote white males (or whomever is the dominant represented employed class in that industry) as well as others. It is, though, still often counter argued that these programs, when institutionalized, tend to hire the less qualified. Moreover, it is contended, any policy that targets specific classes of people violates the principle of equal opportunity, since the dominant employed class, usually white males in our country, are not given equal chances at job opportunities.

How is it possible to defend this third form of affirmative action or diversity initiative? It is important first to clarify the term "equally qualified." There is an assumption underlying the phrase that is somewhat misconceived. The assumption is that we can create and implement objective selective criteria and processes ranking applicants as the first best, the second best, and so on, in rank order just as we can rank lengths of sticks. This, in fact, reflects misguided thinking. With new hires, for example, there is sometimes a temptation to rank them according to school grades. Different schools grade differently, though, and school performance is not the only, or always the best, indicator of workplace success. In the selection of almost any candidate, there is a large pool of qualified people from which any number could be selected who would succeed. No one candidate is exactly like any other. Additionally, what we mean by "qualified" is not limited to the individual school or work record, but also includes how the potential employee will interact with others, for the organization's performance often results from team-based efforts. Take, by analogy, a fish bowl. A fish bowl of guppies is fairly uninteresting, and "drawing straws" would be the best selection process. Let us suppose, though, that you have a tropical fish bowl. Then it might be more beneficial to obtain a selection of fish (perhaps avoiding the beta fish, which eat the others). In that pool there are a number of diverse but qualified applicants, none of whom is identical to the others.

But why should an employer target the underrepresented "fish?" What is wrong with a fish bowl full of guppies or one beta fish? It is often argued that affirmative action programs can be justified as compensating previously discriminated classes or as retribution for past injustices. While there is some merit to such arguments, most firms hiring today will not, in fact, be able hire those they discriminated against in the past, and most of those that were discriminated against are no longer in the workforce (Sher, 1999). A second argument goes as follows. Suppose there is a public tennis course in your neighborhood and Andre Agassi lives near you. Because he is the best player in your neighborhood, should he be allowed first choice of court times when there are other eager and good players? What about court times for those of us who have good potential but need time to learn to play (Wasserstrom, 1978)?

There is also the argument that affirmative action and diversity initiatives are justifiable because the classes of persons they target were not given equal opportunities in the past. They thus tend to start the employment race several steps back from the starting line. In the case of women, for example, the issue is not gender, but the lack of opportunities as a result of gender, an irrelevant qualification for most jobs. Affirmative action programs are therefore designed to get everyone up to the same starting line, particularly those who have traditionally had no opportunity to compete (Nickel, 1974).

The most tenable set of arguments is based on the idea of fairness. Discrimination is not fair play. It is like tripping a competitive opponent when you are in a race. When we hire and promote people who look like us without considering difference, even when this is not malicious, we at least implicitly perpetuate the myth that we are hiring the most qualified. The idea, as we said earlier, is to break habits of discrimination that neglect considering qualified minorities and women. To do that, the ideal would be to find a color-blind, slightly physically handicapped, mixed-race, eunuch personnel officer to conduct all hiring and promotion. None of us, though, is in fact, or can be, perfectly objective. Our culture, upbringing, education, and social interactions create mindsets that do discriminate. Diversity initiatives, properly conceived, try to counteract these blind spots in our judgment by targeting equally qualified people of diverse backgrounds thus helping all of us to break our discriminatory habits. The goal is to eliminate the necessity for affirmative action, but we have not yet achieved that end.

Still, do such programs discriminate against the dominant applicant population? Are they forms of preferential treatment? Yes and no. Except in a full employment economy where there is a scarcity of candidates, all hiring and promotion practices must discriminate, since no company can hire everyone, even all those who are extremely qualified. Targeting specific populations who are qualified is no more discriminatory than any employment practice that cannot hire all worthwhile candidates. Moreover, if the pluralism we espouse as a nation is of value, creating a diverse workplace at all levels should also be a worthwhile goal for its own sake as well as being a fair employment practice.

Recent trends

There is evidence that the legal protection afforded to diversity in the workplace continues to expand. In 1999, the governor of Iowa took a monumental step as the first to issue an executive order prohibiting discrimination against state employees on the basis of gender identity (i.e., protection for transsexuals) (Marvin Dunson, 2001). There are additional signs that sexual orientation is becoming viewed as a protectable category of diversity. Although there is still no official federal ban against discrimination on the basis of sexual preference, localities and firms have begun to value diversity by making allowances for the needs of homosexuals. While husbands and wives of employees receive benefits from firms, the needs of homosexual partners have traditionally been ignored. This is changing. A number of cities (including Berkeley, CA, Los Angeles, CA; Cambridge, MA; Tacoma Park, MD; Ann Arbor, MI; Minneapolis, MN; Ithaca, NY; New York City, NY; Seattle, WA; and Madison, WI), a state (Vermont), and a number of firms and universities (including Apple Computer, Ben and Jerry's, Columbia University, HBO, IBM, Microsoft, Levi Strauss and Company, Lotus, University of Colorado, Walt Disney, and Princeton University) now offer benefits to committed partners of homosexual employees (Robbennolt and Johnson, 1999).

In 2001, a New York court denounced discrimination on the basis of sexual preference. *Simonton* v. *Runyon*, 50 F. Supp. 2d 159 (E.D.N.Y. 1999), *aff'd* 232 F.3d 33, involved a former postal service employee who was the victim of "ridicule, harassment and disparate treatment based upon his sexual orientation" (*Simonton* at 160). Although the specific plaintiff involved was not successful, the court did uphold the cause of action. The court of appeals upheld the dismissal of the employee's discrimination claim, but held that such a situation could state a cause of action that could be successfully litigated. According to the court in *Simonton*, it was not clear "that Simonton behaved in a stereotypically feminine manner and that the harassment he endured was, in fact, based on his non-conformity with gender norms" (*Simonton* at 37–8). Had the record included evidence that discrimination against the employee was based on behavior linked to his sexual orientation, the court indicated that it would have found in his favor. This – the mere possibility of legal protection against discrimination on the basis of sexual orientation – is a significant step for homosexuals and transsexuals.

ECONOMIC ADVANTAGES OF DIVERSITY 

We would *like* to argue that it is always the case that a carefully constructed diverse workforce, where there is a diversity of ideas as well as difference in gender, color, ethnicity and/or national origin, creates more economic value that a homogeneous workplace. According to various studies, race and gender diversity initiatives *can* create competitive advantages for firms (Cox and Blake, 1991; Gilbert et al., 1999). Such initiatives, if managed with care, can be successful in attracting and retaining the best-qualified employees. This in turn, contributes to increased creativity in decision-making and in problem solving by introducing new perspectives. It improves marketing by adding sensitivity to needs and wants of diverse consumers, and increases firm flexibility (Cox and Blake, 1991).

For proponents of diversity, these are lovely conclusions. Such conclusions are, however, tentative at best, and must be qualified. To begin, there are numerous counterexamples. American companies before 1964, most of which were run by white males, were also highly successful. Japanese firms, which are highly homogeneous, have, until recently, been extremely creative and competitive in global markets.

It is essential to keep in mind that diversity is not necessarily visible. Backgrounds and personal philosophies can contribute to diversity in the workplace. Imagine, for example, a firm that continuously hired, retained, and promoted a diverse looking workforce that included employees and managers from around the world. But this firm only hired employees, professionals, and MBAs from one university, albeit a university that had a highly diverse student body. Since all the student hirees would be trained by a similar cohort of faculty, one could imagine that while this firm *looked* diverse, and while a number of languages were spoken in the cafeteria, it was fairly homogeneous and monolithic in its ideas. In a changing global economic and political environment, such a firm might fail to be creative or competitive enough to capture the increasing rapidity and variety of changes taking place. It might actually atrophy even though it was "diverse" in appearance and non-educational background.

A stronger argument is to conclude that, in the global political economies in which most firms operate, and considering the growing diversity and pluralism in the United States, not working toward the goal of a diverse workforce, where the aim is to include people from different backgrounds and educational institutions as well as diverse surface characteristics, is likely not to be conducive to long-term corporate sustainability. With the increasing diversity of our population and our educational institutions, acting discriminatorily in a negative sense of not seeking qualified underrepresented classes of employees is usually disadvantageous. If it is true that, by 2005, only 15–20 percent of all new job applications entering the market will be white male, it is likely that historical discriminatory hiring practices will prevent those firms from taking advantage of the most qualified potential employees – either they will be overlooked or they will not be willing to accept positions. Moreover, companies who hire a token woman or minority or who do not promote qualified persons to supervisory positions often are subject to the "revolving door" phenomenon, since the climate at that company is not conducive to retention. In addition to creating a perception of unfairness that might be perpetuated throughout a corporate culture, this is costly from a training perspective and because, again, one often loses talented personnel who go elsewhere.

Other important considerations involve the diversity of firms' relevant stakeholders. There is a diverse customer and supplier population in this country alone. Customers and suppliers themselves may discriminate against a company whose products, sales force, or marketing is not representative of their gender, race, or ethnic background or interests. So while a homogeneous company can be successful, and many have been, in this changing climate of pluralism, besides being most propitious to respecting equal rights, diversity can add to the bottom line.

In a recent study, Hambrick, Cho, and Chen demonstrated that factors other than surface characteristics played a positive role in competitive behaviors and management decision-making in the airline industry. This study limited heterogeneity to "functional backgrounds, educational experiences and firm tenures" (Hambrick et al., 1996: 661). The hypothesis was that these characteristics "serve as proxies for [someone's] perspectives, belief systems, and networks and affiliations" (Jackson and Alvarez, 1992; Hambrick et al., 1996).

Out of this sort of diversity, the hypothesis continued, there was a good possibility that there would be a diversity of perspectives and ideas. In studying competitive behaviors in the top management in a number of airlines, Hambrick, Cho, and Chen showed that the existence of these characteristics of heterogeneity among top managers in particular firms led to bolder, more creative competitive actions by these firms. Although more work needs to be done in this area, this was a promising study.

It is obvious that surface differences in race, gender, ethnicity, and so on will not guarantee a diversity of ideas. It is also doubtful that background heterogeneity (deep characteristics) will always result in employee creativity. The presence of diverse surface characteristics among significant numbers of employees and managers, however, can help to shake other employees and managers out of habitual discriminatory mindsets and thus enable them to be more open to new ideas and more accepting of a variety of perspectives. In the tough global competitive climate of this new century, new ideas are critical for innovation and adaptability. While surface diversity is no guarantee of innovation, a diverse workforce, diverse only in appearance and gender, goes some way to break old habits. When women and minorities succeed and make a positive difference in a company, color and gender biases tend to slip into the background of our judgments.

There is a caveat to "diversity talk," though. According to Sharon Davie, "As a positive goal for organizations, achieving diversity usually refers not only to numerical inclusion, but also to the creation of an organizational climate in which diverse individuals are able to perform optimally as individuals, in teams, and as a community of the whole" (Davie, 1997: 173). "Climate" is hard to define, but recent studies point out that the mere presence of a workforce that *looks* diverse may not be enough to add economic value, and it could actually create dysfunctionality. The promotion and acceptance of diverse ideas must be encouraged and integrated throughout the organization and in its divisions and teams, and there must be communication throughout the organization that recognizes, respects, and responds to diverse ideas and innovations. Without that climate of openness, transparency, and reciprocity of ideas, and without diversity at the top as well as at the bottom of the organization, diversity initiatives will fail, and firms will be worse for that failure (Hamilton, forthcoming; Jackson and Alvarez, 1992).

SOME WORKPLACE INITIATIVES 

Many firms are recognizing that diversity needs to be confronted head on, not just through piecemeal initiatives. Firms such as WorkPlus.com, a firm that assists other firms in putting their employee benefits communications online, have designed programs that enable firms to reach diverse audiences more effectively (Burzawa, 1999). By narrowing the audience through targeted messages, for example, firms can assist employees in weeding through the overwhelming amount of information available so that they can obtain the messages with greatest relevance to them. In addition, WorkPlus.com personalizes communication, by matching messages with the profiles of the packages.

Other firms have opened their doors to initiatives begun by outside agencies. The Arc, for example, is a nonprofit organization that has formed partnerships with employers to provide jobs to the handicapped. Among the Arc's partners are Wal-Mart, Walgreen, Kmart, Sears, Montgomery Ward, McDonald's, Burger King, Country Buffet, Pepsi, Taco Bell, KFC, Chili's, TGI Fridays, Brinker Corp., Safeway, Kroger, Albertson's, Marriott, Hilton, Holiday Inn, Best Western, Radisson, JoAnn Fabrics and Crafts, and N.Y. Clothworld (Agoratus, 1999).

Texas Instruments (TI) has created a workplace that is physically and psychologically supportive of employees with disabilities. People with disabilities have been employed at every level up to Vice President at TI. In addition, the firm has made structural changes to its facilities in order to accommodate the needs of a physically diverse workforce. Such changes include electronic access to job postings for hearing-impaired employees, frost-free and skid-proof entry ramps and automatic doors, lower ATMs and water fountains and cafeteria accommodations, talking computers for people with visual impairments, and TDD phones at most sites (Agoratus, 1999).

The aging of the baby boomers is changing workplace dynamics. There is a larger number of older workers on the market today, and this number is increasing. These candidates have the same right to a job as the candidates just out of school. They are not, though, considered equally attractive by most employers. Older employees cost more: they have less time to recoup their training costs and investment, and their benefits (such as healthcare and insurance) are more expensive. At the same time, these people hold a wealth of skills, experience, maturity, and professionalism. Not only do they have an equal right to be considered for employment or continued employment, but they can be valuable assets as well (Masera, 1999).

Gay, lesbian, bisexual, and transgender employees are a rich source for talent. While some firms are hostile to people based on sexual orientation, the most successful are not. More than 50 percent of the *Fortune* 500 companies, 75 percent of the *Fortune* 100 companies, and 82 percent of the *Fortune* 50 include sexual orientation in their nondiscrimination policies (Melymuka, 2001).

Business practices parallel changes in legal thinking. Although sexual orientation has traditionally represented a non-protected area of employment discrimination, this changed significantly in 2000, when the federal appeals court in New York held in *Simonton* that the *Civil Rights Act of 1964* could protect people who confront "discrimination based on sexual stereotypes," such as the "gender norms" that some gay individuals defy through their demeanors, dress, and tendencies. According to Judge John M. Walker, Jr. of the Second Circuit Court, "This would not bootstrap protection for sexual orientation into Title VII . . . because not all homosexual men are stereotypically feminine, and not all heterosexual men are stereotypically masculine" (Bravin, 2000). According to the Human Rights Campaign, a gay advocacy group, 11 states and 116 cities and counties now bar employment discrimination based on sexual orientation.

CHALLENGES OF DIVERSITY: MOTHERHOOD AND MOMMY TRACKS: AN EXAMPLE

Accepting diversity as an asset is an important first step, but it becomes complicated even after a diverse workforce is in place. A diverse workforce might include a workforce with a varied set of abilities and needs, and some of those needs translate into complications for employers, such as time away from work and special facilities. Recognizing the benefits of diversity has thus prompted many businesses to take steps to accommodate these needs. It is not always easy to figure out which initiatives are appropriate, though, and there is often a lingering perception that respecting the rights of one category of employees inevitably interferes with the rights of another group.

Motherhood has presented an imposing challenge to many companies. The plain and simple fact is that women give birth to children. At a bare minimum, this means that some women must take time off from work, at the very least to give birth and, possibly, participate in the early stages of nursing.

If a woman chooses to have a child, it can be argued that she must accept the consequences of that choice. Without getting bogged down in tangential arguments (of which there are many), if a woman does not interfere with her pregnancy, even if she did not intentionally become pregnant, this can be considered a *choice* that results in the birth of a child. Since the woman is the one who gives birth, and, often, has already had to take time off from work during the pregnancy, she has traditionally been expected to remain the primary caregiver.

A common counterargument is that either the man or the woman *can* serve as the primary caregiver. Many people argue that the problem exists between the couple. If a mother is upset because she is not able to pursue a career, she is focusing her energy in the wrong direction. Instead of pressuring the firm, it is contended, she should work within the family to find another suitable caregiver, such as her husband or her parents.

Whether or not the woman chooses to remain the primary caregiver is not the pivotal issue, however. The more important question is whether the firm should be allowed to penalize caregivers – male or female. Should we compel firms, morally if not legally, to be considerate of their employees' parental responsibilities to their children? Or should we continue to accept intentional blindness to the fact that employees have connections outside the workplace that can affect their workplace performance?

Let us return to the notion of motherhood as choice. In law, motherhood is considered a *right*. The right to bear children is protected by the Constitution. Similarly, the right to work is protected. How, then, can we justify penalizing mothers in the workplace? And how do we balance these conflicting rights? The typical firm answer is that women are not prohibited from working. If they are not able to rise within the firm, it is only because their external commitments inhibit their workplace performance. That is a *personal* problem, not a problem for the firm.

Interestingly, some companies argue that they would be remiss if they made allowances for mothers. This would be unfair to nonmothers (men and women), and could potentially jeopardize other stakeholder interests. If a mother is not focused on her workplace responsibilities, she could place firm business at risk. If a non-mother performs unsatisfactorily in the workplace, the firm punishes him or her, such as through reprimands, warnings, or even termination. Why, then, should a mother who performs similarly – such as through absences, tardiness, or personal distractions – be rewarded?

In providing special treatment to one category of employees, other employees can be harmed. For example, where there is a certain amount of work that has to be done, if the mother on the team has to leave to tend to her child, it means that the other members of the team will have to fulfill her responsibilities as well as their own. It is often difficult to justify the work balance inequities imposed on non-mothers as a result of benefits given to mothers. If certain employees – mothers – are given special privileges that enable them to escape some work-related responsibilities, then someone else has to fill in for them to make sure the work is handled properly. The problem is that there is often little reciprocity. The mother is given privileges, while others are not.

Some firms have thus introduced "mommy tracks," an expression coined by Felice Schwartz in a controversial article, "Women and the New Facts of Life," which appeared in *Harvard Business Review* (Schwartz, 1989). Schwartz defends mommy tracks as viable options for working mothers who cannot devote continuous full time to their careers. These tracks provide alternatives for working mothers, in that they are provided a different set of expectations that will entitle them to different rewards. It might take longer, for example, for mommy track employees to receive promotions, or to become managers or partners. In some companies those on mommy tracks are not expected to reach top management or partner levels.

While such programs may be appreciated by some "mommies," they do not entirely rectify the wrong they seek to combat. While motherhood is clearly an important consideration, it is not the only one, and providing this alternative track for mommies, other categories of employees are implicitly treated unequally. What about fathers? There is an easy answer to that, through "daddy tracks" or "parent tracks." What about adults taking care of elderly parents or disabled siblings? As one commentator wrote, "The two-track approach does a disservice to all employees and forces both men and women into predefined roles that are inappropriate today" (Biondolillo, 1989: 183). One of the purposes of diversity initiatives is to change our mindsets about traditional social roles we have assigned women and some minorities. The mommy track reinforces old stereotypes, these tracks do not respect equal rights of men and women to choose, and, as with other forms of discrimination, valued talent will be lost as more and more women leave corporate America to start their own businesses.[2]

CONCLUSION

The goal of a diverse workplace with surface and deep heterogeneity in management and leadership as well as throughout the organization, is worthwhile not merely for equal opportunity, not merely to achieve equal rights, and not only because it is an important competitive strategy so that firms can interact with a variety of peoples and cultures in the ever shrinking globe. More importantly, diversity has value for its own sake, and companies are poorer, morally, intellectually, and culturally, in a homogeneous community. Diversity across and up and down in leadership helps each of us to be more creative, to break out of ingrained mindsets, to take multiple perspectives, to challenge each other, and to challenge ourselves.

In a study described in *Built to Last*, James Collins and Jerry Porras demonstrate that the best companies – the ones that have survived for the longest time, through adversity and change, and the ones that were and still are the most profitable – are driven not primarily by the goal of maximizing shareholder wealth, but by a core values-based ideology that pervades the company and its decision-making. They concluded that a values-orientation creates distinctive and desirable outcomes that cannot be achieved by an outcomes-oriented focus on profits (Collins and Porras, 1994).

By analogy, if we think of diversity as a core value that unifies company employment practices and other activities, a company might be better able to achieve other ends without having to count numbers, or worry too much about whether they are complying to a confusing set of laws and public policies. If a company is merely outcomes-oriented or compliance-driven, it might not succeed in that mission. If a corporate culture develops a shared core ideology that includes the espoused value of diversity as well as excellence, and if that drives what the company does as it deals with employees, customers, shareholders, and other stakeholders, it is likely to succeed in the challenging climate of global competition and change.

NOTES

1. Interestingly, in the airline industry males brought suits against the airlines, claiming they were discriminated against in the hiring of flight attendants (called, then, stewardesses). The courts ruled against the airlines and today we have "flight attendants."
2. According to *Catalyst* almost twice as many women as men start their own businesses. (www.catalystwomen.org Press_Room/press_releases/1999)

REFERENCES

Articles, books, and other similar publications

Agoratus, Lauren. 1999. "Working Together: Corporations and Special Needs Organizations Open Doors to a Diverse Workplace." *Exceptional Parent*, vol. 29, no. 12: 34.

Biondolillo, Deborah. 1989. "Letters to the Editor." *Harvard Business Review*, May–June: 182–3.

Bravin, Jess. 2000. "Courts Open Alternate Route to Extend Job-Bias Laws to Homosexuals." *Wall Street Journal*, September 22: B1.

Burzawa, Sue. 1999. "Workplace Trends Enhance Value of Personalized Communications, Online Technologies." *Employee Benefit Plan Review*, vol. 54, no. 6: 28–30.

Collins, James C. and Porras, Jerry I. 1994. *Built to Last*. New York: Harper Business.

Cox, Meg. 2001. "Wal*Martyrs." *Ms*, October/November.

Cox, T. H. and Blake, S. 1991. "Managing Cultural Diversity: Implications for Organizational Competitiveness." *Academy of Management Executive*, vol. 5: 34–47.

Davie, Sharon L. 1997. "Diversity." In P. H. Werhane and R. E. Freeman, eds., *Encyclopedic Dictionary of Business Ethics*. Oxford: Blackwell: 173–7.

Dumond, Dwight Lowell. 1966. *Antislavery: The Crusade for Freedom in America*. New York: Norton.

Dunson, Marvin, III. 2001. "Sex, Gender, and Transgender: The Present and Future of Employment Discrimination Law." *Berkeley Journal of Employment and Labor Law*, vol. 22: 465–505.

General Accounting Office. 2002. *A New Look Through the Glass Ceiling: Where Are the Women? The Status of Women in Management in Ten Selected Industries*.

Gilbert, Jacqueline A., Stead, Bette Ann, and Ivancevich, John M. 1999. "Diversity Management: A New Organizational Paradigm." *Journal of Business Ethics*, vol. 21: 61–76.

Ginsburg, Ruth Bader. 2001b. *Ruth Bader Ginsburg.* Supreme Court History. www.supremecourthistory.org/justice/ginsburg.htm

Graves, Earl G., Sr. 2002. "Excellence in Leadership." *Black Enterprise*, February: 14.

Hambrick, Donald C., Cho, Theresa Seung, and Chen, Ming-Jer. 1996. "The Influence of Top Management Team Heterogeneity on Firms: Competitive Moves." *Administrative Science Quarterly*, vol. 41: 659–84.

Hamilton, Mary. Forthcoming. "The Performance of Difference: Heterogeneous Decision Networks."

Hutchinson, Earl Ofari. 2001. "Due Respect." *Los Angeles Business Journal*, January 15: 47.

"Is the Glass Ceiling Cracking?" *Asian American Issues*, October. 20: 32.

Jackson, S. E. and Alvarez, E. B. 1992. "Working Through Diversity as a Strategic Imperative." In S. E. Jackson, ed., *Diversity in the Workplace.* New York: Guilford Press, 13–29.

Lewis, Diane E. 2002. "Business and Money: Amid Boom, Widening Gender Wage Gap Seen." *Boston Globe*, January 27: E1.

Masera, Kathy. 1999. "Baby Boomers Force More Workplace Maturity." *Human Resource Professional*, vol. 12, no. 5: 3–5.

McLennan, Kenneth. 2001. "Worker Representation and Participation in Business Decisions Through Employee Involvement Programs." *University of Pennsylvania Journal of Labor and Employment Law*, vol. 3: 563–83.

Melymuka, Kathleen. 2001. "The Growing Gay Workforce." *Computerworld*, vol. 35, no. 30: 34–5.

Nickel, James W. 1974. "Classification by Race in Compensatory Programs." *Ethics*: 84: 146–50.

O'Connor, Sandra Day. 1996. "The History of the Women's Suffrage Movement." *Vanderbilt Law Review*, 657–75.

Paltrow, Lynn M. 1999. "Pregnant Drug Users, Fetal Persons, and the Threat to *Roe* v. *Wade.*" *Albany Law Review*, vol. 62: 999–1055.

Perry, Phillip M. 2001. "Retaining Your Asian Talent (The Human Side)." *Research Technology Management*, vol. 44: 56–8.

Robbennolt, Jennifer K. and Johnson, Monica Kirkpatrick. 1999. "Legal Planning for Unmarried Committed Partners: Empirical Lessons for a Preventive and Therapeutic Approach." *Arizona Law Review*, vol. 41: 417–57.

Schwartz, Felice. 1989. "Management Women and the New Facts of Life." *Harvard Business Review* (January/February): 65–76.

Sher, George. 1999. "Diversity." *Philosophy and Public Affairs*, vol. 28: 85–104.

Taylor, Paul W. 1995; 2002. "Reverse Discrimination and Compensatory Justice." In Steven M. Cahn, ed., *The Affirmative Action Debate*. New York: Routledge, 11–16.

Wasserstrom, Richard. 1978. "A Defense of Programs of Preferential Treatment." *Phi Beta Kappa Journal*, vol. 58: 15–18.

Cases

Brown v. *Board of Education*, 347 U.S. 483 (1954).
Simonton v. *Runyon*, 50 F. Supp. 2d 159 (E.D.N.Y. 1999), *aff'd* 232 F.3d 33.

Legislation

Age Discrimination in Employment Act of 1967 (ADEA), 29 U.S.C. 621 (2000).
Americans with Disabilities Act of 1990 (ADA), 42 U.S.C. 12101 (2000).
Equal Pay Act, 77 Stat. 56 (1963) (current version at 29 U.S.C. 206(d) (2000)).
Family and Medical Leave Act of 1993 (FMLA), 107 Stat. 7 (1993) (current version at 29 U.S.C. 2611 (2000)).
Pregnancy Discrimination Act of 1978, 42 U.S.C. 2000e(k) (2000).
Title VII of the Civil Rights Act of 1964, 42 U.S.C. 2000e-2(a).

chapter nine

Future Directions for Employment

This book has presented a series of argument defending employee rights and the importance of employee contributions to firm success. We have approached employment issues through the perspective of rights theory, we have critiqued EAW, we have pointed out the limits of role morality, and we have explored the concept of meaningful work. We have contended that a diverse workplace is both fair and competitively advantageous, and argued that prioritizing employee development and well-being adds firm value.

In this chapter we will review the strengths and weakness of some of these arguments. To date, these arguments and the empirical data that supports them have not dramatically succeeded in changing the mindset of EAW nor employment practices in all American companies – Enron is only one, albeit it the most egregious, example of management practices that created massive layoffs and pension losses without any avenues for employee redress. Because of the failure of such arguments to change the philosophy of EAW, we will conclude the book with the outline of some new models for employment that suggest ways in which employee rights can be asserted regardless of the default rule: the citizenship metaphor, the thesis that employment is part of a political-economic system, and finally, a model of the employee as a professional. This last model, the model of profession or craft, is one that improves employee self-worth and dignity and redefines employee–employer relationships while it also creates economic value for firms.

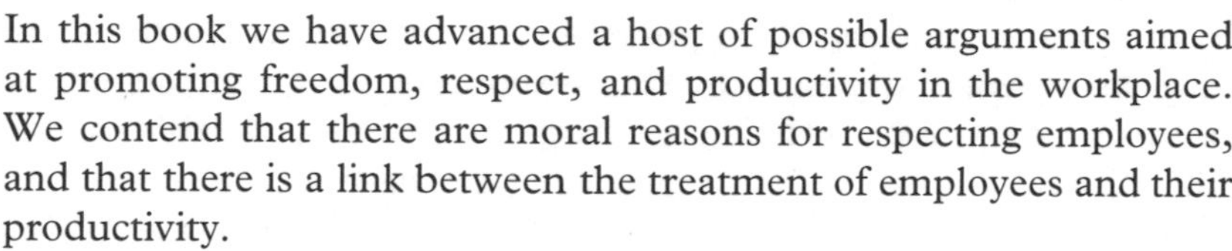

THE ARGUMENTS

In this book we have advanced a host of possible arguments aimed at promoting freedom, respect, and productivity in the workplace. We contend that there are moral reasons for respecting employees, and that there is a link between the treatment of employees and their productivity.

Rights talk and employee rights

The first set of arguments, in chapter 1, has grounded our defense of employee rights on a commonly held theory of moral rights, that is, the proposal that human beings have moral claims to a set of basic rights vis-à-vis their being human. Even if rights talk is a historically late, Western, socially-constructed set of ideas, we concluded that moral rights are candidates for universal principles and serve as justifiable evaluative mechanisms commonly accepted in Western democratic societies such as our own as well as elsewhere around the world. This set of arguments makes three points. First, principles governing employment practices that interfere with commonly guaranteed political rights, such as free speech (including legitimate whistleblowing), privacy, due process, and democratic participation, would appear to be questionable principles and practices from a rights perspective. Second, justifiable rights claims are generalizable. It thus follows that, if employers and managers have certain rights, say, to respect, free speech, and choice, employees should also have equal claims to those rights. Third, if property rights are constitutionally guaranteed, it would appear to follow that employees should have some proprietary rights to their work contributions, just as companies or managers, as representatives of companies, have rights to exercise property claims.

As we discovered, however, there are at least three countervailing arguments against these conclusions. In the United States, constitutional guarantees apply to interactions between persons or institutions and the state, but they do not extend to the private sector or to the home, except in cases of egregious acts. Claims to employee rights are not, therefore, guaranteed by the Constitution. Second, employment agreements are contractual agreements between consenting adults. Unless a person is forced to work or to work under egregious conditions, EAW protects liberty rights in allowing a person freely to enter into and leave contracts of his or her own choosing. Third, property rights protect companies and their owners, so that companies and their managers should be free to hire and fire as they see fit. Indeed, as we pointed out, McMahon, a defender of employee rights, argues that although employers and managers do not have any moral justification for ignoring employee rights claims, including, for example, free speech, due process, and rights to participate in corporate decision-making, as property owners or agents they do have rights to hire and fire "at will."

EAW and due process

Our second set of arguments, in chapters 2, 3, and 4, focused on EAW, the common law practice that permits either the employer or the employee to terminate the employment relationship at any time for virtually any reason or for no reason at all. As we have illustrated, the practice of EAW results in numerous challenges to individual rights. While progress has been made in eroding many of the workplace practices based on EAW, the principle still governs the philosophical presuppositions underlying employment practices in the United States, and, indeed, EAW has been promulgated as one of the ways to address economic ills in other countries.

While EAW remains the default rule, we mounted a variety of arguments that employees should not be treated "at will." Most of these arguments fall within two broad categories: those that relate to rights, which we have just reviewed, and those that relate to fairness. EAW has, on numerous occasions, seemingly translated into a license for employers and employees to treat one another *amorally*, if not *immorally* or unfairly. " 'Why are you firing me, Mr. Ford?' asked Lee Iacocca, president of Ford Motor Company. Henry, looking at Iacocca, said: 'I just don't like you!' " (Abodaher, 1982: 202). While EAW demands ostensibly *equal* treatment of both employers and employees, the result is often not inherently *fair* to either (Werhane and Radin, 1996, 1999). A requirement of "equal" treatment, therefore, is not sufficient or even applicable. Good employment practices should aim for treating each individual as an equal, while, at the same time, allowing for different, though comparable, treatment where relevant differences exist. For example, while it would not necessarily represent a good, or sound, employment practice to demand *equal* pay for all employees and managers, a good practice would be to demand equal pay for employees in similar positions doing similar tasks, and *comparable* pay for others, after taking into account relevant differences, such as in experience, position, tenure at the company, and special skills.

We argued that, except under conditions of very low unemployment or when there is a scarcity of skills in a particular industry, employers ordinarily stand in a position of power relative to prospective employees, and most employees, at any level, are replaceable with others. At a minimum, though, employees deserve to be given reasons for employment decisions that involve them. Unjustified dismissals are not appropriate in light of employees' considerable investment of time and effort. This is not to say that inadequate employees should not be replaced with better performers, but employees at least deserve to find out the reasons underlying employment changes. And if employees are to take charge of their careers, they should receive good reasons for employment decisions and full information. From a management point of view as well, employees should be given *good* reasons for employment decisions. Otherwise there is a perception that at least some management decisions are arbitrary, and this sort of behavior is not in keeping with good management practice. Even if it were possible to defend EAW on the basis of freedom of contracts, in practice, EAW permits inconsistent, even irrational, management behavior by permitting arbitrary, not work-related, treatment of employees – behavior that is not considered a good management practice (Radin and Werhane, 1996; Werhane, 1999). Since arbitrary accounting, marketing, and investment practices are not tolerated, arbitrary human resource practices should be considered equally questionable.

We have therefore concluded that due process procedures should be instituted as mandatory procedures in every workplace. On the other side, employers suffer when employees simply walk of jobs without notice. In a much earlier work, Werhane therefore argued that employees *and* employers have equal rights, rights that would entail reciprocal obligations to inform each other about firing or quitting and to give justifiable reasons for these actions (Werhane, 1985).

Due process procedures have become mandatory guarantees for employees in the public sectors of the economy, on the federal, state, and local levels, but not in the private sector. Again, on the basis of the fairness of equal treatment for all workers, we have concluded that this appears to be unfair. The inapplicability of constitutional guarantees in the private sector of the economy nevertheless prevails in employment (Radin and Werhane, 1996). This is not to suggest that there are no relevant differences between employment in the public and private sectors. In fact, there are a number of significant variations, including, but not limited to, salary differentials. Considering the degree of similarity between public and private work, and the breakdown of the public/private distinction in most areas of our political economy, however, we concluded that it only makes sense that due process be afforded to employees in both sectors.

Rethinking employment relationships

In chapters 5 and 6 we presented a third set of arguments involving the employment relationships themselves. Because employers and employees are engaged in relationships with one another, rights and responsibilities result from the respective reliance of each on the other. The ongoing interaction between employers and employees demands that certain rights be respected, or the relationships will fail.

Roles play an important part in these relationships. People in society fill various roles, or socially-constructed assignments, which assist in defining the relationships in which they are involved. Employment role responsibilities serve as a source of accountability in the workplace. When people are involved in employment relationships, as either employers or employees, they develop sorts of collegial obligations that emerge out of the reciprocity inherent in the relationships. When employment takes place, both employers and employees assume the responsibilities connected with their jobs – responsibilities often only implicitly stated, if stated at all, in verbal contracts. The reciprocity underlying these contracts demands that employees act for the benefit of their employers, and that employers then treat employees with similar respect. People engaged in relationships with one another naturally develop inherently reciprocal interpersonal obligations and responsibilities. Employee rights thus evolve from demands for mutual employee and employer responsibility, loyalty, and respect.

The nature of work is an essential element of employment relationships. It is possible to argue that employees seek meaningful work – work that fulfills their personal needs – in their professional roles. Although it is not always possible for employers to fulfill promises of meaningful work for every manager and employee at all times, efforts toward the provision of meaningful work suggest ways of motivating employees that are not degrading and that simultaneously create both worthwhile work and employer satisfaction. Employer responses to the demand for meaningful work, such as employability training, serve to strengthen the workplace by enriching employment relationships.

Economic value added

A fourth set of arguments, those developed in chapter 7, introduced some new models for thinking about employment. Without attacking or circumventing EAW, it is possible to discern signs of a changing mindset about employment, a mindset that values the competitive advantage of the contributions of good employees and managers. The extensive work of scholars such as Jeffrey Pfeffer and Norman Bowie illustrate this change. Pfeffer argued that a "people first" strategy could serve as an economic advantage for companies. In other words, it is not just for the benefit of employees, but also for the benefit of firm employers, to treat employees with respect. Pfeffer and Bowie conclude that the most successful companies – those that have sustained long-term economic profitability and growth – work carefully to engage in employment practices that include selective hiring, employment security, high compensation, decentralization, empowerment and self-managed teams, training, open information, and fair treatment of all of their employees (Pfeffer, 1994, Pfeffer, 1998; Bowie, 2000).

Building upon Pfeffer's and Bowie's thinking, we determined that from an organizational perspective, contrary to some points of view, it is a mistake to sort out employees, customers, products, services, shareholders, and so on, as if each represented an autonomous set of concerns. For example, a firm cannot do business without people, products, finance and accounting, markets, and a strategy. In times of economic exigency, a merger, or corporate change, it is, therefore, generally *not* to the advantage of a company merely to lop off employees (even if they are the "low hanging [most easily disposable] fruit"), without thinking carefully about their employees as *people*, and recognizing *their* contributions to the long-term survival and success of the company. In uncertain times, no company would simply quit doing accounting, and it would be to its peril to quit marketing its products and services. Similarly, to get rid of too many employees would not serve a company's long-term viability very well.

Long-term, well-trained, and well-compensated employees thus offer economic value added to the firm.

As a result of findings such as Pfeffer's, we were able to link the idea that employees are economic value added with a notion of employee rights, and this allows us to propose new ways to think about employment. If meaningful work has something to do with autonomy and respect, we can then re-envision the mindset of employment to consider each job applicant, employee, manager, or CEO as a unique individual. In addition, it prompts us to begin to rethink employment, not in terms of employees as merely economic value added, but in terms of employees as *individuals* – unique and particularized individuals. Indeed, a cost/asset employee assessment should be abandoned. This is not a prescription for corporate guarantees of lifetime employment, but it does suggest that Kanter's notion of employability should be part of the moral equation of employee rights.

THE BOTTOM LINE

Despite developments toward the erosion of EAW through law and public policy, changing mindsets regarding the value of employment and employment practices, and the contributions of Pfeffer and others toward demonstrating the worth of good employment practices for long-term profitability and success, the principle of EAW continues to underlie management practice in the United States. The language of rights, or employee rights, still evades popular management thinking about employment, at least in the private sectors of the economy. This is most clearly demonstrated by three sets of phenomena. First, there has been a consistent demise of unions and unionism in this country. Since the 1950s, union membership has dropped from about 33 percent of all workers to barely 10 percent today. This demise not only reflects the philosophy of corporations, but it is also the result of a series of public policy initiatives. In addition, it reflects interests of workers, even low-wage workers who toil under strenuous or dangerous conditions, who are nevertheless reluctant to unionize.[1]

Second, despite the enlightened focus on employability and even during the almost full employment economy of the late 1990s, layoffs have continued to dominate the ways in which corporations think about employment when making changes in their strategic direction.

In 2000 alone, there were more than a million people laid off.[2] Admittedly, during times of low unemployment, most of these folks found new jobs, but this often requires relocation and, sometimes, even in this economy, taking less desirable jobs for lower wages. This is particularly true for unskilled workers.

Third, one of the criticisms of Northern Europe's high unemployment and Japan's recent economic difficulties is that these countries have massive legal restrictions on the ability of their companies to engage in flexible employment practices. We are thus exporting our EAW mindset, sometimes as a panacea for economic difficulties that are not always traceable to overemployment. It is important for us to think carefully about the practices we export, particularly considering their questionable success here.

NEW MODELS FOR EMPLOYMENT

Given the failure of such arguments to erode the underpinnings of EAW, in what follows we will conclude the book by proposing some new avenues for approaching employment issues to achieve the desirable end of employee dignity and respect, without our having to defeat EAW or shift completely workplace assumptions about legal and moral issues. We contend that, by reconfiguring our thinking about and expectations of workplace norms, it is possible to give employers new reasons to respect employees and their productivity and employees the impetus to manage their own careers.

A "citizen" metaphor

One way of developing an individualized analysis of employment that recognizes and respects employee rights is through a citizen metaphor. "Citizenship" is a designation that links people to rights and duties relative to their membership in a larger community, such as a political community. There is a growing body of literature addressing this notion of "corporate citizenship" (Waddock, 2001; Wood and Logsdon, 2002). According to Sandra Waddock,

> Good corporate citizens live up to clear constructive visions and core values. They treat well the entire range of stakeholders who risk capital in, have an interest in, or are linked to the firm through

> primary and secondary impacts through developing respectful, mutually beneficial operating practices and by working to maximize sustainability of the natural environment. (2001: 5)

Replacing the view that corporations are, or should be, socially responsible, the corporate citizenship model argues that a firm's membership in complex cultural, national, and global communities accords it, like an individual, rights and responsibilities comparable to those accorded to individuals through national citizenship. The belief is that if corporations are to enjoy operational privileges they must then honor their responsibilities to the communities in which they operate and belong. This model of corporate citizenship describes and evaluates corporate relationships with external stakeholders, such as customers, communities, governmental entities, and the environment (Waddock, 2001).

The citizen metaphor is also a tool to be applied to and address corporate responsibilities to internal stakeholders, such as managers and employees, and in particular, to managerial–employee relationships. This process entails portraying employees as citizens, corporate citizens, who have rights and responsibilities within the firm just has they have in their political lives. This citizen metaphor is not complicated; it requires, simply, "treating workers like adults" (Ciulla, 2000: 233). Treating people as adults translates into acknowledging their dignity and respecting their relevant legal and moral rights and duties. Rights and duties connected to "citizenship" reflect the coexistence of people in a common space, and endeavor to help delineate how people can best interact with the fewest conflicts. This space does not have to be a global or semi-global community, but could also refer to the context of a firm. Within the firm context, the citizen metaphor links people to one another in such a way that they inevitably take responsibility for working together for the benefit of the firm. At the same time, the metaphor of citizenship requires that each "citizen" has equal rights, and requires that all citizens as individuals be treated with respect and dignity. According to such a model, employees thus serve as participants in and members of a firm community.

As applied to employment, a citizenship model would take into account productivity and performance, and it would also require rethinking hiring in terms of long-time employment. This would not entail keeping every employee hired, or even guaranteeing lifetime employment. It would, however, at a minimum, require due process for all employment changes, employability training, protection of fundamental rights such as free speech and privacy, and the provision of adequate information to employees about their future and the future of the company. The employability requirement would enable employees to serve as good corporate citizens in the broad sense of being able to contribute in a number of areas in the economy, and, if Pfeffer's data is correct, such measures add economic value to shareholders as well. At the same time productivity, loyalty, and good performance would be expected from all employees just as responsible community interaction is expected from citizens in a community.

In sum, if a company's core values were to drive the assumption that each employee is a corporate citizen analogous to a national citizen with similar rights and duties, our mental models of employment, both from the employer and the employee point of view, would change. Indeed, we might even adopt a McMahonian model of participatory democracy without reducing the economic development of firms.

Systems thinking and employment

Systems thinking, a way of looking at business that is becoming increasingly in the forefront of management thinking, operates similarly to the citizenship model in challenging traditional views of employment. Pfeffer's conclusion, that employees are critical to corporate success, is grounded in a systems approach, which views employees, as well as products, services, and customers, as all interrelated and contributory to the strategic advantage of the company. By analyzing corporate results, he demonstrates that without good employees a company will fail, just as it will fail without customers, and fail if it does not think strategically about its products and services.

A system is a complex of interacting components together with formal and informal networks of interrelationships between various stakeholders (Laszlo and Krippner, 1998: 51). "A system involves interactions extending over time, a complex set of interrelated decision points, an array of [individual, institutional, and governmental] actors with conflicting interests . . . and a number of feedback loops" (Wolf, 1999: 1675). According to a systems thinking approach, employment is a phenomenon embedded in a complex set of interrelationships, between employees and managers or employers, between workers and labor organizations such as unions, and between employment and public policy. It involves customer relationships, human resource policies, and, given employee stock option plans, often employee/owner relationships with management. Employees are one of many stakeholders who affect and are affected by the companies in which they work. Moreover, companies, and, indeed, industries and the system of commerce, are embedded within a complex structure of laws, regulations, regulatory agencies, public policy, media interaction, and public opinion. And this system – employment – is part of a global economy of exchange, ownership, and trade (Mitroff and Linstone, 1993).

Employees, as "players" in these overlapping sets of systems, are at the same time individuals, members of a company, and embroiled in a system of commerce. Their interests are important, but they are not the only interests that must be taken into account. Like the phenomenon of employment, employee rights and responsibilities are embedded in a complex social system of rights and responsibilities. Employee rights claims thus are not merely individual manifesto claims to certain privileges, but also entail reciprocal respect for others' rights and responsibilities, as we argued in chapter 1.

If employment relationships are embedded in a set of systems or subsystems, then it is important – strategically important – for managers and employees to attack employment issues systemically from a fact-finding perspective, from an organizational or social perspective, and from the perspective of the individuals involved, in this case, employees and managers. Conceptualizing employment systemically may help to reconsider its importance in the underlying system of which they are a contributing part. This sort of analysis will neither eliminate nor replace the principle of EAW, but it does represent another step in the process of reconceptualizing employment.

In thinking about employment and employees, it is tempting to become preoccupied with managerial/employer responsibilities to employees, as if employees were merely pawns in the system. It is, though, important to note that a systems approach does not preclude individual autonomy. No individual in a free commercial society is defined completely by the set of systems in which he or she participates. Interestingly, a systematic approach actually looks beyond protection of employee rights, and also emphasizes employee responsibilities – to themselves as well as to the firm. As part of the workforce, each of us has claims to certain rights, such as free choice, free speech, rights to strike, and rights to work contributions or compensation for those contributions, rights to information, and rights to a safe workplace. As a consequence of claiming such rights, every worker, employee, or manager, in every sector of the economy, has responsibilities as well – responsibilities not merely to employers, but to him- or herself and his or her future, and to manage that future as he or she is able and sees fit (Werhane, 1999).

A systems thinking approach implies that employees are, or should be, responsible for their own lives and careers, and, they need to take the steps necessary to research and explore mobility options. Thinking about employment systemically and thinking about personal responsibilities as well as responsibilities to others within that system can help employees take charge of their own working lives, professions, and careers.

The view of employment as part of the political/economic system is consistent with the notion of corporate citizenship. The systemic conceptualization of employment gives rise to employee rights and duties that animate the employment system. In other words, the rights employees enjoy, and the duties they must bear, are those that ensure the continued existence of the system. Similarly, through the lens of corporate citizenship, employee rights and duties include those that contribute to the firm. Employees have rights to engage in behavior that allows for their development within the system, or firm, and have duties to enable others to develop as well.

A professional model

A systems approach, while serving as an obvious description of the complex nature of employment in advanced political economies such as our own, is not internalized in employment thinking today – at least not in the United States. The citizen metaphor requires an expansion of notions of trust and solidarity within firms, and, considering the mobility of the workforce, the ease with which companies can lay off employees and hire new ones, and the preoccupation with short-term bottom lines, it is unlikely that this metaphor will be universally adopted. Given these conclusions, namely, the persistence of the principle of EAW, the argument that employees have rights and that employees and managers have moral responsibilities to each other, the economic value added of employees to firms, and the questionable adaptability of the citizen metaphor, we are challenged to try to reformulate the notion of employment proactively from an employee perspective – that of the employee as *professional*.

The popular literature is replete with laments that the "good old days" of alleged employee–employer lifetime employment contracts, company paternalism, and lifetime benefits are under threat of extinction (Werhane, 1999). So, too, are the expectations of loyalty, total commitment, company-first sacrifices, and perhaps, even, obedience and trust. Whether or not there ever were "good old days," such laments could be used to change thinking in a positive way, in that they indicate that we have alternatives – the way that we view work is not necessarily the only way. This realization should prompt employees and managers to rethink who they are – to manage their own careers and to rejoice in the demise of paternalism such that they can no longer even imagine that a person is dependent upon, or co-dependent upon, a particular employer, training program, or authority. It demands changes in what we have called elsewhere the "boss" mental model, so aptly exploited by Dilbert, and to alter our vision of ourselves from that of "just an employee" to that of an independent worker or manager with commitments to self-development (Hirsch, 1987).

How, though, in the twenty-first century, is a person to develop this sort of independence and independent thinking about his or her work, when the vast majority of us work for others? A new model of employment is required, and this model requires developing different mindsets about employment that takes into account the fact that most of us are, and will be, employees. There appears to be little in our backgrounds to assist us in thinking of ourselves as free laborers rather than wage earners.

Historically that is not true. One of the great debates in the United States during and after the Industrial Revolution concerned the status of "free labor" versus "wage labor." Free labor was considered "labor carried out under conditions likely to cultivate the qualities of character that suit citizens to self-government" (Sandel, 1996: 169). Such conditions included economic independence, and thinkers such as Thomas Jefferson thus associated free labor with independent farming. Wage earning was thought by some to be equivalent to slavery since it "denied [workers] economic and political independence essential to republican citizenship" (Sandel, 1996: 172). The authors of *Rerum Novarum* (Leo XII, 1892), the first Papal social encyclical, subsequently qualified the admonition about wage labor, and proposed that wage labor was not a form of slavery when workers were paid adequately. By "adequately," the encyclical did not mean merely a living wage, but a wage that would provide enough "left over" so that the laborer could become a property owner as well. Thus the notion of free labor and worker independence is not without precedent.

The model we propose is that of employees as professionals. "Profession" refers to "any group of individuals with particular skills who work from a shared knowledge base" (Spencer et al., 2000: 71). A professional is a person who has trained skills in certain areas that position that person as employable in his or her area of expertise. A professional is identified with, and has a commitment to, his or her professional work. It is the work and its achievements that are important, even more important than the workplace setting. Indeed, for some professionals it is the work and its contributions that are more important than its monetary reward. Additionally, most professionals belong to independent associations that have their own codes of professional ethics and standards for expertise and certification or licensure. Engineering codes include the edict that public safety is the primary value or first commitment of an engineer. The code for the American Institute of Certified Public Accountants (AICPA), interestingly, includes the requirement of independence from clients and the requirement to "blow the whistle" when fraud is committed, even if by an employer or a client. Some of the codes, in particular legal and medical professional codes, include the requirement of a commitment to public service in the area of a person's profession (Bayles, 1981).

The responsibilities of a professional are first to his or her expertise, second to the profession and the code of that profession, and only third to the employer. This is not a model of the "loyal servant," but, rather, of people who manage themselves with employable and retrainable skills that they market, even as they may simultaneously be in the employment of others. These are people who commit to excellence and a particular set of professionally defined moral values in whatever employment situations they encounter, but are not wedded to one employer or one particular job. Professionals are persons who can work in many settings that draw on their expertise. Indeed, it is the expertise that they carry from job to job that distinguishes their work as "free labor."

Outside the traditional professions the professional model is one that has developed primarily in the high tech and dot.com industries, as people with specialized skills have built firms around those skills.

In a recent article Alan Hyde, a student of what he calls "high velocity labor markets" (where employees change jobs regularly) such as in Silicon Valley, outlines the professional model in that industry. While Silicon Valley employees have not officially organized themselves into professional organizations, a number of qualities distinguish this set of employees. Although they are well-trained and well-compensated, the turnover rate at most of these companies is up to 35 percent per year. Employees switch between company and company, exchange informal information through a vast Internet network, and carry their knowledge base with them to the next position.

Hyde indicates that Silicon Valley employees manage their own careers within a network of companies, instead of focusing on just one. According to him,

> Silicon Valley has a regional network-based industrial system that promotes collective learning and flexible adjustment among specialist producers of a complex of related technologies. The region's dense social networks and open labor markets encourage experimentation and entrepreneurship, companies compete intensely while at the same time learning from one another about changing markets and technologies through information communication and collaborative practices. . . . High labor mobility among firms is central to the formation of these ties. (Saxenian, 1994: 3–4, reprinted in Hyde, 1998: 223)

Hyde posed a question to these professional employees:

> Suppose . . . that there were an organization of Silicon Valley professionals . . . that did the following things. It contracted with the large health maintenance organizations in your area for coverage for you and your family whether or not you were employed at that minute. It provided advice and perhaps administrative services on your 401(k) retirement plan. It lobbied in Washington and Sacramento on issues related to professional employment, such as tax aspects of 401(k) plans. It maintained a web site, user lists, and chat groups for exchange of information about employers, where the jobs were, what was the employer's reputation, did it sue department employees. Finally, it might provide training or offer other courses. (1998: 227)

According to Hyde, most said they would join such an organization, and the model he sets up is that of the employee as an independent professional associated with, and protected by, an association of like professionals.

While the model Hyde postulates is formulated within a particular context, it is one that easily could, and should, be emulated elsewhere, as Hyde himself suggests. The growth of high tech firms offers an excellent example because, through these ventures, people have been able to focus on their talents, even as employees have moved from company to company, because employees are valued for their skills rather than their loyalty. High tech firms are not models for all employment, since they are often narrowly tailored to offering particularized products and services, but they do stand as potential models for other areas of employment.

There are other opportunities for professionalism as well, particularly with regard to contingent workers. During the past 20 years we have witnessed what some label as an alarming trend, the increase in contingent workers – workers who work part time, or full time on a contract basis without insurance, pensions, or other benefits. Contingent workers include self-employed, voluntary part-time workers, contract workers and consultants, and home-bound workers. These workers range from dishwashers to professionals and managers. Many have chosen this sort of employment arrangement. Some of these people have benefits independently or through spouses, and they thus appreciate the enhanced flexibility and higher salaries as compared to their full-time counterparts. The problem is that many others resent their "contingency." There are many who, according to Brockner and Wiesenfeld, see themselves as "peripheral" to the organization, particularly those who are part-time, contract, short-term, or "disposable" workers (Brockner and Wiesenfeld, 1992).

These workers are independent contractors – "free labor" in Jefferson's sense of the term – even though many of them do not revel in that. They are thought of, often, as "disposable," and some are involuntarily contingent workers, subject to a number of injustices: (1) the involuntary nature of the employment position; (2) the two-tier wage system (a) with unequal compensation, and (b) where many of these workers are psychologically, economically, and socially mistreated, and think of themselves as second-class workers. Adding to these injustices is (3) the fact that women and minorities account for a greater percentage of contingent workers than white males, even taking into account skills, those who opt for part-time and mommy-track employment, and those who cannot speak English or are otherwise disadvantaged. The further decline in union membership and the shift in the composition of the workforce indicate that, by the year 2005, only 20 percent of new hires, both part-time and permanent employees, will be white males. This data appears to suggest that we will see increased exploitation of new labor and greater utilization of contingent workers.

There is yet another dimension to what might already be considered a gloomy picture. Given the psychological pressures and perception of second-class citizenry, involuntary contingent workers in companies tend to be less loyal, less productive, and exhibit lower morale – all of which hurts the long-term productivity and well-being of the company for which they work. At the same time, contingent works are not as vulnerable to some of the problems that hinder full-time workers. Contingent workers are less likely to be absent, drink or use drugs on the job, complain, snooze, schmooze, or engage in time-consuming office or work floor politics. Moreover, without the shadow of union protection they are unencumbered by work rules or traditions. They are, therefore, more flexible.

As the number of contingent workers increases, those who choose this path as well as those who are involuntarily forced into it should be able to develop a sense of independence, engendered by redefining themselves in relation to their work. Using Hyde's model, this could translate into a rise of professionalism. Because contingent workers are no longer linked to particular companies, it could lead to a shift of loyalty from the company to work and to the profession. In addition, it could lead to the formation of new professional associations – associations, not necessarily industry- or position-specific, which develop guidelines for skills, licensing, and conduct, form employment contracts, develop codes of conduct, and protect members, just as the legal, medical, academic, and, to some extent, the engineering professions do today. These professions, then, could gain leverage, just as unions have done in the past, with employers, with leverage translated into equal pay for equal work and professionally provided benefits and pensions.

But what about unskilled low-wage workers? In a recent provocative book, *Nickel and Dimed*, Barbara Ehrenreich describes her venture into the unskilled work field. Working at under $10 an hour, Ms. Ehrenreich was a waitress, a cleaning woman for a cleaning service, an aide in a nursing home, and a stock person at Wal-Mart. In describing this odyssey in which she lived, with a great deal of hardship, on her wages,[3] she points out that one of the indignities suffered by allegedly "unskilled" workers is that their skills are not treated as such. Virtually all work entails some sort of skills – it is just that the "skills" required by this sort of work are not respected by many of us. Sorting clothes for Wal-Mart racks, for example, requires a great deal of skill, and waitressing is a much under-appreciated talent. Another indignity associated with much of low-wage work is that the workers tend not to be respected or treated with dignity, even by their fellow workers (Ehrenreich, 2001).

Ehrenreich herself recognizes that offering incentives to low-wage workers to take control of their lives and their careers is not easy. Her attempt to unionize Wal-Mart workers, for example, was an abject failure. No one wanted to "make waves" or jeopardize their fragile employment. Most workers there assumed it was their fate to be underpaid and underrepresented. Interestingly, however, in studies by Dorothy Sue Cobble, waitresses who organized themselves by craft, even though waitressing is relatively unskilled, developed a sense of dignity and pride in their work (Cobble, 1991, 1994; Wial, 1993). While these writers primarily propose a model for craft development or what we call professionalism, their suggestions give us hope that such organization is possible.

To accomplish this end, unskilled workers, like many managers today, would have to change their own mindsets about employment. It would require rethinking themselves as independent contractors with trained or trainable skills that are transferable to a number of job settings, rather than as mere wage earners. By taking their work and productivity contributions seriously and banding together, workers with such mindsets would create economic value added for firms and a sense of self-worth.

This model of professionalism requires changing mindsets of employers as well. In a recent article in *Across the Board*, a journal aimed at CEOs and boards of *Fortune* 1000 companies, Thomas Davenport argues that this mindset revision is necessary and valuable for employers as well as employees. Davenport is critical of measuring employees as costs or as assets. That metaphor, he argues, is outdated (if it ever applied at all) and creates a vision of employees as passive phenomena to be deployed, like the assets we buy and sell. Davenport's model is to view employees as investors who make a human-capital investment of their productivity into a particular company. Reinforcing our analysis in chapter 5 of roles and role responsibilities as reciprocal agreements, Davenport argues, "[v]iewing workers as investors underscores an essential fact of workplace life – work is a two-way exchange of value, not a one-way exploitation of an asset by its owner" (Davenport, 2000: 34).

According to Davenport,

> Conceiving of workers as investors rather than assets emphasizes that the link between employee and company depends not on ownership, paternalism, or blind loyalty. Instead, the cord binding organizations and people derives form the ability and willingness of each to provide benefits to the other. The relationship assumes mutual benefit, with neither party elevated at the expense of the other. (2000: 32–3)

Our argument is that professionalization of employees, all employees, helps management to conceive of employees as value creators, as creating specified kinds of value that they "invest" in companies, companies in which they may or may not choose to invest for a lifetime. In return, companies will get better trained, more efficient and productive employees who take their professional expertise seriously as a life commitment.

CONCLUSION

We are a country that has thrived on individualism in our political democracy. Although we have made progress in dispelling the public/private division, it will undoubtedly continue to influence Constitutional rights that in turn reinforce it. We have failed, and probably will continue to fail, to adopt new metaphors that challenge that individualism and the public/private distinction, such as a systems approach or a citizen metaphor for employment.

This is not where the story ends, though. While EAW remains the default rule for employment in most of the United States, new models are emerging that encourage and motivate both employers and employees to create a more satisfying workplace, which, at the same time, can boast higher performance. Hope for a workplace in which both employers and employees enjoy equal respect lies in variations of models such as the professional model. Interestingly, the professional model serves as a link between the individualism that cripples other models and the fair employment principles espoused by all of these models. The professional model is a form of, and reinforcement for, individualism. It will be interesting to see how that idea plays out in the workplace. The model of the worker, the employee, the manager, and the executive as professionals offers a paradigm for thinking about oneself as *both* independent and part of a political economy. With the pending end of implied job security in every sector of the economy, with global demands on management skills, and with the loss of union representation, this is a model for the future – a model that would circumvent EAW and take us fittingly into a new millennium of global capitalism.

Ironically, recent events surrounding the horrific destruction of the twin towers of the World Trade Center on September 11, 2001, underscore the values that underlie the American workplace, which are about professionals, not robots engaged in routine tasks. Although terrorists attempted to attack capitalism, they were only able to break apart the buildings that housed the tremendous values. As Howard Lutnick, CEO of Cantor Fitzgerald, explained, even in the wake of disaster, his people were anxious to get back to work. They felt a need to be part of something, and that something was work. And Lutnick, like many of the surviving business executives, was and is struggling to find ways to help support the survivors and the families of those lost – not because they have to, but because they want to do something to assist those who were part of their workplaces.

It may no longer make sense to waste words arguing against EAW. It is important for us now to accept EAW for what it is – a mere default – and to move forward by emphasizing models, such as that of professionalism, which help to show where the desirable values already exist, and to motivate more employers and employees to adopt similar practices. The firms that not only *survive*, but *succeed*, in the decades to come are going to be those that adopt such models.

EPILOGUE

George Washington once took scruffy groups of farmers and laborers from 13 independent colonies each with its own ethnic background, culture, and customs, and transformed that motley collection into the undisciplined, ill-paid, and poorly uniformed Revolutionary Army. This army lost most of its battles against the better-equipped and well-trained mercenary British troops, but it eventually defeated them. Washington did not train his soldiers to march in straight lines, salute properly, or even in the art of good fighting. Rather, he inspired that crew of dissidents around the core values of individual liberty and defeat of the British (Keeley, 1995:

72–3). Given this legacy, it does not seem that a revolution of the mental model of employment, from wage earner to free professional, is impossible.

NOTES

1. For example, less than 40 percent of all chicken catchers are unionized, despite the fact that they are exposed to pecking and chicken feather dust all day and work under very dangerous and stressful conditions (Goodman, 1999: A23).
2. According to "Extended Mass Layoffs in the Second Quarter of 2000" (USDL 00–266, released September 20, 2000, http://stats.bls.gov/newsrels.htm), 1,099,267 people were separated from their jobs for more than 30 days in 1999, and 971,612 people filed initial claims for unemployment insurance during a consecutive five-week period. During the second quarter of 2000, there were 227,114 separations, and 162,726 initial claimants.
3. As Ehrenreich points out, most people cannot live on a minimum-wage salary so that those working at minimum wage usually have two jobs or a supporting family.

REFERENCES

Articles, books, and other similar publications

Abodaher, D. 1982. *Iacocca: A Biography*. New York: Harper Collins.

Bayles, Michael. 1981. *Professional Ethics*. Belmont, CA: Wadsworth Publishing.

Bowie, Norman. 2000. *Kantian Capitalism*. Malden, MA: Blackwell.

Brockner, J. and Wiesenfeld, B. M. 1992. "Living on the Edge (of Social and Organizational Psychology): The Effects of Job Layoffs on Those Who Remain." In J. Keith Murnighan, ed., *Social Psychology in Organizations: Advances in Theory and Research*. Englewood, NJ: Prentice Hall, 195–215.

Ciulla, Joanne. 2000. *The Working Life*. New York: Random House Times Books.

Cobble, Dorothy Sue. 1991. *Dishing it Out: Waitresses and Their Unions in the Twentieth Century*. Urbana: University of Illinois Press.

Cobble, Dorothy Sue. 1994. "Making Post-Industrial Unionism Possible." In Sheldon Friedman, Richard W. Hurd, Rudolph A. Oswald, and Roland L. Seeber, eds., *Restoring the Promises of American Labor Law*. Ithaca, NY: ILR Press, 285–302.

Davenport, Thomas O. 2000. "Workers are *Not* Assets." *Across the Board*, June: 30–4.

Ehrenreich, Barbara. 2001. *Nickel and Dimed.* New York: Henry Holt and Company.

Goodman, Peter S. 1999. "Eating Chicken Dust." *Washington Post*, November 28. A23–5.

Hirsch, Paul. 1987. *Pack Your Own Parachute.* Reading, MA: Addison-Wesley Publishing.

Hyde, Alan. 1998. "Employee Organization in High-Velocity Labor Markets." In Samuel Estrreicher, ed., *Employee Representation in the Emerging Workplace: Alternatives/Supplements to Collective Bargaining*. Boston: Kluwer Law International, 209–33.

Keeley, Michael. 1995. "The Trouble with Transformational Leadership: Toward a Federalist Ethics for Organizations." *Business Ethics Quarterly*, vol. 5: 67–96.

Laszlo, Alexander and Krippner, Stanley. 1998. "Systems Theories: Their Origins, Foundations and Development." In J. Scott Jordan, ed., *Systems Theories and a Priori Aspects of Perception*. Amsterdam: Elsevier, 47–74.

Leo XII. 1892. *Rerum Novarum.*

Mitroff, Ian I. and Linstone, Harold. 1993. *The Unbounded Mind.* New York: Oxford University Press.

Pfeffer, Jeffrey. 1994. *The Competitive Advantage Through People.* Boston: Harvard Business School Press.

Pfeffer, Jeffrey. 1998. *The Human Equation.* Boston: Harvard Business School Press.

Radin, Tara J. and Werhane, Patricia H. 1996. "The Public/Private Distinction and the Political Status of Employment." *American Business Law Journal*, vol. 34, no. 2: 245–60.

Sandel, Michael J. 1996. *Democracy's Discontent.* Cambridge, MA: Harvard University Press.

Saxenian, Anna Lee. 1994. *Regional Advantage: Culture and Competition in Silicon Valley and Route 128.* Cambridge, MA: Harvard University Press.

Spencer, Edward W., Mills, Ann E. Rorty, Mary V., and Werhane Patricia H., 2000. *Organization Ethics in Health Care.* New York: Oxford University Press.

Waddock, Sandra. 2001. *Leading Corporate Citizens: Meeting the Business in Society Challenge.* New York: Irvin/McGraw Hill.

Werhane, Patricia H. 1985. *Persons, Rights, and Corporations.* Englewood Cliffs, New Jersey: Prentice-Hall, Inc.

Werhane, Patricia H. 1999. "Justice and Trust," *Journal of Business Ethics*, vol. 21: 237–249.

Werhane, Patricia H. and Radin, Tara J. 1996, 1999. "Employment at Will and Due Process." In Thomas Donaldson and Patricia H. Werhane, eds., *Ethical Issues in Business: A Philosophical Approach*, 5th edn. Englewood Cliffs, New Jersey: Prentice Hall, 364–73.

Wial, Howard. 1993. "The Emerging Organizational Structure of Unionism in Low-Wage Services." *Rutgers Law Review*, 671.

Wolf, Susan. 1999. "Toward a Systemic Theory of Informed Consent in Managed Care." *Houston Law Review*, vol. 35: 1631–81.

Wood, Donna J. and Logsdon, Jeanne M. 2002. "Business Citizenship: From Individuals to Organizations." *Society for Business Ethics Ruffin Monograph Series*, no. 3.

Index